# The Duckham's Story

# The *Duckham's* Story

## A CENTURY OF FIGHTING FRICTION

# ROBIN WAGER

## Foreword by John Surtees MBE

**Haynes Publishing**

First published in July 1999

British Library Cataloguing in Publication Data:
A catalogue record for this book is
available from the British Library

ISBN 1 85960 639 3

Haynes Publishing, Sparkford, Nr Yeovil,
Somerset, BA22 7JJ.
Tel: 01963 440635 Fax: 01963 440001
Int. tel: +44 1963 440635 Fax: +44 1963 440001
E-mail: sales@haynes-manuals.co.uk
Web site: http://www.haynes.com

Designed & typeset by
G&M, Raunds, Northamptonshire
Printed and bound in Great Britain by
J.H. Haynes & Co. Ltd, Sparkford

Unless otherwise credited, all photographs are
from the Duckhams archive.

# CONTENTS

# FOREWORD

by John Surtees MBE

If we look back over the past 100 years it would, I believe, be fair to say that it has been the age of the internal combustion engine and motorised transport, whether by land, sea or air. Alexander Duckham was a part of that new era. A chemist by profession, he founded his company on products connected with aircraft and with the vehicles that were being developed for both the First World War and the turn to motor vehicles that followed it.

The company expanded and again the war years came, followed by new management and direction, with Jack Duckham taking over from Alexander who died in 1945. Product involvement in speed records with Goldie Gardner, and a friendship and business relationship with Lord Nuffield, brought about further growth.

However, 1951 was the year that Duckhams really made a great surge forward. The decision was made that multigrade was the oil of the future; and so the product was launched that was to be used universally in all forms of transport and motorsport – the famous Duckhams Q20-50, with its distinctive green colour. It is with the success of this product, and an attempt by the company to prove a point, that I come into the story.

Duckhams had moved to West Wickham, and had started a competitions programme largely based around the Mini, which had become such a giant-killer in saloon car racing. Motorcycles were to follow shortly, and the little Duckhams caravan was to be seen around all the British national circuits providing that back-up with Q20-50.

In 1971, in the second year of my own Formula One race team, I had a call to say that Duckhams would like to test their oil in a Formula One engine, and could I help? My answer was yes, and we provided one of our Surtees team cars to carry out an RAC-observed test at Silverstone, using Duckhams oil purchased from a garage by the RAC scrutineer. The test was over 201.96 miles at an average speed of 123.8mph, and the engine was subsequently dismantled and pronounced to be in a totally satisfactory condition.

The team were delighted and it sparked an increased involvement in motorsport that was to cover Grand Prix support for Team Surtees, Team Lotus, Graham Hill, Embassy and Hesketh. Also, Van Diemen and their Formula Fords have been a success story in their working relationship over the years. If you list the names of drivers who have had support in their early years, it reads like a Who's Who: Hill, Coulthard, Irvine, Mansell, Brundle and Senna, to name just a few on four wheels.

On two wheels, Paul Smart, John Cooper, Ray Pickerell, Dave Crockford – and we mustn't forget the 1995 British Championship-winning rotary-engined Duckhams Norton. Renold Chains went to Duckhams to have the lubrication problems solved with their racing motorcycle chains; BMC did the same with their constant-velocity joints.

As this book relates, the Duckhams story is one of constant development and success on the back of the technology, expertise and enthusiasm that has supported its products, now into a new phase with the Mobil and Duckhams lubricant brands under the BP umbrella. I look forward to a long continuation of the unique niche, and the support that Duckhams have been able to give with their products, in both two- and four-wheel motorsport, at both national and club level.

**John Surtees MBE**
**1999**

# ACKNOWLEDGEMENTS

Compiling the fascinating story of this unique company in the relatively brief time available would have been considerably more daunting even than it appeared, had it not been for the research already documented by Roger Soper, formerly technical and logistics manager at Duckhams. Roger has also patiently helped with my subsequent queries and provided invaluable assistance in unearthing illustrative material.

Former competitions manager Ron Carnell gave an extra dimension to the motorsport connection with his memories, and the loan of some photographs from his personal collection. Additional help was provided by Pat Lelliott, whose official post for many years was technical manager, but who also happily acted as unofficial press relations manager. A number of the current management and staff at Duckhams Oils have also been of great assistance on a day-to-day basis.

Useful pointers on the family side were given by Neill Foster, grandson of the company's founder Alexander Duckham and the last family director.

Michael Adams, Chairman of the Governors of the Alexander Duckham Memorial Schools Trust, was most helpful in providing information relating to the origins of the Trust, and arranging the loan of the painting of Vanbrugh Castle.

The people specifically referred to in the text are those who happen, for whatever reason, to have had a higher profile. I am very conscious that there have, over the years, been many others whose dedication to the company justifies inclusion; similarly there are undoubtedly other events in the company's history that probably should have been mentioned. For such omissions I can only plead constraints of space.

I should also point out that, in asking for certain illustrations to be reproduced from very old photographs, and particularly from old company magazines, I have asked the publishers to perform a near miracle; they must be absolved from any shortfall in the resulting quality!

**Robin Wager**
**Cheltenham**

## Chapter 1

# THE EARLY DAYS

This is the story of a name that, for much of the 20th century, has meant 'engine oil', even to people with no particular interest in motor vehicles. It is also inextricably linked to one man, spurred on by a fascination for engineering and technological progress.

Alexander Duckham was the founder in 1899 of the company that, 100 years later, still enjoys a remarkable enthusiasm and loyalty for its products among engineers and laymen alike.

The 20th century has been a remarkable one for so many reasons, bringing, like every century before it, its share of good and bad. But as we enter the next millennium, history will record the past 100 years as being notable for the amazing advances they saw in two major areas, each to some extent reliant upon the other. Those areas are communications and technology, and it is in the latter field that Alexander Duckham's company has played an important part.

Alexander was born in Blackheath, South London, on 11 March 1877, at the culmination of the Victorian era. In the wake of the Industrial Revolution, science and technology were already taking the major strides that would see them galloping into the next century, gradually improving living standards; but in many ways social conditions were still in the Dark Ages. To help put things in perspective, the London Underground had already been open for 15 years, while children could still legally be sent down the coal mines at the age of 12.

With steam and electricity providing the current forms of mechanical propulsion, the internal combustion engine, with which the

*Alexander Duckham, founder of the company 100 years ago.*

Duckhams story is closely connected, had only just been invented, and Alexander would be in his teens before the first cars started to appear.

Alexander Duckham was fortunate in his parentage. His father Frederick, a Cornishman by birth, was manager of the Millwall Dock Company, one of the oldest and most important sections of London's docks; his mother Maud was a philanthropic woman and a member of the McDougall family, of flour and chemicals fame.

A brilliant engineer, with an inventive bent and a painstaking capacity to achieve results, Frederick apparently tended to lose sight of financial matters when engrossed in a project. It is said that Maud, who was keen to see her seven children prosper, often tried unsuccessfully to persuade her husband to turn his skills to something more lucrative than the dredgers and elevators that were his everyday concern.

Recalling his childhood in later life, Alexander wrote:

'The whole of the married life of this fine couple was, I think, an example of what matrimony should be. They both had brains, kind hearts, a great love and respect for each other. They delighted in good work so long as they could indulge in it hidden and unseen. Each put the life and happiness of the other and the children above everything.

'We were always comparatively poor, mainly because my father was one of the most generous men and was satisfied with the simplest living. I think we all sympathised with my mother whose lot was made a good deal harder than it need have been.

'She was, however, a wonderful manager with a certain amount of cunning which she often used, quite legitimately, to deceive my father. She developed a system of asking him for £10 when she only needed five, spending what she needed and putting the remainder into her banking account. As a result of this she saved over £20,000 up to her death, which

followed my father's by some few years, while he left only £10,000.

'His generosity could be very aggravating to his family though. On one occasion he was given a fine job as arbitrator in the Manchester Ship Canal case. This paid 50 guineas a day as a retainer and 200 guineas when the court was sitting. The case went on for months, and we lived in legitimate expectations of some kind of real beano, perhaps a few tricycles or ponies when he received his emoluments.

'What actually happened was that he gave his helpmate £10 to buy a new hat. Then, with unfeigned pleasure and without any swank, expected us to share his joy in having been able to send a cheque for many thousands of pounds to the London Hospital.'

When Alexander was four the family moved to The White Cottage in Maze Hill, Blackheath. Just across the road stood Vanbrugh Castle, a large, imposing house with battlement-style walls, which, unbeknown to the young Alexander, would later become a testament to the fact that he had inherited his father's charitable nature.

Now a built-up suburb of London, Blackheath at this time was quite rural, and Alexander recorded that the family's new home '... secured a more or less country life within reasonable distance of my father's job ... to get to which he walked to the Greenwich Pier near the Ship Hotel, famous for its whitebait dinners, and then he crossed in a rowboat or one of those funny old paddle steamers.'

Entering a dame school at a young age, Alexander progressed to Blackheath Preparatory School (from which subsequently developed the famous Blackheath Rugby Club) where he gained both a junior and a senior scholarship.

Matriculating at just 16, he went on to University College, London, where his brilliant mind gained him the Goldsmith's Scholarship and the Exhibition of the Cloth Workers' Company. His original ambition had been to become a surgeon, but a fascination with chemistry enticed him away, bringing him the Senior Gold Medal of the university in that subject. He also took the PhD degree of the University of Heidelberg, Germany, but never used the formal title of Doctor.

He was studying at University College under Sir William Ramsay (discoverer of the inert gas argon) at the time of the discovery of X-rays by Röntgen in 1895. Within a couple of hours of the announcement of this in the press, despite the fact that no details of the equipment used by Röntgen were given, Alexander had succeeded with very primitive apparatus in producing what is thought to have been the first X-ray photograph ever

*Frederick and Maud Duckham and their family. Young Alexander is standing, on the left of the picture.*

taken in Britain – of the bones in his own foot. The work was carried on by one of the teaching staff and contributed to some of the earliest published papers on the subject.

Most of Alexander's siblings appear to have inherited a share of their parents' special genes. His elder brother Frederick ('F. W.') Duckham became a distinguished civil engineer, counting among his projects London's George V Dock and Dover Harbour as well as docks and ports around the world.

Younger brother Arthur – for some reason always known as 'Bob' to family and friends – also took up engineering, specialising in furnaces and the gas industry, his experimental work resulting in the formation of a group of companies set up to exploit his specialist products and expertise.

Frederick Duckham Snr, closely involved in various developments of the Industrial Revolution, was a friend or business acquaintance of many of the movers and shakers of the late 19th century. One such was Alfred (later Sir Alfred) Yarrow, of the powerful shipbuilding and engineering family, who had become godfather to the young Alexander. Yarrow took his duties seriously, influencing his newly graduated godson to take up the study of lubrication – hardly a science at all at this time, but a subject in its infancy and using the crudest materials.

In the early 1890s Britain's personal transport was still catered for by the horse and the bicycle, and such cars as existed were all imported. Despite this, and the fact that they were legally restricted to walking pace, Henry Sturmey, editor of *The Cyclist*, was prompted to launch a weekly magazine about cars, which he titled *The Autocar*, a name he created as an alternative to the increasingly common 'automobile'.

A British motor industry was born more or

*Alexander's mother Maud was a kindly and capable woman who learned to live with her husband's casual attitude to the family finances.*

less instantly when in 1895 flamboyant entrepreneur Harry Lawson, who had built a fortune from cycles and tyres, formed the British Motor Syndicate to buy up all existing and future motor vehicle patents. He went on to form the Motor Car Club, with the object of protecting motorists' interests.

Taking his first job in 1897 as a chemist with Fleming's Oil Company in Millwall, Alexander Duckham found himself on a pittance of 15 shillings (75p) a week. Like father, like son – the money was not as important to him as the additional skills he was gaining. Allied to his theoretical knowledge, these practical lessons were to prove invaluable in his business life; not only the tricks of the particular trade that he induced the various workers to teach him, but also, for example, the demoralising effects of working for an employer who did not appreciate the virtues he undoubtedly possessed.

At the age of 21 Alexander was made deputy works manager, to cover for Fleming's manager who was away for a long period in the Rumanian oilfields. Such was his skill in cost-saving, especially in waste products, that the company was able to pay its first ever dividend. It was also the last, for after receiving a gift of £5 for this achievement, Alexander resigned and the company closed.

Seeing little hope of the advancement he so impatiently sought, he had decided that the only solution was to set up on his own. With £200 donated by his father, he acquired a two-roomed, wooden building in premises at Phoenix Wharf, in the familiar Millwall area of docklands.

First naming his business somewhat diffidently 'Alexander & Co', he then, perhaps as an afterthought, affixed a brass plate inscribed 'A. Duckham FCS, Analytical Chemist'. Numbering about 10 in total, the rest of the staff shared one room as a general office while

*Alexander as a young boy: he enjoyed outdoor pursuits including swimming, cycling and rugby.*

Alexander used the other as both his office and research laboratory.

It was the end of the 'Naughty Nineties', with a new century about to dawn. The Boer War had broken out in South Africa, and an ad in *The Sphere* proclaimed that 'the quantity of Liebig's Meat Extract already supplied to the British Forces there amounted to the product of 4,000 bullocks or sufficient to make 5,128,192 breakfast cups'.

The 'no nonsense' literary school of Kipling and W. E. Henley was on the way out, to be replaced by the likes of Oscar Wilde and Aubrey Beardsley. Carlyle and Samuel Smiles were passé; the influence of new thinkers like Shaw and Havelock Ellis was growing. Art Nouveau was at its peak, and the era of advertising had begun.

The theatre too was booming, and every city had several, all well attended, plus a selection of music halls. London itself had over 50 recognised music halls (the Hammersmith Palace was perhaps the best known) as well as hundreds of 'song and drink saloons'. The entertainment at these was of dazzling variety, with often as many as 20 first-class acts on the bill, and a seat cost 6d (2.5p).

In Germany Count Zeppelin was busy with his airships and in Ohio the Wright Brothers were experimenting with their gliders. The electric light and the telephone were new, while the horseless carriage was regarded by most as a crackpot contraption, although its endorsement by Prince Albert was bringing a new respectability.

The Light Locomotives Act of 1896 not only repealed the 'Red Flag' Act of 1865, which required any self-propelled vehicle to be preceded by a man on foot, but also raised the speed limit from 4mph to a dizzy 14 (although this was promptly reduced to 12mph under a clause giving such powers to the Local Government Board!). The date of this relative 'freedom', 14 November 1896, saw the first London to Brighton Run, celebrated annually to this day under the auspices of the RAC.

Spurred on perhaps by this gradual emancipation of the motorist, at the time he set up his company Alexander Duckham also acquired his first car, a Germain. This was effectively a Daimler, built under licence in Belgium, lending extra credibility to the story that Alexander had been taken for his first drive in a motor vehicle by none other than Gottlieb Daimler himself.

Unfortunately the motor car had already come to be perceived by the majority of the population as a social evil – and on grounds that are only too familiar today. The first was speeding: all kinds of ways of catching motorists were tried, but in the end it came down to the good old speed trap involving two constables and a stopwatch. With conviction relying on the word of the police (none of whom could afford a car themselves), and with some local magistrates clearly resolved to hound motorists out of existence, drivers became only more determined to fight back.

The second objection was pollution. In bad weather the primitive, poorly made roads became quagmires as they were churned up by the cars' wheels, while in times of drought the neighbourhood was soon choking in a thick cloud of dust.

Motoring, however, was here to stay, and Alexander Duckham motored on, mainly for business purposes. Fired by an all-consuming interest in problem-solving and developing new techniques, his capacity for tireless work was apparent even then, as his own description of his daily schedule reveals:

'Did laboratory work, saw Works Foreman, washed, shaved and had breakfast. Opened small mail and then dolled up to go out and cadge for orders. Came back in the afternoon to put things in trim. Devoted the evening to laboratory and testing work and often slept on the laboratory table.'

The phrase 'cadge for orders' suggests a certain embarrassment, based on the feeling among business people of the time that it was undignified to tout for trade. In fact this would not prove necessary for long. By 1902 the small business was thriving, and the boss was able to note, '… finding that I had no reason to be ashamed of trade as a profession I called the firm Alexander Duckham & Co.'

The fledgling works carried out basic oil and compound blending. Its products went primarily to serve the various developing forms of mechanised production, but also to the local shipbuilders. Millwall was in the centre of naval shipbuilding, with Yarrow & Co on the Isle of Dogs, and also the Thames Ironworks, the largest of the old firms, who built *Thunderer*, last of the men-of-war to be built on the Thames, and to whom Duckhams supplied tallow for the launch slipways (at some £500 per time), and oils for engine trials.

Almost alone in his chosen field, and with the help of Alfred Yarrow in introducing him to other engineers and companies with specialist lubrication needs, Alexander was quickly able to establish a reputation for himself as an expert on the subject. Never happier than when challenged with solving a difficult problem, he was, perhaps unwittingly, setting the philosophy to which Duckhams would adhere to this day. He recalled that his father's honest nature, too, clearly helped him in these early days of the business:

'I found … when I started in business that his reputation for integrity, ability and kindness of heart were of the greatest value to me. Indeed on more than one occasion it was conveyed to me by those whom I was approaching for business that in view of my parentage they were going to take it for granted that I could be relied upon.'

Queen Victoria's 64-year reign ended with her

*Keenly interested in 'The New Motoring' from an early age, Alexander acquired his first car, a Germain, on founding his company in 1899.*

death in 1901, aged 82, and the accession of Edward VII. As the Edwardian era progressed, so too did Duckham & Co: new offices and laboratories were built at the road end of the works, additional chemists were engaged to handle the intensified research into practical lubrication and associated problems, and the first lady typist was employed. With the arrival in 1904 of a chartered engineer, P. N. Hooper, a further cornerstone of the company's later success was cemented: the partnership between the chemist and the engineer, the laboratory and the technical applications of the science. Hooper became a director soon afterwards.

The growing popularity – at least with drivers – of the automobile (in America, Henry Ford founded his Ford Motor Company in 1903 to produce the two-cylinder Model A, setting the scene for the mass-production that was to follow) presented Alexander Duckham & Co with plenty of business, from two main points of view. First, the rather basic oils available needed developing with a view to improving, for example, the control of carbon formation and engine starting. Second, with the country's fuel and oil needs increasing rapidly, Alexander's expertise was called upon at a high level (where the new importance of oil in the event of war had also not gone unnoticed) to investigate prospecting for oil in British dominions abroad.

Trinidad was soon identified as a major oil source, and new exploration produced an extremely high-class crude, much superior to the asphaltic variety produced by wells elsewhere on the island. In the early 1900s Alexander set up the Trinidad Central Oilfields Company (TCO), which, not surprisingly, found a ready marketing agent for the new oil and its products in Alexander Duckham & Co Ltd of London. So important was this side of Duckhams activities that TCO (later to become Tricentrol) appears to have become the tail that wagged the dog of his British company for a time.

Despite the ready market for cars, social conditions were improving only very slowly. The working week averaged 55 hours, and one person in every 40 still lived below the poverty line (although in 1906 David Lloyd George declared that 60 per cent of the poverty that existed could be blamed on the demon drink!).

By 1907 the Duckham company head-count had grown to around 25, most of the general office staff being teenagers. Weekly remuneration ranged from 25 shillings (£1.25) for the chief clerk to just 8 shillings (40p) for the new arrival, office boy George Joyce. Destined to become a key figure, Joyce would remain with the company all his working life and rise to become joint managing director, one of many staff over the years whose contribution to the company's growth and reputation was invaluable.

Packaging for liquid products did not have access to the sophisticated materials of today, the commonest form of container being the wooden barrel, in which raw materials were received. The company set up its own cooper's shop where new barrels were turned out on piecework, ensuring more than adequate output, and these would be filled and loaded on to horse-drawn carts for delivery to customers.

It was not only land-based transport, as represented by the motor car, that was concentrating the minds of contemporary engineers; so too was the aeroplane. Despite the Wright Brothers' breakthrough in covering 852 feet in their petrol-engined craft in 1903, progress in powered flight was painfully slow for the next few years. By 1908 a number of aircraft were regularly taking to the skies, with France leading the way in the study and practice of aeronautics.

*Alexander spent much time in Trinidad, where he played a major part in developing the 'pitch lakes' as a source of excellent crude oil. He is seen here crossing the Ortoire River in an MG Midget and supervising pumping of oil from pipeline to tanker.*

The French aviator Louis Blériot made a flight of 33 miles over land in 1909, and his pioneering flight across the Channel that same year in a twin-cylinder Anzani-engined monoplane had been witnessed by F. W. Duckham, by whose courtesy a stand-by rescue boat had been provided for the contestants in the challenge. F. W. introduced Blériot to his younger brother, who clearly found the flyer a man after his own heart. Indeed, the successful flight so fired Alexander's imagination that he had a granite memorial, in the shape of the aircraft, inlaid at the spot on the Dover cliffs where the intrepid aviator's machine had landed.

The following year, after making a number

*Seen here accompanied by Alexander Duckham (left), the French aviator Louis Blériot made the first powered cross-Channel flight in 1909 and achieved a new record altitude the following year.*

of flights with Blériot, Alexander was invited at the Bournemouth Flying Meeting to accompany the Frenchman in an attempt on the British altitude record for an aircraft carrying two persons. In a machine fitted with the new 100hp Gnome-Blériot engine, they reached a new record height of 1,600 feet – a great achievement at that time. This early involvement with flying was also significant, with Duckhams formulating and supplying lubricants for many of the early aircraft. The year also marked the death of the King, with George V crowned in 1911.

As both the research and production aspects of the business diversified, among the situations to which the Duckham team provided answers were overcoming sludging in the oil systems of electrical turbines and transformers; the simultaneous cooling and lubrication of machine tools (requiring the development of stable emulsions); the treatment and prevention of skin diseases arising from the

# ALEXANDER DUCKHAM & CO. LTD.
## Motor Oils Price List
# 1912

## Standard Oil

40 gallon barrel
1s. 5d. per gallon

20 gallon barrel
1s. 7d. per gallon

10 gallon drum
1s. 9d. per gallon

5 gallon drum
1s. 10d. per gallon

### POLICE WARNINGS

★
★
★

In each section, we indicate the principal Police Traps that have been worked in the Area since 1909. We have left space for the insertion of new traps as Notification appears in the Press. Ten mile limits and traps in large Towns have not been included.

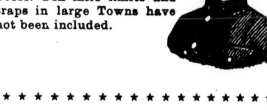

★ ★ ★ ★ ★ ★ ★ ★ ★ ★ ★ ★ ★ ★ ★ ★ ★ ★ ★ ★ ★ ★ ★ ★ ★ ★

 **DUCKHAM'S STEAM CAR OILS ARE UNEQUALLED**

Testimonial:

"I have used nothing else but your Special Superheated Steam Oil for the lubrication of my White Steam Car the whole of this season, during which time I have done over 500 miles. I overhauled the Engine last week to see exactly what condition it was in, and was delighted at the Beautiful State of the Cylinders and Pistons, these being practically as new, a result largely to be attributed to the Quality of your Lubricating Oil."

Signed, Will Clayton.

★ ★ ★ ★ ★ ★ ★ ★ ★ ★ ★ ★ ★ ★ ★ ★ ★ ★ ★ ★ ★ ★ ★ ★ ★ ★

*Part of an early price list issued by Alexander Duckham & Co Ltd.*

use of petroleum-based products; the protection of ball-bearing races against corrosion; and the formulation of non-separating greases and non-emulsifying oils capable of withstanding water.

Products of the Phoenix Wharf works included greases, industrial cutting oils, special oils for horse-drawn vehicles including harness oil, preservatives, petroleum jellies, cleansers and soaps. A new product, Concrete Mould Oil, as used in the building of Dover Harbour between 1903 and 1909, was set to grow in importance with the construction industry. This not only enabled the clean release of moulds, which could thus be re-used many times over, but also imparted a smooth surface to the resulting concrete structure.

By now the business was clearly making some money, and Alexander had courted and married Violet Ethel Narraway. Not only could he indulge his desire to own different motor cars, but around 1910 he bought Vanbrugh Castle, the stately building near his old family home on Maze Hill, where he set up a private laboratory away from the somewhat chaotic conditions of Phoenix Wharf.

The 'Castle' eventually became home to the couple's family of three daughters (Millicent, Joan and Ruth) and two sons (Jack and Alec). Jack later recalled how, one night, they awoke to find smoke billowing into their bedrooms after one of father's experiments ended in a fire!

Largely as a result of becoming one of the earliest owners of a motor car, Alexander had befriended the Australian motoring enthusiast and racing driver S. F. Edge, whose British Motor Syndicate acquired the sole agencies for Napier, de Dion and Gladiator cars for its London showroom, and with whom he shared the same hunger for technological progress. It seems that the Millwall works became Edge's unofficial service station, where he called on almost a weekly basis to drain his car's sump and refill with fresh oil, while discussing with Alexander the finer points of engine lubrication.

Winner of the legendary Gordon Bennett race in 1902, Edge had gone on to carry out early research into the aerodynamics of racing cars, and four years later was involved in the design of Brooklands, the world's first banked high-speed test track, where he was accompanied on some of his record-breaking attempts by Alexander. These included a notable 24-hour marathon, driven entirely by Edge at an average speed of over 60mph, with the circuit lit at night by storm lanterns.

In an early example of the company's wider services to motorists, a motor oil price list distributed by Duckhams in 1912 (the year of the *Titanic* disaster) carried a section detailing the principal speed traps worked by the police over the previous three years. Also included was a testimonial from a customer, a certain Will Clayton:

'I have used nothing else but your Special Superheated Steam Oil for the lubrication of my White Steam Car the whole of this season, during which time I have done over 500 miles. I overhauled the Engine last week to see exactly what condition it was in, and was delighted at the Beautiful State ...'

In addition to lubricants, a further spin-off from the growing involvement with motoring at this time was Duckhams 'Motorist Cleansing Oil', a mixture of hydrocarbon solvent, soap and water. Users were directed to 'Rub a little of the Motorist Cleansing Oil on the soiled (dry) hands then rub in about the same amount of water from the tap. Now rinse thoroughly under the tap'. This product was the forerunner of many specialist Duckhams formulations that served both the motorist and the industrial worker.

Had the Health & Safety Executive existed at the time, they could no doubt have had a field day, for production methods at Millwall

*The early chain-driven Commer lorries had problems with the muddy Phoenix Wharf site.*

were not without their hazards. Flammable 'slush' oils (preservative products, often dyed with bright colorants) were manufactured in an isolated corner, near the main gates, using old-fashioned tar boilers heated by burning the wooden staves of resin casks. Hardly a week went by without one of these volatile mixtures boiling over, so the local fire brigade became regular visitors to Phoenix Wharf.

Entrance to the works involved negotiating a steep, unsurfaced slope, which in bad weather was a quagmire and a severe challenge to horse-drawn transport. The motorised kind didn't fare much better: when the company bought its first lorry, a chain-drive Commer, in 1913, it was only just about able, on a good day, to get up this driveway without stalling.

With the outbreak of the First World War the following year, a number of staff left for the armed services, while at home Alexander's expertise was called upon in earnest. He found his newly developed lubricants increasingly in demand by industry, particularly where metal

machining was concerned. The work he had done on cutting fluids resulted in a contract to supply the Royal Ordnance factories, where guns and other weaponry were being turned out as fast as possible to supply Britain's forces.

The war brought about rapid advances in the development of the aeroplane, which in turn played a large part in the warfare, in a variety of roles: reconnaissance, artillery spotting and bombing, as well as through the formation of the first fighter squadrons. The concept of the aircraft carrier came into being; flying boats had also been developed and were used for spotting submarines and for longer reconnaissance flights, while seaplanes carrying torpedoes attacked surface shipping.

Alexander and his brothers devoted themselves wholeheartedly to war work. He and Arthur were both appointed to high office in the Ministry of Munitions, for which

*The early laboratory at Millwall. The building was draughty and leaked when it rained!*

services Arthur was knighted in 1917. 'F. W.' became Director of Tank Design, ending up in the USA to take control of tank production there.

Not content with doing one important job, however, Alexander more or less simultaneously held the posts of Deputy Director, General Ordnance, Controller of National Aircraft Factories and Controller of American Aircraft Assembly, while it would hardly be unreasonable to assume that he also continued to maintain some involvement in the activities of his own business! It is nevertheless a tribute to the calibre of the remaining staff that it both survived and prospered. Production work continued unabated, with an oil-fired vacuum still being installed in 1916 to replace the hazardous wood-fired heating methods.

It seems that Alexander was keen to play an even greater part in the war effort, which he sought from the coalition government's munitions minister at the time, a certain Winston Churchill. A reply dated 10 November 1917 reads:

**Dear Mr Alexander Duckham**
I am very much obliged to you for your kind letter.

I am very sensible of the fact that your activities will not be fully occupied in the sphere of work which it is in my power at present to assign to you. At the same time the production of machine guns and the development of the new factory constitute tasks of the highest importance to the Army in the future campaign.

It is my desire that you should continue your care of the Government Rolling Mills, and I hope on my return from abroad to revive your connection with the enquiry into the organisation and staffing of the Department. If, at any time, I feel that there is no work of first rate importance available

for you, I will not fail to let you know, but that is certainly not the case at present.
**Believe me,**
**Yours very truly,**
**Winston Churchill**

There is anecdotal evidence that Alexander may have declined honours offered to him for his public service during the war. Following the end of hostilities, the story goes, someone expressed surprise that he had received no

*Alexander's elder brother Sir Arthur Duckham GBE KCB held a number of high-ranking official posts before his untimely death in 1932.*

# THE ALEXANDER DUCKHAM MEMORIAL SCHOOLS TRUST

In 1920 Alexander Duckham presented his former family home, Vanbrugh Castle in Maze Hill, Blackheath, south-east London, to the RAF Benevolent Fund, to provide a school for the children of RAF airmen killed during service.

Made in memory of Alexander's daughter Dinah, who had died at the age of 18 months, this original gift was augmented at the beginning of the Second World War by the donation of another of his properties, Rooks Hill House and the surrounding 200-acre estate, for similar purposes. The latter was eventually sold in 1961, the proceeds of £15,600 being added to the existing £12,317 in the Alexander Duckham Memorial Fund to form an endowment for Vanbrugh Castle School.

Having served the educational and spiritual needs of the children of two World Wars, in 1976, with the agreement of the Charity Commissioners, Vanbrugh Castle too was sold and the school amalgamated with Woolpit School at Ewhurst, Surrey. The new school, now owned and controlled by the RAF Benevolent Fund, was renamed Duke of Kent School, in honour of the President of the Fund.

With the numbers of needy service children decreasing following 50 mainly peaceful years in Europe, the Commissioners in 1997 decreed that the school should be constituted as a separate charity outside the RAF Benevolent Fund (although the two bodies continue to maintain close relations).

The Alexander Duckham Memorial Fund and the Rooks Hill Fund, identified as being for the benefit of service families in need, together with the whole of the Duke of Kent School Estate, were embodied within the new charity, named the Alexander Duckham Memorial Schools Trust, the present value of which now runs into millions of pounds.

Situated in a beautiful wooded setting between Guildford and Cranleigh, the Duke of Kent School in Ewhurst is a flourishing co-educational preparatory and pre-prep school for both boarding and day pupils, whose interests are controlled by the Alexander Duckham Trust. Six trustees and nine governors, under the chairmanship of Air Vice-Marshal Michael Adams CB, AFC, FRAeS, oversee the Trust and the school affairs respectively.

The current Charity Commission Scheme provides that, in allocating places at the school, the trustees shall give priority to children of serving and former members of the RAF (to include the WRAF, WAAF, Auxiliary Air Force, RAF Reserves and Commonwealth Air Forces) who are in need of financial assistance. Any remaining

vacancies may then be filled by RAF children who are not deemed to be in financial need, followed by children of serving and former members of any other branch of the armed forces.

Pupils currently number some 190, including 70 boarders. Headmaster Roger Wilson MA retires in August 1999 and is succeeded by Dr Alan Cameron, under whom the school will continue its aims of providing a stable, ordered, caring and above all happy environment in which each child is given the opportunity to discover and develop as far as possible his or her own skills, providing the confidence necessary for success in later life. Considerable emphasis is laid on pastoral care and each child is the special responsibility of one of six pastoral tutors, all of whom are readily available to the children.

*Vanbrugh Castle, pictured in the late 1970s.*

recognition from the British Government. His reported reply is typical: 'It was suggested to me, and I am flattered, but somehow it goes against the grain. Not only did I have a splendid time performing the duties which it was my privilege to carry out, but what's more – I was spared the trenches!'

Sir Arthur Duckham, always actively involved in public affairs, went on to pursue a special interest in economics as they affected both Britain and the Empire. A member of the 1919 Sankey Coal Commission, he was responsible for the minority report it issued. He led a British Economic Mission to Australia in 1928, receiving on his return the honour of GBE to add to his KCB.

Wartime and its fuel shortages clearly had an effect on private motoring, and therefore on Duckhams' domestic sales. While in Britain the Government urged drivers not to use cars for non-essential journeys, some converted their vehicles to run on coal gas and other petrol substitutes, entailing huge gas-bags mounted on the roof, or towed behind in a trailer. Another interesting effect, however, resulted from the shortage of men in the community. This made it necessary for women to take over many formerly male jobs, many working in car production or becoming mechanics in garages, which fostered a new market for cars after the war.

Such had been the progress made in aviation that, immediately following the war in 1919, Alcock and Brown were able to complete their historic crossing of the Atlantic, from St John's (Newfoundland) to Ireland in a twin-engined Vickers Vimy aircraft, in 15hrs 57min. That same year Ross Smith flew a similar plane in stages from England to Australia in 124 hours.

It was perhaps a mixture of the appreciation of his privileged position during the war, and of admiration for the job done by the 'magnificent men in their flying machines', with whom he already enjoyed an enduring affinity, that in 1920 inspired Alexander, who now lived in Kent, to donate the former family home, Vanbrugh Castle, to the newly formed RAF Benevolent Fund, for use as a school for the children of airmen killed in service.

The gift is recorded as commemorating Alexander's fourth daughter, Dinah, who had recently died from the 'Spanish flu' at the age of 18 months; he continued to assist the Fund throughout his life, raising large sums of money in addition to his own major donations.

The end of the First World War seems to have inspired a major reorganisation of Alexander Duckham & Co Ltd, with improved management systems and records. It was possibly to disentangle its affairs from those of Trinidad Central Oilfields that the original company went into voluntary liquidation in 1920, a new one of the same name being incorporated. New premises were acquired in Broad Street Place, near London's Liverpool Street Station, into which the sales department moved.

As peace returned to Europe, Britain entered the era of the 'flappers', and for a younger generation – at least for those with money in their pockets – the accent was on having a good time. The prospect of increasing markets, both at home and abroad, meant that Duckhams was poised for major growth …

# Chapter 2

# FAME AND FORTUNE

Following the First World War the American economy entered what was undoubtedly a boom period, often referred to as the 'Roaring Twenties'. The US Prohibition laws, which banned alcohol, caused the upsurge of 'speak-easies' in which it could, albeit illegally, be obtained. During this era the vibrant US pop culture of the time rubbed off on Europe by way of radio, gramophone records and movies, although it would not be until 1927 that Al Jolson in *The Jazz Singer* brought the voice soundtrack to the silver screen for the first time.

At the start of the decade, however, Britain also felt the draught of an economic 'blip' in the USA, with labour unrest on both sides of the Atlantic. Miners' strikes, beginning in 1920 and renewed the next spring, caused a state of emergency to be declared and the food rationing (still in force from the war) to become even more stringent.

Although the miners' stranglehold was broken in April 1921, when the anticipated support from the rail and transport unions within the 'triple alliance' failed to materialise, supply problems already created in the motor industry had killed sales and caused a black market to spring up. William Morris (later Lord Nuffield), who had begun producing his own cars in Oxford before the war and continued to do so throughout the hostilities, held out for as long as possible before being forced to gamble on cutting the price of his Cowley model by a third to below £350.

The move paid off, considerably stimulating sales and persuading other companies that the small, economical family saloon was the way forward. Alexander Duckham & Co Ltd was already collaborating with the works on the special lubrication requirements of Morris's chassis, and this proved to be the preamble to a long and mutually beneficial relationship.

The more sophisticated management style prevailing at Duckhams as it entered the 1920s caused the company to take a long, hard look at the cost-effectiveness of its structure. The lease on Phoenix Wharf was nearing expiry and overheads at the site, especially rates, were high given the mediocre facilities. Memories of Millwall from some former employees give an insight into conditions; pensioner Harry Wood wrote in 1969:

'When I joined Duckhams in 1922 at Millwall as a driver, there were two other drivers besides myself. Wages were £2 10s (£2.50) per week and no driver was paid for any overtime. Hours were 7.30am to 4.30pm Monday to Friday and 7.30am to 12 noon Saturday, although most days finished at 6.00 to 6.30pm and 2.00 to 2.30pm on Saturday. You had to be with the company for three years before being entitled to one week's holiday.'

Another pensioner, A. E. Pearson, recalls:

'I started with Duckhams in January 1922 at a salary of around £3 per week, and considered

*Glimpses of life at
Phoenix Wharf circa
1920: employees
Standring and Bennett
on the loading stage;
barrel-making in the
cooperage section;
and a works outing.*

myself very fortunate to have a job. However, conditions were primitive, the office was a wooden hut and 5-gallon drums were often used to catch rivulets of rainwater that came through the roof …'

While typical of those prevailing at the time, these working conditions certainly sound less than ideal, so the entire staff must have been delighted when the decision was taken to move to new purpose-built premises. In 1921 a freehold Thames-side site was purchased at a cost of £14,000 at Hammersmith, building work commencing almost immediately.

With the sales staff already relocated to the City, the laboratory was moved to a building in Johnson Street, Minories. At around this time also, the employees must have gained further encouragement when the company instituted a profit-sharing and bonus scheme, a concept well ahead of its time.

Although Alexander Duckham, perhaps by his own wish, received no honours for his war services, his company had probably reaped its

own rewards as a result of the intensive research that had been dictated by military requirements. Continuing concentration on motor oil development enabled Duckhams in 1922 to launch its revolutionary New Process Oils, the outstanding feature of which promised the answer to the contemporary motorist's prayer – the control of carbon deposits.

So great was the carbon bugbear that any antidote was destined to be grabbed with both hands by the motoring classes. And so it was: within a year New Process Oils were specified by the makers of more than 60 British cars. Even the special lubrication problems of the air-cooled engines, like those of the contemporary Rover 8 and Vauxhall, proved to be overcome by specially formulated grades.

Here can be seen perhaps the first indica-

*Duckhams' exceptionally pure 'New Process Oils' were increasingly adopted by vehicle manufacturers whose names became attached to their specific blends.*

tions of the modern-day concept of 'own-branding', with the marketing of, for example, 'Duckhams Trojan Oil' and 'Duckhams Vauxhall Oil'. So rapid was the uptake of the new oils that it also marks the setting up within the company of two distinct divisions, one to service the still important industrial sector, and the other to look after the mushrooming motor industry market.

One of the major features that distinguished Duckhams New Process Oils was the exceptionally thorough filtration to which they were subjected, which included a straining through Fullers Earth. This, however, produced a paler

*William Morris (later Lord Nuffield), the British pioneer of family car mass-production, became a personal friend of Alexander, and Duckhams collaborated on suitable lubricants for Morris cars from their earliest days. Pictured is the Cowley assembly line for the 'Bullnose' Morris of 1925.*

than usual product, and there is evidence of some sales resistance on the part of conservative motorists as a result.

It was more important than ever that they should be able to have complete faith in the product, so great emphasis was placed on ensuring that viscosity characteristics were maintained. The oil was chilled to below 0°F to solidify substances that would normally cause it to congeal; these could then be extracted, leaving it 'clear, limpid and as nearly as may be unaffected by changes to temperature'. An elaborate system of quality control included tests for oxidation and coking.

Amazingly, given the unprecedented demand for the new oils and the upheavals of the various moves, production began at the Hammersmith works in 1923, with Millwall being vacated. The new plant included a 5-ton, coal-fired grease autoclave, to Duckhams' own specification; this was quickly converted to gas heating when better temperature control was found to be needed.

Over the next few years demand for New Process Oils continued to grow and a proper brand name was sought. After some deliberation, from 1926 the name Adcol was decided upon for one section of the motor oils range, this and its variations figuring prominently for many years afterwards.

That year, however, was a black one for Britain, with the long-rumbling dispute between the miners and their employers escalating into the General Strike, in which many thousands of other workers came out in sympathy. As had happened earlier in the decade, a central food and milk depot was opened in London's Hyde Park, and volunteers joined soldiers in maintaining essential services. The strike lasted only a short time, but, with a demoralised and dissatisfied workforce, Britain remained in poor shape for the even greater economic tribulations to come.

From the letter to shareholders in 1927 we

*Duckhams 'Morrisol' became the official recommendation for Morris and Wolseley vehicles from 1931.*

learn that the annual profits of Alexander Duckham & Co over the five years ended 31 December 1926 had averaged a satisfactory £11,921. Trinidad Central Oilfields had now become, temporarily, the major shareholder in Alexander Duckham & Co, the main reason apparently being to satisfy the Trinidad Government of its solid financial base.

The Western World, however, was about to be gripped by the worst economic depression ever seen, as the decade that had come in with a roar ended in tears. On 24 October 1929 almost 13 million shares were offloaded at virtually any price on the New York Stock Exchange as panic swept through the market, and both large and small investors were left ruined.

The fallout from the crash was rapidly exported to a Britain that had itself already been sliding into depression. Pensioner H. E. Price recalls:

'I joined the company in July 1929 in Broad Street, EC, as area sales manager for the Midlands region, and was paid £400 per year plus small commissions on the sales of oil in my area ... bankruptcies were rising daily and old-established firms of all sizes were sacking staff. Duckhams profits fell to the point where no dividend could be paid. The sales force was reduced to an absolute minimum and paid commission only; senior sales staff were given the same treatment and were put "on the road".'

While unemployment and poverty were once again rife into the early 1930s, and industrial production was at rock-bottom, the better off continued to drive their motor cars, maintaining at least some demand for the company's lubricants.

And cars continued to sell. If New Process Oils needed any further testimonial, they were to receive it in 1931 when Sir William Morris selected one of the grades as the sole recommended oil for his Morris and Wolseley marques, as well as for Morris Commercial vehicles, and the brand 'Morrisol' was launched.

This brought a legal letter from a certain Matthew Wells & Co, who had been marketing an oil under the same name. Morris, undeterred, decreed that henceforth the Duckhams oil would be known as 'Morrisol "Sirrom" regd' (thus incorporating his name spelt both forwards and backwards), and that this was 'the only oil recommended by Morris Motors Ltd and Wolseley Motors (1927) Ltd'.

Just one variety of the by now famous Duckhams New Process Oils, Morrisol 'Sirrom', was to hold 'sole recommended' status for Morris and Wolseley right up to 1946, with all lubricants for the Cowley plant also being supplied by Duckhams. Oil from Duckhams NP range was now actually specified by the makers of more than 90 per cent of British cars, including all Austin models, Bentley and Invicta; New Process Oils also enjoyed 'approved' status from Rolls-Royce, Humber and Rover.

The year 1931 also saw more major expansion and reorganisation and, with the workforce now numbering some 250, Alexander's son Jack Duckham was appointed to the board of directors. Jack's childhood spent at Vanbrugh Castle, living above his father's laboratory, had ensured an early initiation into the workings of the firm.

From school at Oundle, he had intended to go directly to university, but Alexander arranged for him to spend a year in Trinidad as an apprentice oil-well driller, maintaining that practical experience in the oil industry was needed before attempting the theory.

Entering Clare College, Cambridge, he studied geology, applied chemistry and engineering before joining the company on the retail side, where he was given responsibility for liaison with customers throughout the country.

Also in 1931 a freehold site for a second works, in Holyport Road, Fulham, was purchased for £9,000, while the sales department was on the move again, this time from the outgrown Broad Street Place premises to new offices in Cannon Street, leased from Prudential Assurance and grandly retitled Duckhams House.

In 1932 Alexander's younger brother Sir Arthur Duckham died unexpectedly, at the height of his career. His place on the board was taken by Professor J. S. S. Brame, an eminent scientist and a past President of the Institute of Petroleum Technologists. (At around the same time, their older brother 'F. W.', hale and hearty at well over 70 years of age, was heard to be organising an expedition to recover the £5 million worth of treasure reputed to be aboard the East Indiaman *Grosvenor*, wrecked off the coast of Pongoland, southern Africa, 150 years earlier!)

Works No 2 opened in Fulham, following reconstruction to provide production facilities as well as offices, laboratories and storage. A sulphurisation plant with fume-scrubbing tower had to be installed for the production of neat sulphurised cutting oils, and shortly afterwards a soda base grease plant was added.

Meanwhile work continued at Hammersmith, with a building erected to house a new filling plant for small packs. The long frontage on to the Thames provided an excellent vantage point for the University Boat Race, and each year many hundreds of

*Alexander's son Jack Duckham joined the company in 1931. He was to take over as chairman following his father's death.* (Navana Vandyk Ltd)

friends and customers joined the directors to watch the event.

An important innovation of 1932 was the launch of Duckhams' first house publication, *Links*. Intended to inform customers rather than staff, it mixed 'general interest' articles, like a piece on the developing aircraft industry, with 'soft sell' technical information. The background message all the time was that

*The prestigious Cannon Street office building occupied by Duckhams in 1931 was destroyed by enemy bombs during the war.*

quality will always give better returns in the long run.

By now Alexander, always interested in something new, had taken up pig-breeding, and this led the company into further product diversification: the development of an oil for grooming and nourishing the skin of animals. The result was Duckhams 'Arkoil', which during the 1930s was being supplied to London and Whipsnade Zoos, among others, where it was used for various applications including treating the shells of tortoises. The dogs at Battersea Dogs' Home were also

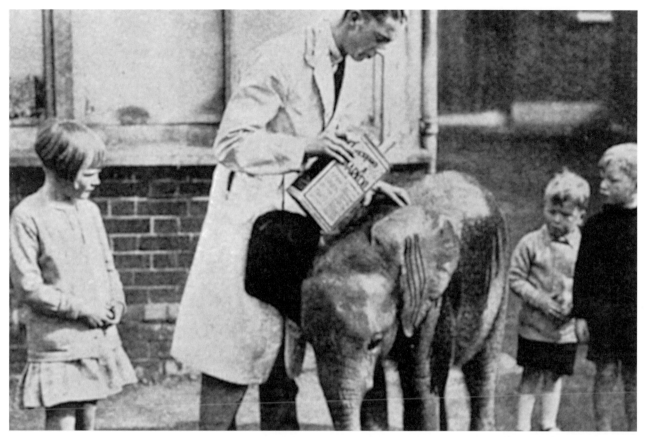

treated regularly with it. An article in the 1932 *Links* describes Arkoil as:

'… unexcelled for cleaning and softening the skin of animals, whilst in the case of dogs, for example, it imparts to the coat a beautifully glossy sheen such as one aims at when showing. It keeps an animal free from all undesirable trespassers, in addition to which it is antiseptic and pleasant to touch and to smell.

'Similar attention [should be] given to the animal internally; and here again Arkoil is particularly effective … so pure and innocuous that it can be used to lubricate internally – a baby, a watch or an elephant. Unlike castor oil, it can be given in any quantity without danger or without any griping or irritating effect – in fact, it soothes inflamed or sensitive membranes.'

Then came a bit of soft sell:

*Duckhams 'Arkoil' was a remarkable unction for treating the skin of animals. Here it is being applied to a baby elephant at London Zoo.*

'The smallest package in which Arkoil is sold is 1-gallon cans at 7s 6d [38p], but we are quite prepared to supply readers of *Links* with special 8-oz samples at 1s 6d [8p] each, post free. Such a sample is quite sufficient to prove to a dog-lover how efficacious is Duckhams Arkoil, but of course, where the need for a larger quantity is felt, it is naturally far more economical to buy in barrels or 5-gallon drums.'

While the quality of today's electronically originated magazines may be visually slick and colourful, much of the content is superficial and shallow when compared to the early editions of the monochrome *Links*, whose articles are well written, carefully edited and informative, even if some of them do reflect

*" I suppose, then . . . you will send me back, making the excuse of ' No demand ' ? "*

*'Monty Morrisol' (seen here) and 'Archie Adcol' featured in an educational product series in* Links *during the 1930s.*

their times in not being particularly 'PC'. Today's sophisticated publicity manager would probably cringe, too, at the quaint sales angles pursued in its pages.

Take, for example, 'Monty Morrisol', the cartoon character employed to relate the story of the oil as it cleans and protects the engine, a theme that ran through the first year of publication:

'Hallo everybody! This is Monty Morrisol speaking and here I am squeezed into a beautifully clean can, parked in soldierly fashion with thousands of other chaps. Pretty dark inside here, of course, but I'm feeling perfectly fit and nothing matters.

'Hallo! What's happening now? I feel myself rudely hauled down, there is a sharp pop followed by a tearing of metal as my sealing cap is burst open and I see daylight. Then gurgle! gurgle! away I go, sliding and

tumbling into a capacious chamber with just a glimmer of daylight above it. What's to happen next I am soon to learn as I feel myself being forcibly drawn through the engine …'

Monty's heroics were clearly deemed to be achieving results, for during the next year he was joined in the pages of *Links* by 'Archie Adcol', promoting the New Process Oils to the few unconverted motor manufacturers.

Both cartoon characters were eventually phased out with the completion of this 'oil education' campaign, but *Links* continued to inform, with regular articles on the industries of the day. Many of the companies concerned were already household names that, usually, had some connections with Duckhams products.

There were, for example, the special type-mould oils supplied to Monotype Corporation. 'Hot metal' typecasting was a precision operation, since the slightest variation in the size of a single character could cause major headaches for compositors in the course of a large block of text. Consequently the moving parts had to be maintained in perfect order, a job for Duckhams Monotype Mould Oil, which both cleaned and lubricated the moulds and was supplied to the Monotype Corporation and its customers for many years. Similarly, in the civil engineering field Wimpey Construction, already prolific users of Duckhams Concrete Mould Oils, would still be a major customer some 50 years later.

The 'quality equals economy' theme was of continuing importance. An article in June 1933 points out the 'extravagance of using inferior lubricants' in commercial vehicles:

'The man in the street and, it may be said, some operators of commercial fleets, cherish the misguided opinion that commercial vehicles do not require the best in motor fuel or the best in oil because – well, they are only commercial vehicles. The older they become, the more confirmed the opinion, hence they reach the scrap heap years before they need do.

'Omnibuses, in particular, are prone to crank case dilution troubles brought about by continual stopping and restarting, the trouble, of course, being aggravated during cold weather operation. An oil which can stand up to a fair percentage of dilution without completely breaking down is, therefore, most desirable if undue wear is to be prevented right throughout the engine.

'... a worm-driven rear axle may not give audible warning of approaching trouble, but, at the same time, quality lubrication is certainly vital to long life. Nothing but the best lubricant is good enough here, and that is why our "D.B.S." Worm Gear Oil is so largely used by fleet owners throughout the country.'

The article is illustrated by photographs of some AEC public service vehicles of the time, all using exclusively Duckhams lubricants:

*Duckhams Concrete Mould Oil was a significant contribution from the industrial products side of the company to the construction industry, aiding clean release from the timber form and enabling its re-use. It was used on this grain silo, seen under construction at London's Royal Victoria Dock in 1933. (*Links *magazine)*

Regent double-deckers owned by Bournemouth and Colchester Corporations, a Regal single-decker coach from the Quest Coaches fleet, and an older double-decker operated by Pro Bono Publico in London.

Export sales were assuming more importance in view of the continuing recession at home, where by 1933 oil consumption had fallen by a quarter since 1929. *Links* helped forge connections with overseas markets, where Duckhams leadership in oil technology provided ready scope for exports. From the 1920s agents had been appointed in strategic locations to provide the necessary local knowledge and product handling, with partic-

ular attention given to the then numerous Commonwealth countries, where British products were held in high esteem.

In Australasia, for example, New Zealand was handled by Hayward Bros & Co Ltd, who had branches in Auckland, Wellington, Dunedin and Lyttelton, while the agents in Melbourne, Victoria, were Ramsay & Treganowan Ltd. Balmer Lawrie & Co Ltd, who took over as main agents in India in 1933, were established back in 1876 and had wide-ranging interests, acting as main agents for some 25 companies operating in the sub-continent, including tea plantations, paper and flour mills, coal companies and construction concerns, and representing many British

*A splendid Duckhams Morris Dictator tanker (built on a bus chassis) pictured in 1932 with an Abingdon-built MG J2 Midget – another marque highly favoured by Alexander and which in fact derived from the Morris stable. (Chas K. Bowers & Sons)*

firms, mainly in the engineering field.

*Links* also provided a social service in covering health topics, and sometimes these were product-related, as in the case of skin care. Alexander's long involvement in industrial metal machining, through cutting fluid development, had brought to his attention the various skin disorders suffered by operatives. Not only did he publish articles and booklets on the subject, but he ensured that Duckhams became leaders in skin cleansers and treatments for workers.

The monotonous drudgery of many workers' jobs, not to mention the cost of heating their homes, found an escape route in the evenings and weekends through the cinema, the popularity of which was soaring. Full houses and queues were the norm, and film shows often included live stage or circus acts; however, with tuberculosis rife at the time, cinema-goers often had to endure being sprayed with disinfectant by the usherettes! On the way home, an amorous lad might treat his girlfriend to a fish supper for 4d (2p).

The recession may have curtailed motoring, but it couldn't stem the desire for ownership of the latest cars, among which were the products of Cecil Kimber's MG Car Company in Abingdon. Alexander had borrowed an MG Midget roadster in Trinidad during one of his sojourns there, and 'so impressed was he with its performance, particularly … the manner in which it handled over some of the none too good roads traversed', that on his return to Britain he immediately placed an order for one of the company's Magnette sports saloons.

Perhaps there was just a hint of currying favour here for, following a laudatory *Links* article on the production at the Abingdon

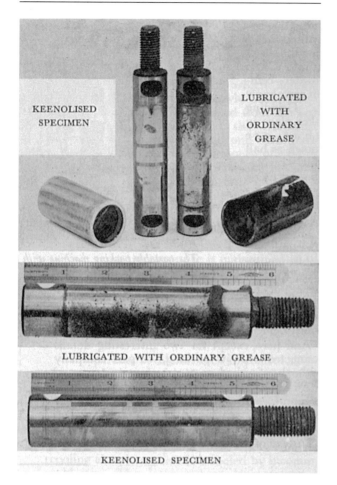

KEENOLISED
SPECIMEN

LUBRICATED
WITH
ORDINARY
GREASE

LUBRICATED WITH ORDINARY GREASE

KEENOLISED SPECIMEN

*'Keenolisation', using Duckhams patented range of lubricants containing colloidal zinc oxide, offered substantial advantages in applications such as highly stressed gears. It formed an adherent film on the metal surface that was continually replaced as wear took place. (*Links* magazine)*

factory, in September 1933 MG gave sole recommendation to Duckhams N.P.5 (Aero) Oil for engine lubrication, and Duckhams Gear Oil 'N' for gearbox and back axle lubrication of all their models. *Links* reported glowingly:

'We think it can be said without reservation that the most popular sports car in this country is the MG ... The reason for its popularity is not far to seek. In appearance the *tout ensemble* of the MG is the materialisation of

the technical artist's conception of what a sports car should be, and, what is more important, its performance is such as to satisfy the most sporting of enthusiasts ... There can be no question that the successful performance of MG cars has been responsible for enhancing the prestige of the British motor industry all over the world.

'... As the makers of these oils we are proud of being so honoured, especially as the oil has been selected, after prolonged and severe tests, on its merits, and still more because the MG Car Company Ltd, in making this selection, has not asked for and are not receiving any financial advantage for such decision ... Lastly, it is yet another triumph for an all-British firm.'

A number of the motor dealers whose names are recognised as major groups today were growing rapidly during this period, like London's principal Morris agents Stewart & Ardern, who opened new, expanded showrooms and workshops featuring lubrication exclusively by Duckhams.

Morris's service agents, like others, were having to cope with continual advances in technology, one of the most important of which was the advent of the synchromesh gearbox. Until its invention, the only method of achieving a clean, silent gear change was to employ a method known as double-declutching. Synchromesh, as its name implies, is a mechanism designed to synchronise the speed of rotation of the gearshafts as they mesh, doing away with the need to double-declutch. The conventional gearbox oils of the time proved unsuitable for the new mechanism; but, naturally, Duckhams had the answer, as *Links* explained in March 1934:

'The introduction of the synchro-mesh gearbox is without doubt due to car manufac-

*Conceived in 1934, Duckhams Tablets became a mainstay of sales for many years.*

turers' efforts to meet the demand of the motoring public for greater mechanical simplicity of control … achieved by a most subtly designed piece of mechanism for the lubrication of which ordinary gear oil is unsuitable.

'To meet those special conditions Alexander Duckham & Co. Ltd. have evolved a new grade which, after exhaustive tests, has been adopted by both Morris Motors and Wolseley Motors as their exclusive recommendation for use with 1934 models to which synchro-mesh gearboxes are fitted. This new grade is known as Morrisol "Sirrom" (Regd.) Brand Synchro-Gear Oil and its use will make easier changing gears work still more easily.'

The 'factory-fill' contracts with the Midlands car industry meant that regular bulk deliveries of oils had to be maintained. At this time deliveries to the Morris and Wolseley works

*After more than 50 cars, Alexander had a love affair with Bentleys. This is BGF 63, his first, a 3.5-litre convertible.*

were being made, not unnaturally, by three Morris tankers – two Morris Commercial Dictators and a Morris-Carrimore. Even more predictably, they ran on Duckhams Morrisol Commercial "Sirrom" (Regd) Brand Oils, Duckhams' own records confirming the sterling performance of their lubricants in these hard-working vehicles.

By now the particular efficacy of Duckhams engine oils in reducing high oil consumption – until now widely regarded as inevitable – was beginning to gain wider acceptance. This was backed up by customers like the Morris Commercial user who wrote:

'Compared with the ordinary oil previously used the consumption of Morrisol is almost negligible and, when we tell you that nothing has been done to the vehicles since Morrisol was put in, you will realise our satisfaction.

'Actually of our previous oil we were using a pint per day per vehicle and we thought that the price of 2s 8d [14p] per gallon was a fair figure. Your Morrisol, however, gives a consumption of one pint per vehicle per week.

Our business demands service and we, in turn, appreciate service when we get it. Hence this letter.'

Apart from the direct automotive applications, the continuing development work on the industrial side resulted in a number of break-throughs. An example is the research into the deterioration of steel surfaces, which culminated in the concept of 'Keenolisation'.

A patented range of lubricants containing colloidal zinc oxide, 'Keenol' offered substantial advantages in applications such as highly stressed gears, where pitting and corrosion were prevalent. On the theory that these were caused by electrical disturbance at the point of contact, the introduction of the zinc compound made the lubricant anodic to the steel, creating an electrolytic couple and forming an adherent film on the metal surface. As wear took place through the stress of operation, this film was instantly replaced. Keenol soon began to be promoted by means of a touring caravan, which housed a display for industrial customers.

Alexander Duckham's prescient chairman's report to the company's 1934 AGM refers to large, foreign combines entering the British market and cutting the prices of lubricants in order to gain sales of petroleum and fuel oils. (This was to be a recurring problem for the company; the majors with their large fuel sales were also able to apply profits from these to subsidise their lubricant prices.) He pointed out that several of the old-established firms had suffered, but that Duckhams remained in a strong position to counter this foreign competition, thanks not only to its modest size but also its policy of concentrating research on solving the problems encountered by industry.

Ironically perhaps, Duckhams' size meant that it remained vulnerable, although the biggest changes that would affect it, later in the century, were to come about through its relations with a British company rather than

*A quayside delivery to SS* Dunbar Castle, *circa 1934.*

one of the foreign giants by whom he felt threatened …

Were these occasional glimpses of xenophobia from the well-travelled Alexander provoked perhaps by the events he could see unfolding on the Continent, where Nazi party leader Adolf Hitler had just become Chancellor of Germany? We cannot tell, but soon afterwards *Links* quoted an article in *The Times* lamenting the diminishing birthrate in the British Empire:

'… this will ultimately lead to a crisis, in that sparsely inhabited Dominions which could not be filled by British stock will be filled sooner or later, peacefully or otherwise, with aliens … Before very long, with improved economic conditions, the Dominions will be clamouring for greater populations, for more British stock of the right kind to fill their unoccupied territories. Are we going to fail them?'

As the effects of recession were gradually supplanted by beneficial ones deriving from preparations for rearmament, the company's most lucrative new product of this inter-war period was again in the motoring field. Duckhams 'Running-in Tablets', simply dropped into the fuel filler neck when taking on petrol, at the rate of one tablet for every 2 gallons, were formulated to keep the upper cylinders and combustion chambers in good order. Based on a blend of additives formed into a waxy, solid cube that dissolved in the fuel to complement the performance of the new oils, the tablets were the subject of a British patent in 1934, when Duckhams exhibited at the Motor Show.

As their effectiveness became recognised, sales of Running-in Tablets soared and their eventual contribution to the growth of Duckhams in the motoring market is enormous. The company's increasing prosperity is reflected in Alexander's acquisition of BGF 63, a 3.5-litre Bentley drophead coupé, with coachwork by Park Ward.

Duckhams engine oils gained a further useful boost when in the same year W. G. Everitt, driving an MG at Brooklands, broke the world record (H class) for the standing-start kilometre and mile, at 69.75mph and 79.88mph respectively, using standard Adcol N.P.5 (Aero) oil. Despite the engine speeds of almost 7,000rpm, this pure mineral oil performed at least as well as the vegetable-based oils normally used for such demanding trials.

Among other records broken that year using Duckhams oils were the fastest time for the London–Copenhagen–London return flight, set by Capt Neville Stack in a Gipsy Major

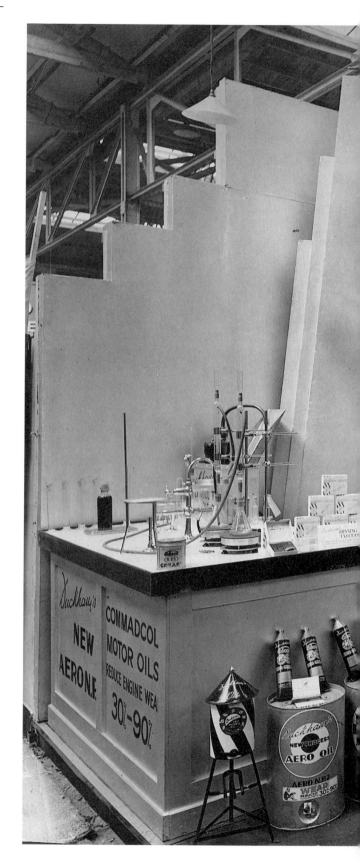

*An exhibition stand circa 1935 featuring N.P. (Aero) and Adcol motor oils together with industrial products. (H. J. Whitlock & Sons Ltd)*

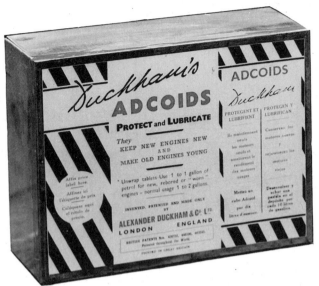

*Those tablets again, in their final incarnation from 1936 as Duckhams Adcoids.*

Miles Hawk aircraft, and a new best time for covering 24 nautical miles (inboard unlimited class boats) achieved by Arthur Bray in his 92hp Chrysler-engined 18-foot Chris Craft.

The latest, uprated Adcol and NP oils were using corrosion inhibitors and, following successful experience in private car engines, these were extended to the commercial vehicle oil range with the launch of Commadcol at the beginning of 1935 – the Silver Jubilee year of King George V and Queen Mary. To compensate for the increasing use of solvent-extracted 'thin' grades, whose advantage of lower viscosity at low temperatures also brought the danger of reduced lubricity, the addition of Adcoid material increased 'oiliness' – the ability of the lubricant to adhere tenaciously to the metal and maintain an unbroken film.

With today's advanced marketing and promotional techniques still in their infancy, Duckhams now began to pioneer the kinds of ideas that still have their devotees among the professionals more than 50 years later. A free life insurance scheme was introduced,

*One of the original wall thermometers commissioned to promote Adcoids.*

designed to promote both sales of oils and the garage trade. Anyone purchasing a 5-gallon drum of Adcol NP Oil through a recognised garage became entitled to £500 worth of free insurance cover against his or her death in a motor accident occurring during use of that oil (defined as six months from the purchase).

Other schemes designed to aid peace of mind included the Duckhams Key Ring Assistance programme (motorists applied for a key ring bearing a unique number, which in the event of the keys being found enabled the company to identify the owner and return them by post) and the Driving Licence Reminder scheme, where drivers registered their licence expiry date with Duckhams and received a reminder in good time to renew, thus avoiding the invalidation of their insurance. Road maps were also published, showing national and urban routes.

The retirement of P. N. Hooper after 30 years' service in 1936 created a board vacancy that was filled by the chief chemist, Stanley Bowrey, who had joined the company in 1910 having previously worked with Alexander in

his private laboratory at Vanbrugh Castle.

With the realisation that Running-in Tablets were widely regarded by motorists as beneficial long after the end of the running-in period, these were cannily renamed 'Duckhams Wear-Cure Tablets'. Advertising under the new name in the national press, and on the currently popular sandwich boards, ensured a further explosion in demand, requiring additional plant to be installed, including automatic wrapping equipment. Such was the 'brand awareness' (as we would now call it) among consumers that the tablets, now packed in boxes of a dozen, could soon be renamed again simply 'Duckhams Tablets'.

While the tablets were designed to dissolve in the fuel tank, a very small number of complaints (literally one in five million sales) were received to the effect that a tank with no filter at the outlet pipe had been blocked by

*The later Thames-side (Works No 1) site at Hammersmith, showing a makeshift 'stand' erected for guests to watch the Boat Race in 1938.*

*Alexander's all-time favourite car, which he named 'Sheer Joy', was CXB 277, this tailor-made Bentley 4.25-litre drophead coupé with Youngs bodywork. (F. N. Birkett)*

fragments of undissolved tablet. A further patent application of 1936 shows that the production technique was modified to incorporate a gas into the tablet, which aided flotation until fully dissolved.

'Envy vandalism', which nowadays often

*Alexander's country mansion Rooks Hill House, near Sevenoaks in Kent, was used by him to provide holidays for needy children, later being gifted to the RAF.*

manifests itself in scraping a key or knife along the paintwork of a new car, is clearly not new: investigation of 'unjustified' complaints about the tablets showed that two of the blockages were caused by sugar in the fuel tank, and another by soap. Something else that has not changed is consumers' failure to read instructions – motorists who omitted to remove the wrappers before putting the tablets into their tank could surely not have been anticipated!

With testimonials declaring that the tablets did indeed provide not only engine protection but also fuel savings, by this time both Duckhams oils and the tablets were being officially recommended by the car manufac-

turers. The Austin Motor Co, for example, specified Duckhams Tablets for the 'top' end and Duckhams NP oil for the 'bottom'.

The American-owned Ford Motor Co, on the other hand, had only just come around to setting its coveted seal of approval on Duckhams NP (Aero) oils for all cars, trucks and tractors. Its caution was hardly justified: that same year Morrisol oil was used in the engine of a six-cylinder Morris 25 by a transnational expedition crew who covered 3,381 miles from Britain to Nigeria in just over seven days.

History does not record whether the team also used Duckhams Tablets, but the sales explosion in these had already sparked one spurious imitation, prompting Duckhams to indulge in a further spot of branding: in their final, most famous incarnation the tablets now became Duckhams Adcoids.

As rearmament peaked during the late 1930s, in response to the increasing threat from Nazi Germany, Alexander Duckham voiced his concern about the 'boom-bust' economy that was becoming the order of the day. With industry now moving into over-capacity, the company had cause to thank the motoring side – and particularly Adcoids – for maintaining turnover levels, and the advertising of the product as an 'engine tonic' was maintained.

As far as we know, Alexander was not a gambling man, but there is constant evidence of his uncanny sense of the right horse to back. In 1936 the company had one of its Morris staff cars fitted with a Perkins 'Wolf' high-speed diesel engine (the term 'high-speed' being relative, as it revved to just over 3,000rpm), racking up many thousands of business miles in it, and prompting an interesting debate as to whether the compression-ignition engine would ever catch on for private cars.

In November 1936 it was reported that the car had just completed its first six months' service, covering 17,000 miles and showing a pronounced saving in fuel costs. Calculated on an annual basis this amounted to around £65, 'more than twice covering the additional depreciation on the more expensive (in first cost only) diesel engine'. At 25,000 miles Jack Duckham reported: 'When one remembers that the stage of development of diesel engines is the same as that, say, for the petrol engine of 10 or 12 years ago, it would appear that there is a rosy future for the former.'

George V passed away in January 1936 and by December his successor, Edward VIII, had

*Some of the constituents of Adcoids were added to New Process Oils from 1937.*

abdicated, resulting in the Coronation in May 1937 of the new monarch, George VI.

Alexander Duckham was still indulging his passion for cars, of which he admitted to having owned 49 in 30 years of motoring. As a 60th birthday present to himself he replaced his 3.5-litre Bentley with a 4.25-litre convertible model, CXB 277, tailored to his own requirements:

'I decided to let myself go and embody those fads and gadgets which I had so often in mind but which I had been too slack to put into effect and therefore accepted the orthodox. So as not to spoil the beauty of line and finish, the car has an all-black body with a grey head and is devoid of excrescences such as "A.A." or other badges and radiator cap mascot. That greatest eye-sore of all – the spare wheel – has also been made to disappear.

'I place on record my appreciation of the patience and real enthusiasm displayed by Mr G. H. Wenham, managing director of Messrs James Young & Co, of Bromley – the body builders – in evolving ways and means for incorporating my unorthodox ideas and for the perfect work turned out.'

The car was indeed a beautiful example. Alexander gave Youngs a selection of the things he always carried (clothes brush, Adcoids, tobacco tin, packet of Ryvita, AA guide, keys, etc) so that the glovebox could be specially built with appropriate compartments. Besides that spare wheel, the boot contained a small refrigerator, built by Duckhams' own laboratory and cooled by solid carbon dioxide, that held four half-pint bottles of beer and a snack. Two pigskin suitcases, fitted into the space behind the seats, held items that might blow around when the hood was lowered, while the rear window blind carried the word 'THANKS' so that it could be temporarily yanked up to acknowledge the courtesy of another driver.

Not that Alexander, who was by now clearly a wealthy man, simply indulged his own whims. Having acquired the beautiful country property Rooks Hill House, near Sevenoaks in Kent, some years previously, he now found it too large for everyday living but loved it too dearly to sell it. Instead he conceived the idea of making the house, with its 200-acre estate, available to provide holidays for children of poor families.

Alexander himself moved into a cottage on the estate, while the house would be occupied by children – boys up to five and girls up to seven – gathered together by the non-denominational body of Infant Care Associations. The house could occupy 60 children and a staff of 15 helpers, with stays lasting three or four weeks. Costs, including those of the helpers, were said to work out at 10 shillings (50p) per child per week, with Alexander liable for rates only during the periods of occupation; and he professed himself amply repaid by the pleasure this arrangement gave him.

In 1937 Duckhams' relationship with the motor industry was set in stone, as it were, when Earl's Court, which for so long afterwards would be the home of the British Motor Show, was constructed – using, naturally, Duckhams Concrete Mould Oils. It was also the year in which George Joyce, who had joined as office junior 30 years earlier, was appointed to the Duckhams board.

Advances in the packaging field are seen later that year when the company began to offer sealed cans for 'small-packaged' oils, as a smart, convenient alternative to the customary glass bottles: 'A sealed can will give the consumer the confidence that he is getting the grade and the brand he asks for, in perfect condition, in quality and quantity exactly as it left the refinery.' To help promote the new packaging the 'Duckhams Canned Oil Cabinet' was introduced, a simple structure holding 36 cans for quick dispensing on the forecourt.

The move coincided with the incorporation

*A 1930s Morris Commercial box van in 'Aero N.P. Oils' livery. (Chas K. Bowers & Sons)*

into the Aero NP Oils of certain components of Adcoids; followed soon afterwards by similarly upgraded Commadcol, these 'Adcoidised' lubricants represented a further important advance towards the sophisticated blends available today.

In 1938 the company acquired a new member of staff in the person of the Hon Ruth Cokayne, daughter of Lord Cullen of Ashbourne (a former Governor of the Bank of England). Well known as a keen pilot, Ruth's scientific bent had led her to invent the SU Thermoil Lubricator, a device for reducing wear in petrol engines when starting from cold.

The initial version, factory-fitted to some of the more powerful Wolseleys, used the SU thermostatic carburettor as a means of introducing special upper cylinder lubricant into the engine only during the warm-up period; a later development, with its own thermostatic control, was suitable for use with any type of carburettor. The upper cylinder lubricant itself was named Duckhams Adcayne, presumably after the system's inventor.

The company was at pains to point out that the device in no way supplanted Adcoids, but was supplementary to them. Sales of Adcoids themselves peaked at some four million packs (or 48 million tablets) in that year when, at the annual salesmen's dinner held at the Langham Hotel in London's West End, Alexander spoke fondly of the product as 'the company's baby' – promptly going on to pronounce it the 'penultimate baby' as he announced another breakthrough, a stay-put grease for leaf springs named Laminoid. Once again the company was on a roll …

*Names to conjure with: many of the makes listed in this early application chart have since disappeared without trace.*

# RECOMMENDED GRADES

## How to Read this Chart :

| | |
|---|---|
| 2. | Means Duckham's AERO N.P.2 (S.A.E.40). |
| 3. | Means Duckham's AERO N.P.3 (S.A.E.50). |
| 5. | Means Duckham's AERO N.P.5 (S.A.E.60). |
| N. | Means Duckham's Gear Oil " N." |
| N2. | Means Duckham's Gear Oil " N2." |
| S. | Means Duckham's Adcol " S " |
| | (for Constant and Synchro-Mesh Gears) |
| DBS. | Means Duckham's Worm Gear Oil. |
| HBB. | Means Duckham's H.B.B. Grease. |

The S.A.E. (U.S.A.) Specifications corresponding to AERO N.P. Grades are given in brackets.

*DUCKHAM'S MORRISOL " SIRROM " (Regd.) Brand ENGINE, TRANS-MISSION, SYNCHRO-GEAR OIL, WOLSELEY SPECIAL REAR AXLE COMPOUND and H.B.B. GREASE, the ONLY lubricants recommended by the makers of MORRIS and WOLSELEY Cars.

When a car engine has completed 20,000 to 30,000 miles and has not had the engine reconditioned, it may be necessary to use the next grade heavier than is recommended on this chart.

| CAR | Engine. | Gear-box. | Back Axle. | CAR | Engine. | Gear-box. | Back Axle |
|---|---|---|---|---|---|---|---|
| A.B.C. | 3 | N | N | Bentley | 3 | 3 | S |
| A.C. | 3 | S | N | Bentley, 1934 | 3 | S | N |
| Acedes Magna | 3 | S | N | Bentley, 8 litre | 3 | 3 | 2 |
| Acedes Magna (Pre-selector) | 3 | 2 | N | Benz | 3 | S | S |
| A.J.S. | 3 | N | N | Berliet | 3 | S | S |
| Albert | 2 | N | N | Bianchi | 3 | N | N |
| Alfa Romeo | 5 | S | N | Bond | 3 | N | N |
| Alpine Steyr | 3 | 3 | S | Bradshaw | 3 | 3 | N |
| Alta | 5 | S | N | Briton | 2 | N | N |
| Alvis 4 and 6 cylinder | 3 | N | N | B.S.A., 10 h.p. | 3 | 2 | N |
| Alvis (FWD and super- | | | | B.S.A. (3-wheeler) | 3 | N | — |
| charged) | 5 | 5 | N | Bugatti | 5 | S | S |
| Alvis (Pre-selector) | 3 | 2 | N | Buick | 2 | S | N |
| Amilcar | 5 | N | N2 | Cadillac | 2 | N | N |
| Angus Sanderson | 3 | N | N | Calcott | 2 | S | S |
| Ansaldo | 3 | S | N | Calthorpe | 3 | N | N |
| Argyle Sleeve Valve | 2 | 2 | N | Ceirano | 3 | N | N |
| Armstrong Siddeley | 3 | N | N | Chandler | 3 | N | N |
| Armstrong Siddeley (Self- | | | | Charron | 2 | N | N |
| change) | 3 | 2 | N | Charron Laycock | 3 | N | N |
| Arrol Aster Straight 8 | 3 | 3 | N | Chenard Walcker | 3 | S | S |
| Arrol Johnston | 3 | N | N | Chevrolet | 2 | N | N |
| Ascot | 3 | N | N | Chrysler (1931 and previous) | 2 | N | N |
| Ashton Evans | 3 | N | N | Chrysler | 2 | 5 | N |
| Aston Martin | 5 | S | N | Citroen | 3 | S | S |
| Auburn | 3 | N | N | Cleveland | 2 | N | N |
| Aurea | 3 | N | N | Cluley | 3 | S | S |
| Austin (all models) | 3 | 3 | N | Clyde | 3 | N | N |
| Austro Daimler | 3 | S | N | Clyno | 3 | N | N |
| Ballot | 3 | DBS | N | Coventry Victor | 3 | S | S |
| Bean | 3 | N | N | Crossley, 10 h.p. | 3 | N | N |
| Beardmore | 3 | S | S | Crossley 10 (Self-change) | 3 | 2 | N |
| Belsize | 3 | N | N | Crossley, 1934, 2 litre | 5 | 2 | N |

*Duckham's* N.P. OILS CARRY MORE EXCLUSIVE RECOM-

## RECOMMENDED GRADES—cont'd.

| CAR | Engine. | Gear-box. | Back Axle. |
|---|---|---|---|
| Crossley, other models .. | 5 | N | N |
| Crouch .. | 3 | S | S |
| Cubitt .. | 2 | S | S |
| Daimler (others) .. | 3 | S | N |
| Daimler (Self-change) .. | 3 | 2 | N |
| Darracq .. | 3 | S | S |
| De Dion .. | 3 | N | N |
| Delage .. | 3 | S | S |
| Delahaye .. | 2 | S | S |
| Delaunay-Belleville .. | 2 | S | S |
| Derby .. | 5 | N | N |
| De Soto .. | 2 | N | N |
| D.F.P. .. | 3 | N | N |
| Diana .. | 2 | N | N |
| Diatto .. | 5 | S | S |
| Dodge .. | 2 | N | N |
| Dodge (Free Wheel Unit) .. | 2 | 5 | N |
| Donnett-Zedal .. | 2 | N | N |
| Durant .. | 2 | S | S |
| Enfield Allday .. | 3 | N | N |
| Eric Campbell .. | 3 | N | N |
| Erskine .. | 3 | N | N |
| Essex (1932 and previous) .. | 2 | N | N |
| Essex, 1933 and 1934 .. | 2 | S | N |
| Falcon Knight .. | 2 | N | N |
| Farman .. | 3 | 3 | 3 |
| F.I.A.T. .. | 3 | S | S |
| Flint .. | 2 | S | S |
| F.N. .. | 3 | S | S |
| Ford, T. model .. | 2 | N | N |
| Ford, 1928-32 .. | 3 | N | N |
| Ford, 1933 and 1934 .. | 3 | S | N |
| Franklin .. | 3 | N | N |
| Frazer Nash .. | 3 | S | N |
| Galloway .. | 3 | S | N |
| G.N. .. | 3 | N | N |
| Graham .. | 2 | N | N |
| Graham Paige .. | 2 | S | S |
| Gregoire .. | 3 | N | N |
| Guy .. | 3 | N | N |
| G.W.K. .. | 3 | — | N |
| Gwynne 8 .. | 3 | N | N |
| Hampton .. | 3 | S | S |
| Hanomag .. | 3 | N | N |
| H.E. .. | 5 | S | S |
| Hillman .. | 3 | 3 | N |
| Hispano Suiza .. | 3 | S | S |
| Hispano Suiza (Sports) .. | 5 | S | S |
| Horch .. | 3 | S | N |
| Horstman .. | 3 | S | S |
| Hotchkiss .. | 2 | S | S |
| Hudson (1932 and previous) .. | 2 | N | N |
| Hudson, 1933 and 1934 .. | 2 | S | N |
| Humber .. | 3 | 3 | N |
| Hupmobile .. | 2 | N | N |
| Hupmobile, 1934 .. | 2 | S | N |
| Hurtu .. | 3 | N | N |
| Imperia .. | 3 | S | S |
| Invicta .. | 5 | S | N |

| CAR | Engine. | Gear-box. | Back Axle. |
|---|---|---|---|
| Invicta (Self-change) .. | 5 | 2 | N |
| Isotta Fraschini .. | 5 | N | N |
| Itala .. | 2 | S | S |
| Jowett .. | 3 | N | N |
| La Buire .. | 2 | N | N |
| Lagonda .. | 5 | 5 | 5 |
| Lagonda (Self-change) .. | 5 | 2 | 5 |
| Lanchester .. | 3 | 2 | N |
| La Salle .. | 2 | N | N |
| Lea Francis .. | 3 | N | N |
| Lea Francis, T.T. model .. | 5 | N | N |
| Lincoln .. | 3 | S | S |
| Lorraine Dietrich .. | 3 | S | S |
| Marendaz Special .. | 3 | N | N |
| Marmon .. | 2 | S | S |
| Marquette .. | 2 | N | N |
| Martini .. | 2 | N | N |
| Mathis .. | 3 | 3 | S |
| Mercedes Benz .. | 3 | S | S |
| Mercedes Benz (Super-charged) .. | 5 | S | S |
| Metallurgique .. | 3 | N | N |
| †M.G. .. | 5 | N | N |
| †M.G. (Pre-selector) .. | 5 | 3 | N |
| Minerva .. | 2 | S | S |
| Morgan, Air-cooled .. | 3 | N | — |
| Morgan, Water-cooled .. | 3 | N | — |
| *Morris, all models .. | Morrisol Standard Recommendation* | | |
| Napier .. | 3 | N | N |
| Nash .. | 2 | S | S |
| Oakland .. | 2 | N | N |
| Oldsmobile .. | 2 | N | N |
| O.M. .. | 3 | S | N |
| Opel .. | 3 | N | N |
| Overland .. | 2 | N | N |
| Packard .. | 2 | S | S |
| Paige .. | 2 | S | N |
| Panhard Levassor .. | 2 | 5 | 5 |
| Peugeot, Sleeve Valve .. | 2 | N | N |
| Peugeot, other models .. | 3 | 3 | N |
| Pierce Arrow .. | 2 | N | N |
| Railton Terraplane .. | 3 | S | N |
| Rally .. | 3 | N | N |
| Renault .. | 3 | N | N |
| Reo Six .. | 2 | N | N |
| Rhode .. | 3 | N | N |
| Riley, 1933-34 .. | 3 | N | N |
| Riley (Self-change) .. | 3 | 2 | N |
| Rockne .. | 3 | N | N |
| Rochet-Schneider .. | 3 | N | N |
| Rolland Pilain .. | 3 | N | N |
| Rolls-Royce .. | 3 | S | S |
| Rover, Air-cooled .. | 3 | S | S |
| Rover, Water-cooled .. | 2 | S | S |
| Rover, 2 litre .. | 3 | S | S |
| Salmson .. | 3 | S | S |
| Salmson Sports .. | 5 | S | S |
| S.C.A.T. .. | 3 | N | N |

† In Winter use N.P.3.

**MENDATIONS FOR BRITISH CARS THAN ANY OTHER OIL**

## RECOMMENDED GRADES—cont'd.

| CAR | GRADE | | | CAR | GRADE | | |
|---|---|---|---|---|---|---|---|
| | Engine. | Gear-box. | Back Axle. | | Engine. | Gear-box. | Back Axle. |
| Senechal .. .. .. .. | 3 | N | N | Sunbeam, 3 litre .. .. | 5 | S | S |
| Schneider .. .. .. .. | 2 | 5 | S | Swift .. .. .. .. | 3 | N | N |
| Sheffield Simplex .. .. | 3 | N | N | Talbot .. .. .. | 5 | 5 | N |
| Singer .. .. .. .. | 3 | N | N | Talbot (Pre-selector) .. | 5 | 2 | N |
| Singer, 9 h.p. Le Mans .. | 5 | N | N | Triumph .. .. .. | 3 | 5 | S |
| Sizaire Berwick .. .. | 2 | N | N | Triumph (Self-change) .. | 3 | 2 | S |
| S.P.A. .. .. .. .. | 2 | N | N | Trojan .. .. .. .. | 3 | 3 | HBB |
| Spyker .. .. .. .. | 2 | N | N | Turner .. .. .. .. | 2 | N | N |
| S.S., 1933 and previous models | 3 | S | N | Vale .. .. .. .. | 5 | R | R |
| S.S., 1934 .. .. .. | 3 | N | N | Vauxhall .. .. .. | 3 | S | S |
| Standard .. .. .. | 3 | N | N | Vermorel .. .. .. | 3 | N | N |
| Standard Avon .. .. | 3 | S | N | Vernon Derby .. .. | 5 | N | N |
| Standard (Self-change) .. | 3 | 2 | N | Vinot .. .. .. .. | 3 | N | N |
| Star .. .. .. .. | 3 | N | S | Voisin .. .. .. .. | 2 | S | S |
| Steyr .. .. .. .. | 3 | N | N | Vulcan .. .. .. .. | 3 | N | N |
| Straker Squire .. .. | 3 | N | N | Whippet (Overland) .. | 2 | N | N |
| Studebaker .. .. .. | 3 | N | N | Willys Knight .. .. | 2 | N | N |
| Studebaker, 1934 models .. | 3 | S | N | Willys Overland .. .. | 2 | N | N |
| Stutz .. .. .. .. | 5 | S | 2 | *Wolseley .. .. .. | ..Morrisol Standard | | |
| Sunbeam, all models except | | | | | *Recommendation* | | |
| 3 litre .. .. .. .. | 3 | S | S | Zebre .. .. .. .. | 3 | N | N |
| Sunbeam (Self-change) .. | 3 | 3 | S | Zedel .. .. .. .. | 2 | N | N |

### * For MORRIS and WOLSELEY CARS—all Models.

See recommendation at top of page 26

―――

## MOTOR CYCLES

| Name of Cycle | N.P. Grade | Name of Cycle | N.P. Grade | Name of Cycle | N.P. Grade |
|---|---|---|---|---|---|
| A.J.S. .. .. .. .. | 5 | Grindlay Peerless .. .. | 5 | N.U.T. .. .. .. .. | 5 |
| A.J.W. .. .. .. .. | 3 | Guzzi .. .. .. .. | 5 | | |
| A.K.D. .. .. .. .. | 3 | | | O.E.C. (Blackburne) .. | 3 |
| Ariel .. .. .. .. | 5 | Harley Davidson .. .. | 3 | O.K. Supreme .. .. | 3 |
| | | H.R.D. .. .. .. .. | 3 | Omega .. .. .. .. | 3 |
| Blackburne Engines .. | 3 | | | | |
| ,, (O.H.V.) .. | 5 | Indian .. .. .. .. | 3 | P. & M. .. .. .. .. | 5 |
| Brough Superior .. .. | 3 | Ivy .. .. .. .. .. | 3 | | |
| B.S.A. .. .. .. .. | 5 | | | Raleigh .. .. .. .. | 3 |
| B.S.A. (O.H.V.) .. .. | 5 | J.A.P. (touring) .. .. | 3 | Royal Enfield .. .. .. | 3 |
| | | ,, (racing) .. .. | 5 | Royal Ruby .. .. .. | 5 |
| Calthorpe .. .. .. | 3 | James .. .. .. .. | 3 | Rudge .. .. .. .. | 5 |
| Cotton .. .. .. .. | 5 | | | | |
| Coventry Eagle .. .. | 3 | Levis (2-stroke) .. .. | 3 | Scott.. .. .. .. .. | 5 |
| | | ,, (4-stroke) .. .. | 5 | Sunbeam .. .. .. .. | 3 |
| Dot .. .. .. .. | 3 | Matchless (S.V.) .. .. | 3 | Triumph (side-valve O.H.V.) .. .. | 5 |
| Douglas .. .. .. .. | 5 | Matchless (O.H.V. and O.H.C.) .. .. .. | 5 | | |
| Dunelt (2-stroke) .. .. | 5 | Montgomery .. .. .. | 3 | Velocette .. .. .. .. | 5 |
| Excelsior .. .. .. .. | 3 | | | Villiers .. .. .. .. | 3 |
| Excelsior (O.H.V.) .. | 5 | New Hudson .. .. .. | 3 | Wolf .. .. .. .. | 3 |
| | | New Imperial .. .. | 5 | | |
| Francis-Barnett .. .. | 3 | Norton (Racing) .. .. | 5 | Zenith .. .. .. .. | 3 |

Should your car or motor cycle not be included above we should be pleased to advise you as to the correct grade of AERO N.P. Oil to use on receipt of particulars of make and model.

## DRAIN FREQUENTLY AND PROTECT YOUR ENGINE

*Duckham's*

**manufacture lubricants of Quality for all types of Industrial Plant and Transport Vehicles including:**

## COMMADCOL

**Branded Oil for Commercial Vehicles, will reduce cylinder wear by at least 30 per cent.**

"Aquicut" Soluble Cutting Oils.

Ball Bearing Lubricants.

Bench Oils.

Chain and Wire Rope Lubricants.

Commadcol Motor Oil for Commercial Vehicles.

Compressor Oils.

Concrete Mould Oil.

Cutting Oils.

Crank Chamber Oils.

Cylinder Oils (Steam).

Diesel Engine Oils.

Dynamo & Electric Motor Oils.

Exhauster Oils.

Floradcol, Floor Dressing Oil.

Gas Engine Oils.

Gas Holder Filming Oil.

Gas Meter Oils.

Gear Box Oils.

Grease for all Purposes.

Hardening & Heat Treatment Oils.

Joint Box Compound.

"Keenol" Surface Building Lubricants.

"Kemcut" Neat Cutting Oils.

Loom Oil.

Marine Engine Oils.

Motor Oils.

Oil Engine Oils.

Petroleum Jellies.

Pneumatic Tool Oil.

Polishing Oil.

Preserving Slushes and Greases.

Quenching Oils.

Refrigerator Oils.

Rolling Oils.

Rust Preventatives and Solvents.

Shafting and Machine Oils.

Spindle Oils.

Stamping Oils.

Turbine Oils.

Worm Drive Lubricants, Etc.

Interesting Staff Leaflets of a technical nature on lubrication subjects will be supplied on application to our Technical Advisory Section.

**Duckham's products are recommended or approved by over 400 manufacturers of Industrial Plant and Commercial Vehicles.**

## QUALITY IS ECONOMY

# Chapter 3

# WAR AND PEACE

Duckhams' 40th anniversary was a memorable one for both good and bad reasons. Already predicted to be a bumper year, 1939 brought greatly increased profits, which, in the eight months to August, had already exceeded those for the whole of the previous 12 months. A 40th anniversary book of maps was commissioned, as a gift for selected customers, copies of which occasionally still come to light at antiquarian booksellers.

But it was also, of course, the year war was again declared, and with Chamberlain's momentous words the export market virtually collapsed owing to the restrictions on oil movements. Worse still, petrol rationing curtailed motoring to the extent that Duckhams motor oil sales fell by 80 per cent, leaving the home industrial business to carry practically the whole of the overheads.

Celebrations were nevertheless considered to be in order. Since it was too late for the full effect of these strictures to be felt during the year, the 1939 final accounts showed another record profit, after tax, of £36,884. The retirement was announced of director and chief chemist Prof J. S. S. Brame; and George Joyce, continuing his rise up the company ladder, was appointed deputy managing director.

The likelihood of air raids on London prompted the board's decision to move the head office out of Cannon Street, and for this purpose the company purchased the freehold of a large house, 'Woodlawn', in Page Heath Lane, Bickley, Kent, for £2,000. Air raid shelters were constructed at the Hammersmith works.

The 1940 Budget, which provided £200m towards the first year's war expenditure, increased income taxes and imposed Purchase Tax for the first time. Rationing was introduced for most commodities – food, clothes, sweets and, of course, petrol. For many people, however, this was not such a new hardship: whereas such items were now restricted by supply, they had previously been effectively rationed by price. The war brought a benefit, too, in that it created virtually full employment for the remaining civilian population.

With wartime constraints biting hard, Duckhams, in common with the rest of business, was forced to make economies. Much of the meticulous record-keeping was abandoned and, with 'poaching' of customers and all other common forms of competition between oil companies suspended by mutual agreement, the largely redundant advertising budgets were slashed.

Now in his 60s, Alexander Duckham was already in failing health, having adapted to a quiet life, much of which was spent pottering in the garden of the small cottage to which he had moved in the grounds of his estate, Rooks Hill. Perhaps because he had seen the plight of some of the orphans whose fathers had died in the First World War, it was at this early stage in the new hostilities, rather than in their aftermath, that he made a further munificent donation, that of Rooks Hill itself, to the RAF Benevolent Fund, together with a settlement of £1,000 per year towards its upkeep.

The role designated for the large house, with its 200-acre estate, was to provide a shelter for the children of officer and non-commissioned pilots killed in action or in flying accidents. Edward Bishop, in his book *The Debt We Owe – The RAF Benevolent Fund 1919–1969*, relates how Alexander, an inexhaustible patron of the RAF, personally raised a further £100,000 from British industrialists for the Benevolent Fund, continuing to work with two business acquaintances, the Sheffield steel magnate Baron Riverdale and a prosperous City man, Bertram Rumble, to establish the Fund on a firm basis.

During the early months of the war Rooks Hill housed 15 children aged between two and seven. Sevenoaks, however, lying as it did under the bomber route to London and close to the South East fighter defences, was soon considered too vulnerable a location, and in August 1940, as the Battle of Britain raged, Rooks Hill was closed and its occupants returned to family members. Vanbrugh Castle School, too, was closed because of its proximity to London's docks. Both properties eventually did suffer bomb damage and neither re-opened until after the end of the war.

With the feared Blitz becoming a reality, the precaution of moving the offices out of Cannon Street was amply justified when these premises were totally destroyed – somewhat ironically, by an oil bomb. Shelter trenches were constructed in the grounds at Bickley, the work continually interrupted by the wail of air raid sirens. Even these temporary offices did not escape the continuing raids, however, sustaining considerable damage from an indirect bomb strike in 1941.

In the same year another distinguished scientist, Cecil Pepper PhD BSc FRIC FCS, was appointed to the board of the company. Dr Pepper, who came from a farming family

*George T. Joyce joined Duckhams as office junior in 1907 and rose to become joint MD.*

but had gained a scholarship that started him on a career in science, was another graduate of London University who, after obtaining his higher degree, joined the research labs of Alexander Duckham & Co, working closely with the founder himself.

During the course of the war he assisted in overcoming the problems posed by shortages of raw materials, plant and labour and became more concerned with the commercial and economic sides of the business. Later, by keeping a careful eye on developments in

*Repairs under way to the temporary offices at Bickley, which were badly damaged (above) in a 1941 air raid.*

other world markets, he was to play an important role in the company's post-war product developments.

Perhaps succumbing to an illogical British feeling that even the Luftwaffe would not dare to destroy the top London hotels, Alexander hired a suite in the Waldorf at £40 per month to serve as his office. The Hammersmith works was clearly vulnerable to the bombs, so to reduce the fire risk it was decided to move the manufacture of products with a low flash point from there to Kent. Formally known as Works No 3, this operation was in fact based in the grounds of Alexander's property at Seal, the temporary arrangement lasting for just over a year.

To prevent a single bomb strike wiping out a huge quantity of product, stocks of oils were dispersed around the country, these 'reserve dump' locations including Birmingham, Bristol, Chard, Glasgow, Goole and Manchester.

For the second time Duckhams had seen its staff reduced by war service, this time from

*Distinguished chemist Dr Cecil Pepper was mainly responsible for Duckhams development of the first European multigrade engine oil, following his fact-finding visits to the USA.*

around 170 to 130, and with a corresponding increase in the proportion of female employees. Among those leaving to do their duty was Alexander's son Jack who, as a Major in the RAOC, was for some time seconded to the 51st Highlanders and saw service in the Low Countries and Germany.

In the petroleum industry, men over 30, and women over 22, were deemed to be in reserved occupations, although working hours were increased. Fire-watching (keeping a look-out for fires started by enemy raids) became compulsory for these male staff, and voluntary for the women.

Transport was becoming a problem owing to war restrictions. Lorries were prohibited from leaving the factory with less than an 80 per cent payload, and deliveries out of London were restricted to a 30-mile radius of Charing Cross (the only exception being bulk tankers, which participated in reciprocal arrangements under the provisions of the Lubrication Oil Pool).

With a major proportion of the company's sales being to Midlands industry, to help overcome the transport restrictions Works No 4 was set up in Birmingham, following the purchase for £6,550 of No 42 Grosvenor Street. This plant, a self-contained unit with its own small laboratory capable of basic quality control, appears to have enjoyed a charmed life, adjacent as it was to the local railway marshalling yards that were targeted many times during the Blitz.

Adcoids production was reduced to a minimum and capacity turned over to neat cutting oils and soluble fluids, as well as hand cleansers, skin ointment and other hygiene aids for industrial workers. The commencement of production of these at Fulham in 1943 required significant changes at Works No 2, where larger volumes of soluble oils had to be stored and raw material storage tanks were turned into blenders.

Although it sustained no direct hits, the continuing air raids of 1944 saw Works No 1 suffer from extensive blast damage; it was nevertheless back in action within two days thanks to tireless work by the staff, already under considerable duress. A memorandum from the works manager to Alexander Duckham refers to 'the air raids, blackout, fire-watching and travelling difficulties … having an impact on staff, causing lack of sleep, strain, fatigue and irritation.'

Referring to packaging problems, he says: 'Due to the shortages of metals we are forced to cut out sales in small packs except for government requirements, and to utilise second-hand packs ordinarily suited only to scrapping.' (The allocation of steel for new packs was under the jurisdiction of the Petroleum Board, which decreed minimum sizes of 10 gallons for oil drums and 28lb for grease.)

With a possible end to the war in sight, it was not all doom and gloom in the latter half of 1944; in any case, the ever-optimistic Alexander found a ready excuse for a celebration. On 25 July he hosted a luncheon at the Waldorf to celebrate the 35th anniversary of Blériot's historic Channel flight, the list of

*The Hammersmith works was vulnerable to bombs during the war, and precautionary blast protection was erected at strategic points around the site.*

*Situated not far from Buckingham Palace, the premises at 12–14 Wilfred Street were the scene of many a cocktail party.*

distinguished guests including Sir F. Handley Page, Mr T. O. M. Sopwith and Lord Brabazon of Tara. Also in attendance was Cdr John Ide USNR.

It is typical of Alexander that, despite the continuing restrictions on the industry, he was already anticipating the Allied victory, and enthusing about the possibility of getting the

company back to something approaching normality, when he died on 1 February 1945, aged 67. The funeral took place at Golders Green Crematorium, followed by a memorial service at St Michael's, Cornhill, on 12 February.

Alexander Duckham had maintained control of his company throughout and, although he was looked upon by many as an autocrat, this was no more than the general management style of the time. Among his many achievements was bringing Duckhams to a leading position in the lubrication industry, with a loyal team of engineers and chemists, supported by sales and administration personnel, who had made the company's philosophy of 'quality and service' their own.

Following Alexander's death his son Jack, although still in the Army, was appointed to take over as chairman of the company.

Jack Duckham is remembered with affection, by both staff and outsiders, for his outgoing personality, which was so useful in winning trade. A distinguished and entertaining character, his natural interest in people, and ability to remember the details of their lives and families, made him a natural 'front man' for the company. The nuts and bolts of business administration did not greatly appeal to him, and it seems that he was never happier than when out visiting customers or socialising at a party or dinner. There will be a few who still recall the supercharged Morris Eight that heralded his arrival, and the tendering of a business card that bore his full name, Jack Eliot Duckham.

It was not until Jack's early discharge later in 1945, however, that he was able to take up the reins in person and oversee the gradual return of the company to its peacetime footing. As the lights came back on all over London, the office at the Waldorf was vacated, a new chairman's office leased in Dover Street, and further freehold office premises in Wilfred Street, off London's Buckingham

# THE DUCKHAM'S STORY IN COLOUR

*This portrait of Alexander Duckham in his 30s accompanied an article about him in a 'Men of the Day' series in the society magazine Mayfair in June 1913, which concluded: 'He is one of the few men today who can claim to have earned a reputation on such original lines – a love of accuracy, an insatiable appetite for hard work, and an inimitable notion of stating his own opinion.'*

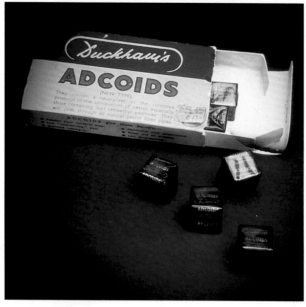

Above *Vanbrugh Castle, Blackheath, the home of Alexander and his family, was gifted to the RAF Benevolent Fund after the First World War.* (Watercolour by Chris Floyd, courtesy Duke of Kent School)

Left *First conceived in 1934, Duckhams Tablets became a best-seller, especially under their later name of Duckhams Adcoids.*

Right *Running on 'off-the-shelf' Q oil, Team Surtees had a successful Formula 1 partnership with Duckhams. Here team boss John Surtees has a last word with Tim Schenken, while his car gets a final oil check before the start of a race.*

*Left* A Range Rover of the successful 1972 British Trans-Americas Expedition gets a little help in crossing one of the deeper rivers of Central America's Darien Gap. (Michael Cross)

*Below left* The privately entered Duckhams-Ford of Alain de Cadenet put up a fine performance in the Le Mans 24-hour race in 1975. (David Oliver)

*Right* Driving the Duckhams-lubricated new Hesketh F1 car, World Champion-to-be James Hunt leads Peter Gethin in the 1974 Race of Champions at Brands Hatch. (David Oliver)

*Below* Winner of the Brands Hatch Race of Champions 1974: Jacky Ickx in the Lotus John Player Special, also racing on Duckhams Q.

Left *Aldridge works, built from scratch in 1967/68, provided additional capacity of 10 million gallons annually. It is seen here with the 1977 extension (top of picture) linked to the main site by a pipe bridge.*

Above *Ronnie Peterson (JPS Lotus 72E) on his way to victory in the 1974 Monaco GP.* (David Oliver)

Above left *Typical of the grass-roots competitors who swear by Duckhams oil is Newburn, Northumberland, garage proprietor Andy Norton. Andy was successful in various branches of motorsport with Duckhams, whose products he has used for nearly 50 years – and his father used them before him!* (Paul Boothroyd)

Left *Forming a 'Q' with the Duckhams support caravans. This attempt at a publicity picture in the 1960s proved abortive; the necessary aerial shot would have made the livery invisible!*

Above *Probably the most successful motorcyclist to team up with Duckhams was the great Sammy Miller. Pictured at the 1977 Scottish Six Days Trial is the Miller Honda Team: (l to r) Nick Jeffries, Marland Whaley, Sammy Miller and Rob Shepherd.* (Nick Nicholls)

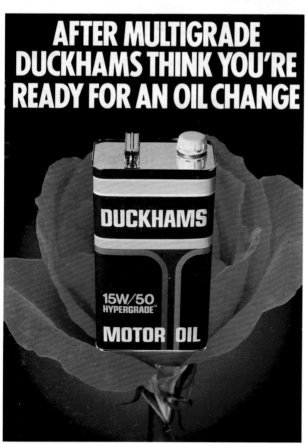

Above left *For the Queen's Silver Jubilee in 1977, Duckhams brought out a special commemorative medallion that was attached to 'Q' packs.*

Left *Hypergrade, a 15W/50 engine oil with improved additive package, was launched in 1982. The can retained the now traditional Q colours.*

Above right *The distinctive graphic that accompanied the ad campaign for Q based around the slogan 'The Utmost Care'.*

Right *QXR was a revolutionary new high-performance oil launched to sell alongside Hypergrade in 1986. Produced in collaboration with parent company BP, it helped convert many motorists to a premium oil.*

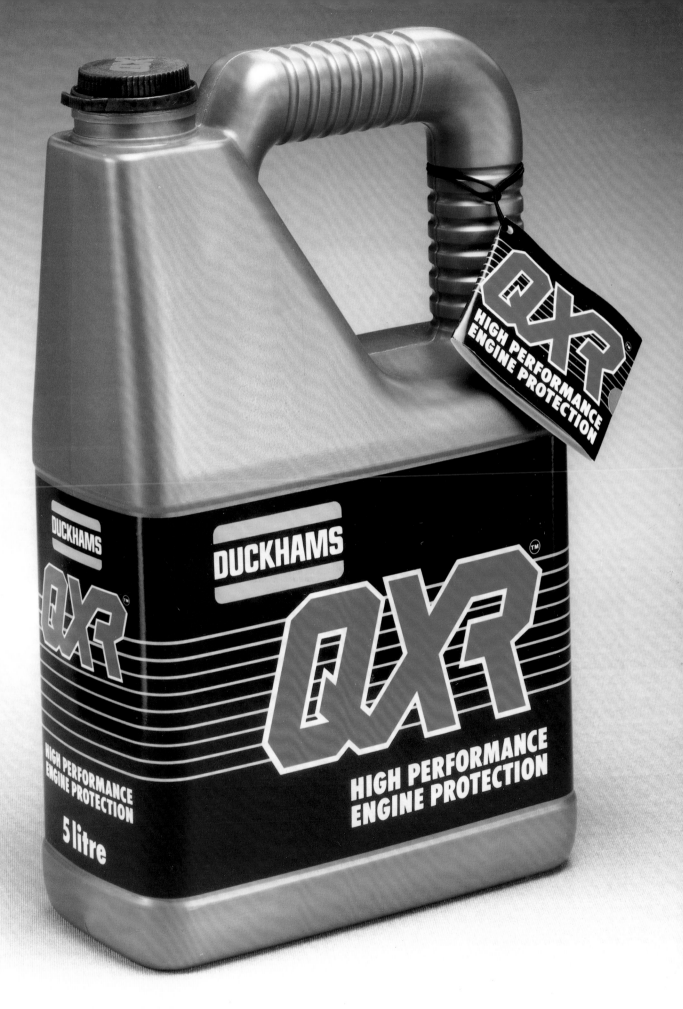

QS was the culmination of concentrated research and development, including pre-launch testing in the British Rally Championship Peugeot 205 of Steve Bennett and Duncan McMath, which went on to take the 1993 BBC Top Gear award for the series. (Transmission magazine)

Above right *Launched in 1995 in conjunction with British Motor Heritage, Duckhams Heritage range included an engine oil blended to the original Q20-50 formula, especially to suit the engines of the 1950s and '60s.*

Right *The QS Metro 6R4 of John Price and John Morgan on the Mewla National Rally in 1997. (Kevin Mashiter)*

Left *Paul Radisich at the wheel of the Duckhams-lubricated works Ford Mondeo Super Touring Car, pictured in the 1997 BTCC Championship.* (Courtesy *Fast Ford* magazine).

Below left *Karl Muggeridge under pressure on his Duckhams-Seeley Honda in the 1998 British Supersport 600 Championship.* (Bryan Turner)

Right *Duckhams long and successful partnership with the Van Diemen Formula Ford racing team continues today. Pictured is Daniel Wheldon whose Duckhams Van Diemen features the latest-style livery for 1999.*

Below *The latest, simplified range of user-friendly motor oils continues a tradition of catering for every car on the road.*

Keeping the football flowing. **DUCKHAMS**

*A scene from the 'break bumper' commercial shown during Sky TV's 1999 Duckhams-sponsored football coverage. The green 'cast' identifies with the unique oil.*

*The old and the new: Duckhams oils of today and 50 years ago.*

Gate, purchased for £12,000. As the company grew, this location came to provide a prestigious venue for receptions, press launches and so on, and is remembered with affection by those who attended functions there.

The large American oil companies had clearly gained significant ground during the war, leaving small British independents like Duckhams with much leeway to make up. Dr Cecil Pepper, now joint managing director, was closely involved in a programme of replacing overworked plant and overhauling production techniques to offset the high cost of labour and materials.

Discussions were soon undertaken with Morris Motors to re-establish the pre-war relationship, resulting in the new specification 'NOL' (Nuffield Official Lubricant) as the exclusive Morris/Wolseley recommendation in 1946. With oil availability improving all the

time, the winding up of the Petroleum Board in 1947 was perhaps the final symbol of normality in the industry, although the damage done to the British economy by the war was made only too clear in Prime Minister Clement Attlee's newly announced austerity measures. 'Work or Want' and 'Export or Die' became official slogans.

That same year new freehold offices were purchased in Kensington for £30,000 and, with a view to boosting exports, overseas trips were embarked upon by senior management, Dr Pepper travelling to the USA and George Joyce to Australia.

The following year brought a prestigious

*After the war the company reinstated its 'lost keys' registration scheme for drivers. The original records had been lost in the bombing of Cannon Street.*

accolade for Duckhams when Lt-Col A. T. 'Goldie' Gardner set a new international car speed record in Belgium, using the company's products. Cabling head office with the good news, Goldie advised: 'Lubrication by Duckhams as ever perfect'.

In 1949 a new era of small cars was heralded by the launch of the Morris Minor, followed closely by the oddball Citroën 2CV. The world's largest aircraft, the Bristol Brabazon, made its maiden flight.

Sadly Alexander, who would have been thrilled at these achievements, had not lived to see them. Neither could he witness the one that would perhaps have made him proudest of all: his company's Golden Jubilee in 1949. The surviving directors, though, made sure this year, in which the prestigious Kensington premises were occupied, was a memorable one, with some company traditions revived and special emphasis placed on customer involvement.

Publication of the *Links* magazine was recommenced, targeted at those in technical and administrative roles in business. Then the 'lost keys' scheme for motorists was re-introduced, after its forced abandonment through the Cannon Street bombing, with both old and new customers invited through the pages of *Links* to write in and register their details in exchange for their engraved Duckhams disc. Re-introduced too were Duckhams road maps in a new bound format.

Two major sporting events saw the contemporary equivalent of 'corporate hospitality'. In June 1949 Duckhams took three coachloads of important customers to the Oaks meeting at Epsom, and the following month representatives of major motor trade groups and manufacturers like Wadhams, Caffyns, Puttocks, Hartwells, Ford Motor Company and Leyland were the company's guests at Henley Regatta.

No jubilee year would have been complete without a formal dinner, so in October a long list of celebrities and customers joined

Duckhams management at the Savoy Hotel, where a message of congratulation from Prime Minister Winston Churchill was read out to the assembled company.

The company received a suitable 50th birthday present from the indefatigable Goldie Gardner who, still running exclusively on Duckhams oils in his new MG Record Car, set new record speeds in international classes E to I.

But times were changing rapidly. As the motor industry entered a new phase of mass-production and relative sophistication, not only were cars like the Morris Minor starting to look more like those we know today, but widening markets and servicing requirements meant that it was increasingly impractical for manufacturers to stick with one brand of oil.

George Joyce was consequently obliged to enter into an outline agreement that would effectively end Duckhams' solus position as suppliers of recommended lubricants to the Nuffield organisation. Perhaps to sweeten the pill, Joyce was asked to act as go-between in the negotiations with the other main oil companies for their inclusion on the 'approved' list, effective from 1 January 1950.

The return of peace had brought plenty of employment for Britain's workers as they faced the huge task of reconstruction following the bombings. Some of the constraints of wartime were slow to disappear, however: it was only in 1950 that petrol rationing, which had been in force for ten years, ended (as did, more bizarrely, the rationing of soap as well), causing record traffic on that Whit Monday.

Gradually, though, a new age of consumerism was created and living standards rose. Commercial television and Premium Bonds were introduced. Council houses

*Jack Duckham breaks out the bubbly with Goldie Gardner to celebrate another successful record speed run in his Duckhams-lubricated MG at Utah in 1951.* (Nuffield USA)

With the return of peacetime, transport was in demand, and Duckhams' fleet encompassed all sorts. Here we see a Morris Eight 5cwt van, a Morris-Commercial box van, an Austin ex-Army 30cwt Austin K30 truck pressed into service as an extra delivery vehicle, a Morris-

Commercial LC series small tanker, and a Rolls-Royce 'van', about which perhaps the less said the better!

sprang up, including the ubiquitous 'prefabs', which could be quickly put together using preconstructed sections to fill the new demand for housing. Those who had previously had no chance of owning their own home could now, with a secure job, buy one on a mortgage for £10 down; indeed, ownership soon became the better bet as private rents started to increase substantially.

In the new atmosphere of affluence, and in anticipation of escalating motoring-related production, Duckhams increased raw material storage capacity at Hammersmith by some 1,000 tons, later expanding the works itself by taking over a portion previously let.

One hundred years after the Victorian Great Exhibition, in 1951 the 'Festival of Britain'

*Crowds line the Hammersmith Works river frontage for the 1951 Boat Race.*

opened on London's South Bank. Like the Millennium Dome that was to follow 50 years later, its 'Dome of Discovery' and cigar-shaped 'Skylon' excrescence proved controversial to a public still suffering from the deprivations of wartime. One of the main complaints was the price of a cup of coffee at the exhibition – 9d (4p).

By now the company had taken the decision to end the sale of New Process Oils, and the NP name, used for 30 years, was incorporated into the NOL brand. Motoring was entering a new era and, thanks to Duckhams, engine oils were more than keeping pace. A new product, Adcoid Liquid Upper Cylinder Lubricant, was now also introduced, trading on the brand name of the product launched 14 years earlier in tablet form.

Dr Pepper again visited the USA to check out developments in motor oils there, and,

despite embargoes on imports by some Continental countries, Duckhams continued efforts to rebuild its brand awareness in post-war Europe. Under an agreement designed to get round import restrictions, production of Adcoids and NOL oil began in France, and new export arrangements were set up through

*The Adcoids formula was introduced as a liquid upper cylinder lubricant in 1950.*

*Duckhams' caravan-based stand displays agricultural lubricants at the 1950 Barnstaple (Devon) Show. Tow vehicle is a Standard Vanguard van.*

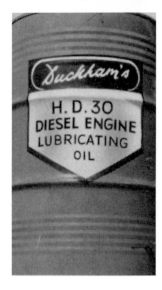

*Duckhams' diverse range of industrial lubricants at the start of the 1950s.*

agents in Belgium, Switzerland, Denmark and Portugal.

The company's major event of 1951, though, was also probably the single most important product launch in its history, destined to put even Adcoids in the shade. Inspired by Dr Pepper's first trip to America, where greater extremes of temperature are the norm and where a new type of engine oil had been introduced, Duckhams unveiled for British motorists the famous 'Q' for the first time. It was Europe's first multigrade engine oil. And it was green …

# Chapter 4

# THE QUEUE FOR 'Q'

The result of intensive laboratory research, Q5500 was a 10W/30 multigrade (an oil whose 'flat viscosity curve' meant improved flow characteristics at all temperatures), which had been undergoing field trials with several hundred motor trade customers for the past year or so. It was claimed to have extreme fluidity at both normal and arctic temperatures, increased film strength and 'oiliness', and a high degree of detergency. Increasing engines' resistance to oxidation and corrosion, its most noticeable practical advantages to motorists were easier starting and quicker getaway.

The distinctive green hue of this original 'Q' brand was introduced into the formulation originally in order to overcome an irrational prejudice on the part of the motoring public against pale-looking oils, which were thought to lack 'body'. Pensioner Jean Walton (née Gould) recalls that, as a technical assistant in Duckhams Works No 2 labs, she mixed the first multigrade (destined to be Q5500) for Dr Pepper. It was so pale that it looked more like mineral or hydraulic oil, so he asked her to add a green dye to make the appearance more acceptable.

The colour used in production derived from a bespoke dye manufactured by Williams of Hounslow for Duckhams. Although the company subsequently attempted, unsuccessfully, to register 'green oil' as a trade mark, it immediately became a well-known feature of Duckhams multigrades, even customers who could not remember the brand name asking for 'that green oil', encouraging 'passing off' by spurious imitators.

Another frequently asked question concerns the derivation of the oil's name, and the answer, though simple, does not disappoint. Duckhams chemists maintained a 'Q' book in which experimental formulations were documented under a 'Q' number prior to being preserved in a more formal way. The new formula's number in the book happened to be 5500 …

Advertised as 'the super lubricant for the motoring connoisseur', over the next three or four years Q5500 steadily gained acceptance, becoming Europe's best-selling multigrade. The motor manufacturers themselves, however, always cautious, continued to specify mainly NOL brand 'straight' lubricants.

The year 1952, in which Princess Elizabeth acceded to the throne on the death of her father King George VI, also brought the death of John Cobb, holder of the World Land Speed Record, when his jet-engined boat disintegrated on Loch Ness at 240mph. The following summer, however, the nation rejoiced as a new Elizabethan era was heralded by the Coronation. And in the same year, after being outdone for a year or two, Ford again claimed to have the world's

*Reflecting oil developments in the USA monitored by Dr Pepper, Q5500 was developed by Duckhams to become the first European multigrade.*

cheapest car with its four-cylinder Popular at £390, beating Austin's new A30 (£475) and Standard's Eight (£481).

As multigrade oils began to catch on for cars like these, competitors introduced their own brands. Naturally, Duckhams had anticipated this and had never reduced the level of commitment to the strong industrial products division of the company, with the lubricants, coolants and associated products continuing to be developed and, of course, promoted.

The increased levels of trading, resulting largely from the sales volumes created by the multigrade breakthrough but also from sustained sales of NOL, required greater working capital, and in 1954 the company announced a conversion and rights issue, doubling the total issued capital to £250,000, comprising 1,000,000 five-shilling (25p) shares.

The growth in volumes for the oil companies was being created by mushrooming car ownership, all the companies seeing extra business despite new levels of competition between them. The majors were engaged in a game of 'tied' service stations, as they attempted to sign up retailers to stock only their brand. The 'carrot' consisted of special trade terms, and back-up by way of signage, hardware, advertising and marketing aids.

The balance between sales of the NOL monograde and Q5500 multigrade brands was gradually changing, thanks to developments in engine design that were largely American-led. With manufacturers slow to change their recommendations, however, it was still a time for hedging bets; Q5500 was advertised for its 'winter' attributes, with NOL being promoted on the 'prevention is better than cure' theme.

The company had to keep a constant eye on the ever-changing requirements in service workshops. Chassis developments meant that many of the newer passenger and commercial vehicles no longer needed the various specialised greases for different components, and in response Duckhams introduced LB 10, a lithium-based all-purpose grease with high water resistance, which considerably simplified life for the mechanic.

In a market where complacency could mean death, Duckhams strove continually to move forward. Whether in the motor or the industrial sector, there was the same strong commitment that has existed throughout the century, to continually upgrading the product to meet the changing needs of users.

Investment in new plant and equipment continued apace, and by 1955, the year in which Churchill (now aged 80) handed over the premiership to Anthony Eden, production capacity was double that of seven years previously. In conjunction with an increase in the numbers of laboratory staff, engine test facilities became more sophisticated, permitting ever more stringent tests to be run, while research into cutting coolants and tool life took a major step forward when Duckhams' laboratory became the first in Europe to begin using radioactive tracer elements in this field. With the company's hand cleansers and skin treatments highly regarded, a dedicated bacteriological laboratory was also installed.

Meanwhile in the lubricants laboratories, while Q5500 was still establishing itself with motorists, Duckhams boffins were already working on its successor …

A bullish start to 1956 saw Duckhams taking a more pragmatic view of its activities. The Adcoids patent was sold to Shell, while an agreement was negotiated with British Sun Oil, of the USA, to market the American company's lubricants in Britain. Capital expenditure continued, too, with a new grease-making plant commissioned for Works No 1.

It soon became clear, however, that the British motor industry was starting to experience another recessionary phase, and this was compounded later in the year by the Suez Crisis, which threatened oil, and therefore petrol, supplies for the first time since the end

*The traditional underbonnet holder in Morris cars could now carry a multigrade oil.*

of the war. As things turned out, 1956 was not to be the best year in which to launch a new oil.

But in true Duckhams spirit, launch they did, even though Q20-50 first saw the light of day as a motorcycle oil. It was a depressingly downbeat time for the birth of what was to become the company's best-known brand of motor oil, the new year dawning against the gloomy background of fuel shortages, with constant queues at filling stations and the precautionary issue of ration coupons to motorists on the basis of need.

Fortunately the downturn was not a sustained one and, with the re-opening of the Suez Canal and the gradual lifting of fuel restrictions, 1957/58 proved to be healthier years than expected.

*Expansion at Hammersmith in the 1950s included new engine test bed facilities.*

Although Britain remained outside the European Common Market, created by the initial six signatories to the Treaty of Rome in 1957, Duckhams' export sales improved, as did those of industrial products, thanks to an extensive range offering everything from commercial engine oils, through press and wire-drawing compounds, to hygiene preparations like soaps, detergents, barrier creams, and skin cleansers including the widely used A.S.C. (Antiseptic Skin Cleanser).

Some of the previous year's sales deficit was made up for by an improvement in turnover of the new motor oils, with Q20-50, Q5500 and NOL 30 all featuring in the range. Despite the competition between the oil majors for 'tied' sites, the vehicle manufacturers obligingly continued to encourage free choice in motor oils, and Duckhams exploited every opportunity to offer its products through

garages and filling stations. The commercial vehicle oils range was also updated, with 20W/50 and 10W/30 rated multigrades, and the concept was even extended to 'multigrade' hydraulic oils.

It was not uncommon for the family car engine of the day to need at least a top overhaul at 30,000 miles and, by 50,000 miles or so, wear in the bores would probably be causing it to burn oil. Although still advertised as a motorcycle oil, Q20-50 was becoming recognised as ideal for car engines that were beginning to suffer oil consumption problems in this way. These would only increase with driving speeds on the imminent motorways, of which a pilot stretch – the Preston By-Pass – opened in 1958.

As motorists recommended 'Q' to friends and neighbours, ads proclaiming 'Complete engine protection' and 'An all year round oil'

made increasing reference to cars as well as bikes. 'Time for an oil change? Change it to Duckhams!' – and thousands did. Combined with High Street availability through Halfords stores, this brought daily converts to the new oil with its mysterious green hue. As sales soared, the company's capitalisation was again increased, by a bonus issue, to £500,000.

It was in 1959 that Duckhams lost an invaluable scientist and administrator in its joint managing director Dr Pepper, who was taken ill and died aboard the *Queen Elizabeth* while returning from a business trip to the USA. It was he who had seen the potential of the multigrade oil concept on an earlier visit to the States. Duckhams had never been averse to copying a good idea, but always endeav-

*New underground raw material storage tanks being craned into position at Hammersmith.*

# DUCKHAM'S Q20-50

## A *NEW* MULTIGRADE OIL

### FOR MOTOR CYCLES

- EASY STARTING

- LOWER FUEL CONSUMPTION

- COMPLETE ENGINE PROTECTION

*The later multigrade, Q20-50, was originally launched in 1956 as a motorcycle oil.*

oured to improve it; and on his return Pepper had overseen the research and manufacture stages of the project that provided the company with the mainstay of its automotive sales over the next half-century.

That year also saw the British Motor Corporation launch its ground-breaking new

*A decade after the Minor, the first Mini (a Morris Mini-Minor) rolled off the line at Cowley, bringing a new lubrication challenge for Duckhams with its revolutionary integral engine/gearbox unit. It is pictured here with designer Sir Alec Issigonis, on the occasion of his retirement in 1971. (Rover Group)*

£500 family car, the Morris Mini-Minor. Issigonis's radical design not only turned BMC's A-series engine through 90 degrees, starting a trend followed by most family hatchbacks today, but also placed the transmission beneath the crankcase, with the gearbox effectively operating in an extension of the sump.

While this was fine for space-saving, it caused problems for the engine oil, which, in addition to suffering the usual contamination from combustion deposits, was suddenly called upon to act as a gear oil as well. Not surprisingly, there were problems. Probably the greatest of these was the 'shearing' effect of the high pressures involved in the gears, which quickly broke down the polymers in ordinary oils causing loss of viscosity and lubrication properties.

Once again, it was Duckhams to the rescue. While monograde NOL had been the manufacturer's original recommendation for the Mini, Q20-50 proved to be in a class of its own in this type of engine, maintaining viscosity and reducing the oil leaks that had started to plague the Mini.

As other front-wheel-drive spin-offs from the Mini concept started to arrive on the scene, their highly stressed constant velocity joints proved vulnerable to rapid wear. Duckhams was called in again, and provided the solution with a special molybdenum disulphide grease.

With Q20-50 still considered unique in the market, widening its availability appeared to be the only obstacle. The question of 'solus' petrol stations, with the associated tied sales of lubricants, was becoming a major issue with the independent and specialist producers; in 1960 they finally succeeded in getting the practice referred to the Monopolies & Mergers Commission, which, in time-honoured fashion, embarked on the lengthy process of taking evidence.

In that year, too, another member of the Duckham family joined the company when Alexander's grandson Neill Duckham Foster, the son of Millicent Duckham and her husband Wilfred Foster, was appointed company secretary.

The Hammersmith plant commenced major expansion, and a new plant was also installed to provide more efficient production of the latest types of grease. Nearby, construction of the Hammersmith Flyover was under way with, naturally, extensive use of Duckhams Concrete Mould Oils.

The Government had, of course, long taken an interest in the country's love affair with the car, and the 1960 Budget saw taxes on oils increased. It was a setback that did little to blunt demand for the product. When, just down the way at Earl's Court, that year's Motor Show opened its doors, Duckhams' associated advertising featured the ditty:

'For starting on a winter's day, or driving on
   the motor way,
For those who can afford the best, and cars
   that pass the ten year test,
For crawling in a traffic stream or driving in a
   rally team,
Use Duckhams Q20-50.'

Perhaps The Beatles, who were making a name for themselves in Liverpool, should have been called in to write the lyrics! Also featuring in the Duckhams ads of the time – and a reminder of the continuing links with Morris – were the Millionth Morris Minor (a celebratory edition finished in a love-it-or-loathe-it lilac shade) and, of course, the 'incredible' Mini.

When joint managing director George Joyce retired in 1962 after 55 years' service with the company (he had joined as office boy in 1907, and his son Ron followed him into Duckhams, becoming the company's technical services manager), sales had more than doubled within

*The answer to the Mini's oil consumption problems? Duckhams Q20-50, of course!*

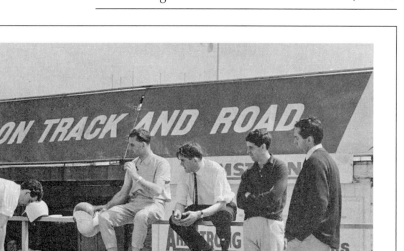

# REMARKABLE OIL CONSUMPTION TEST AT SILVERSTONE

**THE TEST**  1001 miles over 347 laps at an average speed of 77.26 m.p.h.

*Drivers:*  Warwick Banks, Harry Ratcliffe, Brian Redman and Bob Smith.

*Scrutineer:*  R. J. Soanes, M.S.A.E., M.I.M.I.
*Time Keepers:*  W. W. Turner and D. W. Bell

**THE CAR**  A Mini-Cooper 1275 S - a performance car used by enthusiasts for fast driving at maximum engine revs, where oil consumption is an important factor.

**THE CONSUMPTION**  2 pints during the whole test.

ONE PINT PER 500 MILES!

**THE OIL**

**DUCKHAM'S** ⬭ 20-50 ⬭ **MOTOR OIL**

*the oil that likes to be driven hard!*

\* Silverstone, 14th July, 1965.

15 years, despite full potential being hampered by the restrictive practice of 'tied' outlets, which remained under consideration by the MMC.

These rapidly growing sales, which were being enjoyed in spite of the trend in the motor industry towards smaller sumps and extended oil drain periods, were to prove something of a problem. Not only were the existing premises in danger of being outgrown in the shorter term, but the company's capital base was constantly under strain as well. This, coupled with the highly competitive trading conditions at the time, tended to create a 'stop-go' regime within the company.

Industrial sales were also buoyant, and re-organisation of this side of the company resulted in the launch of the Duckhams Industrial Lubrication Service. Duckhams was now in the enviable position of being the only independent to offer a full-range, nationwide lubrication service covering industry, transport and private motoring.

There was more good news soon afterwards when, following collaboration between the

*A BMC-badged delivery van at Hammersmith in the late 1950s.*

technical staffs of Duckhams and Vauxhall Motors, the contract was gained for the supply of production line fill-up supplies, with Duckhams products to appear in the approved listing in the handbook of the new Vauxhall Viva HB.

In August 1963 Lord Nuffield, a fellow philanthropist, business colleague and friend of Alexander Duckham and Britain's most successful motor industry figure, died aged 85. Having given up his directorships 10 years previously, he had set about disposing of his fortune charitably, including allocating £10m to set up the Nuffield Foundation. Also that year, US President John F. Kennedy died at the hands of a gunman in Dallas, Texas.

Such were Duckhams' sales levels by now that even the squeezed profit margins were able to absorb the overheads associated with the setting up of regional sales offices. By the year end large field forces were operating in both retail motor and industrial sectors, and were getting results.

Having been available on the UK market for some 12 years, multigrades were at last replacing the traditional monogrades as the recommendation in manufacturers' literature. With car production booming as consumer affluence grew, competition for the increased business was severe, but Duckhams held its own with renewed marketing and promotional effort, the emphasis now firmly on 'Q20-50 Multigrade Engine Oil for every car on any road at any time of the year!' – a simple-to-understand message that caught on with motorists.

The house colours were changed from green (originally conceived to represent the colour of Q) to the first incarnation of the now familiar blue and yellow logo. Such was the loyalty and recognition by this time that large numbers of garages and fuel stations continued to defy the move to 'tied' outlets, and the regional field staff were poised to provide a ready response to their demands to stock Duckhams. Together with the countless

*Joining as company secretary in 1960, Alexander's grandson Neill Foster was the last Duckham family link. Later becoming MD and vice-chairman, he left in 1974. (The Ullage magazine)*

motorists who bought their cans in High Street stores, they helped make it Britain's fastest-expanding brand by 1964, when the newly formed British Motor Corporation approved Q20-50 for the engine of its new 3-litre, Rolls-Royce-powered Princess R saloon.

The increased brand awareness among the motoring population can only have helped the 'pull-through' effect on industrial sales. From production engineering right through to local authority sewage works, Duckhams had a substantial share of the market, aided by specialities such as the aerosol silicone spray Adsil.

In October 1964, as Harold Wilson's Labour Government squeezed to power with a majority of four, the purchase was completed of a Manchester works from United Lubricants to ease the pressure on existing facilities. A nucleus of retained staff helped effect a rapid start-up, with production under way within a few months.

The burgeoning packaging industry of the new consumer age was identified as a likely

*Hammersmith works saw further major expansion in 1961/62, to provide new offices, packaging facilities and vehicle workshops.*

target for diversification into wax production, with Duckhams expertise in hydrocarbon compounds ideally suited to the requirements of impregnating, laminating and coating paper. A couple of sales representatives were appointed, but delays in the supply of equipment meant a slow start in 1965.

The new year brought a landmark for the British motor industry with the production of the millionth Mini, but this was overshadowed as the nation mourned Winston Churchill, who died aged 90.

Following a further increase in Duckhams share capital to £750,000, June of that year also saw the opening of leased premises in Hounslow, as a filling and distribution depot,

capable of automatic filling of gallon, quart and pint cans.

With industrial sales now showing a decline, war was declared on overheads, with the closure of some regional offices, much to the regret of chairman Jack Duckham, who was very conscious of the key role played by the field forces. A corresponding upturn in European sales, however, meant that it became cost-effective for local manufacture of some products to be licensed, thus avoiding import restrictions.

With the benefit of hindsight, the brake on costs was perhaps an over-reaction. While it certainly improved the profitability of the industrial department, demand for motor oils

*The millionth Morris Minor in 1961 inspired both BMC and Duckhams to celebratory promotions.*

# DUCKHAM'S
*Congratulate*
# MORRIS

## on producing the millionth MINOR

**Duckham's oils
have been officially
recommended by
Morris Motors Ltd.,
for 30 years**

**ALEXANDER DUCKHAM
& CO. LTD.,
LONDON, W.6**

*In 1963 the company changed its design for packaging and publicity, abandoning the script-style name (although the apostrophe survived for a while) and adopting the familiar blue, yellow and white colour scheme.*

continued to soar. By 1966 not only had Q20-50's market share doubled within a 12-month period, but so had Duckhams profits, with the company established as the UK's third largest supplier of engine oils – no mean feat when its size is compared to that of the competition.

A new advertising slogan, 'The oil with the perfect body', caused a stir during this period. A picture of the Louvre's Venus de Milo sculpture, used in the campaign, was deemed

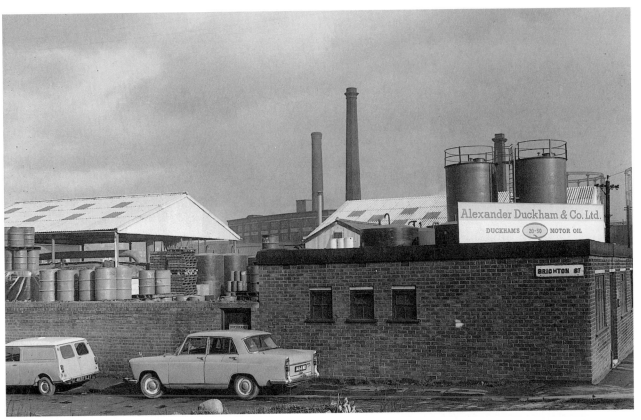

*As a fast means of increasing capacity, the Manchester works was acquired from United Lubricants in 1964 with a nucleus of existing staff.* (Trevor D. Wainwright)

unacceptable by some people, one North London clergyman writing to the press to complain about 'the desecration of art'. It was a case of any publicity being good publicity, however, from which Duckhams (unlike the Venus statue) derived plenty of coverage!

The continuing rapid sales growth in motor oils was causing severe pressure on facilities, alleviated to some extent by the coming on stream in March 1966 of the Manchester Works. A couple of months later the sales and publicity departments, with some other admin staff, moved from Hammersmith to new offices at Summit House, West Wickham. Additional space was created by leasing extra warehousing in the Hammersmith area, and purchasing a private house in Skelwith Road, next to the works, for security purposes. New depots opened in Norwich and Newcastle-upon-Tyne, followed later in the year by another in Newry, Co Down, to serve the company's recently established Irish arm, Duckhams Oils (Ireland) Ltd.

With staff numbers now increasing almost daily, working conditions were improved at Hammersmith by the purchase of the cargo barge *Ipswich*, to be moored alongside the works. Refitted and renamed *Aphrodite* (the Greek name for Venus), it fulfilled a multiple role as staff restaurant, social club and training centre.

The efficacy of 'Q' in dealing with the oil consumption problems of contemporary cars was becoming legendary. Quite apart from the increasingly professional advertising, many of the company's best salesmen were ordinary motorists who spread the word to friends and relations. It was also at around this time, however, that the company fully realised the impact on publicity of maintaining a presence in motorsport, and marketing director Cyril

*The leased Hounslow depot not only brought extra distribution facilities, but was also equipped for rapid automated filling of smaller packs of oil.*

Ford gave the task of setting up the appropriate department to Ron Carnell, whose reminiscences appear elsewhere in this book.

Nor was it just at home that the phenomenal growth was being experienced. Duckhams' European agents were also seeing unprecedented demand for Q20-50. When the financial press were briefed in March 1967 on the company's excellent 1966 results, they learned that exports had risen by 75 per cent in that year alone. And prospects received another fillip when, after years of cogitation, the Monopolies Commission ruled in favour of independent suppliers and against the practice of 'tied' outlets.

Still the roller-coaster had not reached the top of its ride. As market share continued to increase, fuelled by aggressive promotion,

further expansion of the field force, and the opening of more new depots, profits would double again in 1967. By July *The Observer* was able to comment: 'Racing away with the motor oil stakes is Alexander Duckham's Q20-50. Their market share has increased from 5 per cent in January 1966 to 12.5 per cent now', while *The Scotsman* reported: 'The Duckham market share has increased from 1.5 per cent to 12.5 per cent in just three years, with sales for the first half of '67 up by 120 per cent'. This UK market share confirmed the company as third largest player, led by Castrol with 35 per cent and Shell with 16 per cent.

While the office staff's snowballing workload – processing of orders, invoices, accounting and statistical records – was relatively easily coped with by replacing the existing punch-card equipment with a new IBM computer-based system, production resources were now at the point where further expansion of the brand was unthinkable without drastic action. The decision was taken

Duckhams - the oil with the perfect body

*This series of ads in the 1960s met with some controversy, one newspaper claiming that they represented a dangerous distraction for motorists!* (Robin Ross)

to build from scratch an additional plant on a canal-side site at Aldridge, Staffordshire, most of the capital to be raised through a combination of a rights issue to ordinary shareholders and the issue of 7 per cent Debenture Stock. Construction work started almost immediately, in May 1967, to provide a projected additional annual capacity of 10 million gallons.

The increase in export turnover was maintained, with southern Africa proving a fast-growing market. To develop this more efficiently, arrangements were made with the South African agents for the setting up of a new subsidiary, Duckhams Oils Africa (Pty) Ltd.

With the employees in the various locations around the country now numbering around 700, a house magazine, *The Ullage* (a term for the wastage or dregs involved in fluid processing industries), was launched to aid communications. A major re-organisation of the technical department was implemented, which

formally divided research from the ongoing activities of quality control and troubleshooting.

From the early 1960s part and parcel of the active promotion that was helping to drive Duckhams' turnover ever upward was the brand's presence at the major shows and motorsport venues. The importance of sponsorship in this type of industry was now fully appreciated by a management initially taken almost unawares by the tremendous demand for its products. The Duckhams Racing Service was established, with the familiar yellow caravans strategically placed at the various race meetings to provide support for the company-backed drivers and riders. Duckhams Oils Ireland negotiated exclusive rights to advertising at the Phoenix

*Summit House, West Wickham, formed the company's main offices from 1966.*

Park circuit, also sponsoring the saloon car meetings there.

With the additional capacity from Aldridge yet to feed in, it was decided to extend the Manchester works, currently blending more than 2 million gallons annually for distribution to the North, Ireland and northern Europe. In the background, industrial sales were quietly holding their own in a declining market, while wax sales were beginning to take off.

The new year brought further acclaim with the completion of a 10,000-mile test in a BMW 1600, observed by the Royal Dutch Automobile Club, that confirmed the effects of Q20-50 on oil consumption. Sales of the

older grades like NOL and Q5500, although they were still available, had now been replaced almost entirely by Q20-50.

With devaluation of the pound in late 1967 further boosting exports, Duckhams products were now sold in 37 countries (most of which had been added in the past few years), and in February 1968 the first international conference was organised, attended by representatives from overseas agents. Recently appointed among these was Harper Gilfillan & Co, who covered Malaysia and Singapore and whose offtake had rapidly grown to 150,000 gallons a year. Closer to home, Duckhams

*To cope with the explosion in demand for 'Q' oils many regional depots were opened, such as this one in Bristol.* (Bromhead Bristol Ltd)

*Moored at Hammersmith, this Thames barge, renamed* Aphrodite, *became the canteen and social club HQ in 1966. (Henry Ellis Photographers Ltd)*

Oils Ireland now claimed an 11 per cent market share.

With the service bay an all-important area in the battle for market share, additional engineers were taken on to back the provision of a free-of-charge planning service for garage workshops.

Three months into 1968, market share had reached 18 per cent with Q20-50 on sale at some 30,000 outlets. Brand loyalty was at its height, with an estimated 2 million motorists specifically asking for Duckhams Q20-50 when buying oil. Still more sales personnel were employed, taking staff numbers to more than 800, and marketing spend was further

increased. Included in that year's publicity budget was the purchase of a 600 cubic metre hydrogen balloon carrying the 'Q' livery. This unfortunately was to survive for less than a year, crashing in flames on the following Easter Monday, though thankfully causing no serious injuries.

Approaches for sponsorship were continually being received, and the company's policy continued to be to support the up-and-coming motorsport drivers and riders, rather than those already in the top echelons. In this way the budget could be spread much wider, and

*The ill-fated 600 cubic metre hydrogen balloon* Venus, *acquired as a novel publicity aid, makes its take-off after the Easter 1969 race meeting at Thruxton Circuit. It was landing near Swindon when venting gas ignited and it crashed in flames. (*The Ullage *magazine)*

*Neill Foster presents Ray Gunter MP with a gallon of Q20-50 at the opening of the Aldridge plant in 1968.* (Birmingham Post)

the brand message constantly renewed at grass-roots level. Organisers of expeditions to various parts of the world could also count on Duckhams support, further aiding brand awareness overseas. With all this background activity in mind, a new publication, *Quest,* was launched to bring motoring enthusiasts full-colour news of Duckhams-backed competitors in motor, motorcycle and powerboat sport, as well as stories of notable journeys, product updates and technical information.

Annual output now exceeded 50 million litres, and with Hounslow depot filling 2 million cans per month a new depot opened at Townmead Road, Fulham. Despite dilution by a scrip issue of a further million shares in May 1968, the share price had bounced back to 61 shillings (£3.05) within a month. Given the high profile and record trade levels enjoyed by Duckhams at this time, it was hardly surprising that rumours should have started to circulate about possible takeover bids, although the board put out the usual disclaimer …

With the installations at Aldridge plant complete, the official opening was performed by Ray Gunter MP in October, production immediately transferring from the old Birmingham works and 30 new jobs being created.

It was an exceptionally healthy company that chairman Jack Duckham handed on in December 1968 when he retired after 37 years as a director. He had latterly been in failing health and, despite suffering considerable pain from arthritis, remained notable for his uncomplaining attitude and solicitude for others. Reflecting a nature acquired from his father, he had made almost a full-time hobby out of devising aids and gadgets for handicapped people.

Jack himself took up the honorary post of president of the company, his nephew Neill Foster and newly appointed chairman Sir Richard Manktelow becoming joint MDs, the former nominally responsible for the marketing function.

Trading profit was set to pass the million-pound barrier for the first time, and Duckhams now held no less than 25 per cent of the retail motor oil market, with exports (although still a small fraction of total sales) up by another 50 per cent. A further boost to turnover came from the waxes and hot-melt compounds, which were now being sold to most UK packaging converters.

The company's 70th anniversary year marked further technological advances, as the supersonic Concorde made its maiden flight and American astronaut Neil Armstrong became the first man on the Moon. Closer to home, oil was discovered in the North Sea.

Vice-chairman Neill Foster declared that, over the previous six years, Duckhams had progressed from an expensive minor brand to the UK's least expensive major brand. As still more new staff joined the technical and field forces, market research in early 1969 showed Duckhams running neck and neck with its

*The Duckhams sales force pose for a snapshot at the opening of the Aldridge works.*

*Sir Richard Manktelow became the first non-family chairman when he took over from Jack Duckham in 1969. (The Ullage magazine)*

main competitor in the public awareness stakes.

By mid-year rumours were rife once more of possible bids for Duckhams from major oil companies. In fact, an approach by Esso had already been made during May but was thwarted, following which the Duckhams

*Further industrial interests were gained in 1969 with the takeover of Jenolite, a company specialising in rustproofing and metal surface treatment. The picture shows a GEC Gas Turbines bedplate being treated at the Egham (Surrey) works of Duckhams Jenolizing Services.*

board entered into confidential negotiations with BP.

Expansion plans, however, continued apace with the cash acquisition in September of the Jenolite organisation, which specialised in metal surface treatments, to supplement Duckhams' industrial activities.

As Duckhams once again flew the flag at the Earl's Court Motor Show, the press carried reports of an imminent bid from BP Oil. BP's current access to the UK lubricants market was confined to its shared interest within the Shell-Mex & BP joint venture, and the acquisition of Duckhams would provide indepen-dent entry. In going public on the bid, BP confirmed its intention to 'maintain Duckhams as a corporate entity trading at arm's length, with freedom to determine its own competitive commercial policy and prices, and to maintain by means of its own sales force its brand image in the market. Duckhams' commercial activities will not be constrained on account of BP's other lubri-cants interests through Shell-Mex & BP.' Following acceptances from holders of 82 per cent of the shares, the acquisition of Duckhams was confirmed on 31 December 1969.

## Chapter 5

# THE SPORTING LIFE

One of the most rewarding and inspiring aspects of Duckhams' activities, linking its continuous programme of research and development with advertising and promotions, was the company's involvement with the competitions side of motoring and motorcycling. There can be few better ways of advertising a product like motor oil – and winning

*Ron Carnell was never happier than when involved in the two-wheel side of the sport. He is seen here with some early beneficiaries of Duckhams support, all top riders of their time – Rob Edwards, Gordon Farley and Dennis Jones – at the 1969 Scottish Six Days Trial. (D. J. Staton)*

friends in the right places at the same time – than by supplying it to drivers and riders for use in the thick of competitive racing, rallying or trialing, together with some well-placed stickers for car, bike or boat.

While the company, from its early associations with drivers like S. F. Edge and Goldie Gardner, had long been involved in various forms of sponsorship, these had generally resulted from personal friendships of Alexander or Jack Duckham; there was no co-ordinated effort until the 1960s, when Cyril Ford was the company's director responsible for sales and marketing.

One of Ford's salesmen, Joe Gardner, an RAC scrutineer and keen motorsport enthusiast, was pushing for Duckhams to get involved in racing. Finally, in 1966 Cyril called in a young man who had just been recruited as a technical writer, and asked him: 'If we got a caravan would you be prepared to give up a few weekends a year to represent the company at motor race meetings?'

The young man was Ron Carnell, who was also a motorsport fan, and he recalls: 'It was a dream come true – I couldn't say yes fast enough!'

'So we got a caravan, painted it in Duckhams colours and off we went. In those days, if we found a couple of cars running with our oils we were very pleased. It seemed to be a useful exercise, so I asked if I could take the caravan to motorcycle meetings when there were no car events on, and this was well received. (In those days, "trade support" was

*Duckhams-backed Ray Pickerell (works BSA) pictured at Mallory Park in 1971.*
(B.R. Nicholls)

permitted at only a limited number of race meetings designated by the SMMT and the tyre companies.)

'By the end of the year I was called in again and asked: "This all seems to be going well – would you like to head up a motorsport department?" Well, to be honest, I wasn't sure I was up to it. All the established motorsport trade representatives seemed such flamboyant characters (even if some of them were pretty successful alcoholics as well!). Anyhow, that's the way I got the job, and so we set about building up contacts.

'Joe Gardner came from Bolton, and introduced us to Chevron Cars and Brian Redman, a young up-and-coming driver who was already running on Duckhams oils. We also got to know Brian Hart, a driver as well as an engine tuner, and were able to show him that BDA engines were better protected by Duckhams 20/50 than they were by the castor

oils then considered *de rigueur* for racing.'

This was just the sort of message the company wanted to get across: by switching to Duckhams, Hart solved the problem of excessive bucket tappet wear on those engines and, of course, the word got around.

From the outset, Ron Carnell's brief was that all such support was to be only with a Duckhams product identical to that available over the counter to the private motorist. The product was supplied free of charge in return for permission to advertise any successes: there were no formal contracts, a handshake being considered sufficient to seal the agreement.

As the support programme became established, it also became more wide-ranging. 'In saloon racing, Ken Costello and Harry Ratcliff were going well in Minis,' recalls Ron, 'but we didn't find real success in single-seaters until Formula Atlantic came along. That brought great drivers like Tony Brise and David Purley, and it was marvellous: almost every finisher used our Q20-50 in those races, and it became practically the Duckhams formula!'

Still climbing the motor racing ladder, Duckhams first entered Formula 5000 with Brian Redman and Sid Taylor, with Alan Rollinson following; then came the first exciting possibilities of involvement in Formula 1. In 1971 the company was in discussions with Team Surtees, who posed the $64,000 question: could a Ford Cosworth DFV F1 engine run successfully on totally standard Duckhams Q20-50?

'Although we had every confidence in the product, nobody knew the answer for certain,' says Ron. 'Quite reasonably, John Surtees wanted the oil fully tested, both on the bench and in a car, before he would commit his team to a contract. The bench test proved satisfactory, which was encouraging, but we still had to test the oil under race conditions, which we did at Silverstone in the November.

'We decided to turn this test into a bit of a publicity exercise. To show it was totally genuine, we asked the RAC to buy some Q20-50 off the shelf somewhere and put it into the Surtees F1 car. Alan Rollinson then drove the full grand prix distance on the circuit. He didn't hang about, either – if I remember correctly, he set a time that day that would have given him fourth place back in that year's British Grand Prix!'

Much to everyone's delight and relief, when the engine of the Surtees was stripped it was found to be in totally sound condition. The go-ahead was given for the 1972 season, with Mike Hailwood and Tim Schenken using Duckhams Q20-50. The exceptional cleanliness of engines raced on 'Q' was noted time and time again as they were worked on by race technicians, and this added further to its reputation.

During that season an approach was made concerning support for Team Lotus the following year. Ron Carnell admits to being concerned at the time that Duckhams might be getting out of its depth, not least from the financial point of view, but he was won over by the team's boss. 'The way Colin Chapman handled it was really impressive. He rang my MD and said: "No strings attached, but the John Player people are coming up for lunch in a couple of days and I thought you'd like to join us. I'll send the plane over to Biggin Hill – pop over and have some lunch, we'd love to see you."

'The plane picked us up right on time at Biggin, and we were soon touching down on the private landing strip at Hethel. Although we were just 100 yards from Colin's private door into the boardroom, a Cadillac (not a Lotus) rolled up to the plane and took us the short distance. We were ushered in and there was Chapman, waiting to shake hands. It was all so impressive, our MD was just thinking, "Where do I sign?"

'So now we were with Lotus, and once we got to know the team I thought, this is it – now we're in with the top professionals, we'll really learn what it's all about. But to my amazement, I found that they were the same as all the others; they'd still change the roll bars, the spring settings *and* something else all at the same time, so they didn't really know which tweak had made the difference! Even so, it was really interesting and I thoroughly enjoyed it. The drivers were Ronnie Peterson and Jacky Ickx, and although Peterson was a terrific driver I don't think he could ever really "sort" a car. He used to pinch Jacky's settings quite a lot, which upset Jacky a bit.'

His close working relationships with the race

*Duckhams was rightly proud of the test that found Alan Rollinson's engine in perfect condition after driving a full F1 distance at Silverstone.*

# The toughest test of oil.

## Silverstone... a Formula 1 Surtees TS9... Duckhams Q20-50

**1** Where could you find a tougher test of a motor oil than in a Formula 1 racing car? Yet this is the test to which Duckhams publicly submitted Q 20-50.

**2** In the presence of an official RAC scrutineer and timekeeper. 20 pints of Duckhams Q 20-50, the same oil the makers recommend for your car, are poured into the engine.

**3** Alan Rollinson is the driver. His brief is to drive the Surtees for 200 miles at Grand Prix speeds. That means speeds topping 160 mph, and maximum revs up to 10,000.

**4** Under conditions far tougher than anything you could possibly meet on the road, the oil temperature remained normal and oil pressure was good throughout the test.

**5** 200 gruelling miles later, Rollinson gets the thumbs up. The test is over. Now the engine is to be stripped and examined by Race Engine Services Limited.

**6** They reported: ''The engine was in first class condition and in our view the test was completely satisfactory.''

The Formula 1 Test is the latest and toughest challenge for Duckhams Q 20-50.

In the world's hardest and fastest motor sport events, Britain's best selling motor oil has been proving itself for years.

With Duckhams Q 20-50 in your engine, you can depend on the oil which has proved it will stand up to anything.

## DUCKHAMS

### One oil. Whatever you drive.

teams left Ron Carnell with a host of reminiscences, and one in particular concerning Team Lotus is worth sharing: 'I think it was the Rothmans 500 – there were Formula 5000 and lots of F1 cars there. We qualified very well, and Peterson got into the lead with Ickx about fourth. Ronnie was going extremely well when some silly electrical thing caused him to retire; Jacky inherited his place and went on to finish something like third.

'The general verdict was, "What a shame

*John Surtees (right) shakes hands with competitions manager Ron Carnell on the deal that would see Team Surtees running successfully on 'off-the-shelf' Q20-50 oil for the 1972 season. (John Stoddart)*

Ickx wasn't in Peterson's car and vice versa, because then we would have won." But I just happened to be standing in the pits as Jacky pulled in at the end of the race. Colin Chapman went over, patted his helmet and said, "Well done, Jacky, nice finish." Jacky replied, "Thanks, Colin, but you might just have a look at that offside front wheel – I think you'll find the pads are in back to front."

'Sure enough, when they removed the wheel they found the mechanics had installed the brake pads inside out: he had driven the whole race with metal-to-metal contact on one brake! Now obviously that was never reported in the press, so who can really say who are the great drivers?'

Duckhams raced with Team Lotus for two

*Lotus boss Colin Chapman has a word with Ronnie Peterson in the JPS Lotus, while James Hunt passes by (top right) with girlfriend of the day.*

seasons, during which engine builders started to see F1 engines coming back in superb shape after running on genuinely standard Duckhams Q20-50. The word went around that, if a driver or team was looking for an oil contract, it was the one to go for, and that brought a number of names into the frame.

'We ended up running Mo Nunn,' recalls Ron, 'who had built a Formula 1 car for Rikki von Opel of Team Ensign. Graham Hill now had his own team, with sponsorship from Embassy – he couldn't run anyone else's stickers on the car so he was on Duckhams oil! Oh, and then there was Lord Hesketh: he, as some will recall, wouldn't run any decals on the car except the little bear; but that was a fabulous deal, I thought, because in return for supplying the lubricants we had permission to use the team in any way we liked for publicity.

'So we had an F1 car with James Hunt driving, and I had a personal deal with James: we would give him £25 for each World Championship point he got. In return for that he wore a very large Duckhams badge on his overalls and two Duckhams helmet stickers. The "mileage" we got out of that was absolutely incredible – women's magazines, obviously the men's magazines too – James appeared everywhere, and I think in the end it cost us about £200. It was another wonderful deal! One way or another, you know, at that time we had virtually half the Formula 1 field running on Duckhams oil.

*Pat Mahoney (Seeley-Kawasaki) races with Duckhams at Silverstone in 1973. (John Stoddart)*

'There's one story we'd have loved to use in an advert, but we couldn't. One of the well-known names in Formula 1 management rang me up and said: "I know I've got a cheek, we can't do anything officially with you because we're under contract to ——, but we're building a brand new F1 car and I've been told that, if we want to lubricate it from front to back, we should use Duckhams and there won't be any problems. We've got enough of those already just building the car, so could you supply us with the lubricants? We'll pay for them, of course, but there's no way you can use this because of our contract with —— !"

'I thought that was such a fantastic recommendation, I gave him the oils free of charge, of course. Although we couldn't use it officially, I knew I could mention it at motor club talks and suchlike, and it was a genuine boost for our products.'

The 1974 season was a good one for Duckhams, and by the end of the year the roll of honour read:

Formula 1: Jacky Ickx wins Race of Champions; Ronnie Peterson wins Monaco, French and Italian GPs; James Hunt wins International Trophy at Silverstone
Formula 5000: 16 out of 19 races won on Q
Formula Atlantic: 23 out of 24 races won on Q
Formula Ford: 43 out of 55 races won on Q

*Ford 'Rallyman of the Month' Malcolm Wilson, with co-driver John Davies, throws his Mk 1 Escort round a corner in the Greystoke Forest en route to victory in a Lakeland Stages Rally of the 1970s. (Tony North)*

That, of course, was the name of the sponsorship game and it was all intended to pay off in heightened brand awareness, leading to increased sales. Ads were run along the lines of 'Ronnie Peterson wins the Monaco Grand Prix using the same oil that you can buy'; another series gave a blow-by-blow account of the Surtees engine testing.

The effect on consumers can be very difficult to measure, though, and in practice the most quantifiable result of all this activity seemed to be simply an increase in the number of approaches for free oil. Certainly, Duckhams had established a reputation for top-quality products, but motor racing sponsorship costs were growing disproportionately, especially at the top of the sport, as the big tobacco companies raised the stakes.

Before any major decisions could be made, Ron Carnell was approached by Alain de Cadenet, who was preparing a Ford DFV-powered car for the 1975 Le Mans 24-hour event. As the DFV unit was known to run well on Duckhams standard oil, would they be interested in sponsoring it?

'Well, our budgets were never that big anyway, and by April/May they were gone,' reports Ron. 'But from our discussions it seemed that Alain was not being taken seriously. Although he had had the car built by

*A delighted Lord Hesketh clasps the trophy while World Champion-to-be James Hunt sprays the champagne after gaining the first Formula 1 victory for Hesketh in 1974. (Mike Keppel)*

Lola, a firm of great repute, people were laughing behind their hands at the thought of it taking on the top-line Matras, Ferraris and Porsches.

'In the end I said: "Alain, I can give you £200 towards your fuel costs, and for that we want decals on the car." He replied: "OK, but what I really need is some practical help – I've got no hospitality vehicle, nowhere for the mechanics to sleep. Could you come over with your caravan and provide a few helpers? If you can I'll put the car in Duckhams colours and we'll call it a Duckhams-Ford."

'I just didn't believe this, but I really took to the guy and we got on well. Anyway, off he went to Le Mans and the car really was painted up in our colours and entered as a Duckhams-Ford, with Chris Craft as the co-driver. So I rustled up a "support crew" who were really a bunch of amateurs – butchers, bakers, candlestick-makers – with a couple of people from the office. We went out to join them and it was just unbelievable. Alain's car was running second or third at one time, due to pit-stops by the works cars! We did reach dizzy heights, but then there was a bit of a shower and Chris slid off and bent the front suspension.

'They banged it straight in the pits but the scrutineers wouldn't let him out again. So Alain had a furious row, as only he can, and in the end they let us out for the last few laps. The car finished 12th overall and won the *Motor* Trophy for the best-placed British entry! It ran on the standard oil, of course – the consumption was quite remarkable – and when they stripped the engine afterwards it was virtually as good as when it started the race. We backed private Le Mans entries again for a couple of years, but that was our best result.'

Another branch of motorsport in which Duckhams featured strongly was rallying; for years the company had been backing some of the best drivers in the lower echelons of the sport. There were always plenty of entrants in the British Rally Championship running on Duckhams, and for some of the major events like the RAC Rally a mobile back-up service was provided, generally for the smaller teams and privateers.

Suddenly, through one of those quirks of fate, Duckhams found its colours on the World Rally Championship Ford Escorts. The Rothmans team, managed by David Sutton, ran in blue, white and gold. The deal originally involved support from Shell, but Rothmans did not want the clash of their red and yellow on the team livery. Shell pulled out and, at a late stage, Sutton rang Duckhams and invited Ron Carnell along to a meeting with the main sponsor. This resulted in a deal that satisfied all parties, and a Drivers' World Championship for Ari Vatanen with Duckhams and 'Q' in 1981.

Following his success with Rothmans, David Sutton gained the contract from Audi to run the Quattro rally cars in the British Championship. In the first season, 1982, the team gained second place for Audi in the makers' section, with Hannu Mikkola third in the drivers' championship, both he and team-mate Waldegard scoring outright victories in individual rounds. Sponsorship for the British Audi team subsequently moved to Duckhams' parent company BP.

This was followed by backing for Team Toyota, which, according to Ron Carnell, cost

*The famous pairing of Hannu Mikkola and Arne Hertz in the Audi Sport UK Quattro. With Duckhams backing, this car was driven to individual victories in the 1982 British Rally Championship by both Mikkola and team-mate Bjorn Waldegard, with Mikkola finishing third in the Drivers' championship and Audi second in the manufacturers' category. (Audi UK)*

*Barry Sheene and girlfriend pictured on a Duckhams-sponsored charity trial in the 1970s. The company had backed him in his early days, riding Bultaco two-strokes prepared by his father.*

about £10,000 in the first year but soon escalated to something like £60,000 for just a small decal on the car.

Two-wheel sport, of course, played a big part in Duckhams promotional activities too, although when it came to racing bikes there was one fundamental difficulty. Whereas the company's policy was to run only on the standard mineral oil, the majority of racing engines of the time were assembled with large tolerances and were designed to run on castor-based oil.

For that reason, involvement with the top riders was small, although a well-known relationship was that with the legendary Sammy Miller, which lasted for some years and saw numerous British Championship wins by Sammy. Another name who was to become legendary, Barry Sheene, was backed by Duckhams when he first started riding competitively.

A certain gentleman by the name of Mike Hailwood also teamed up with Duckhams on a couple of occasions. Ron recalls: 'He could ride anything; I always felt he could have made it big in Formula 1 if he had just knuckled down and done what he was told.

'I remember once another extremely successful rider, Phil Read, said he would take on Mike in the Oulton Park Gold Cup race if they were both riding British single-cylinder machines. Mike, true to form, rose to the challenge and asked a friend of mine, Colin Seeley (who was being backed by Duckhams at the time) to build a bike for him.

'We all went off to Oulton Park and Mike went out to practise on this single-cylinder 500. He was doing pretty well but eventually he came in and said: "It's gone off a bit and it's making funny noises as well." The engineer said the big-end had gone, so I went off to Bill Smith, the local racing dealer, and he said: "I bought one of those bikes in a few months ago – it's up the back of the workshop. I don't know what the engine's like but you're welcome to take it." I rang Colin with the news.

'So I was in the Duckhams caravan when Mike Hailwood came in and said, "Everything OK?" Colin told him there was no problem but we were going to take a bit of a gamble on the race. "I've got a works development engine that we brought as a spare. It's never been raced but it's showing good power on the brake. I'm confident it'll do the business." Mike looked delighted.

'Meanwhile this filthy old engine was in a dustbin having a couple of gallons of petrol poured over it to clean it before we rushed it back to Oulton Park, just in time to be fitted and wheeled out for the race. Mike beat Phil Read, won the race and, giving his garland and trophy to Colin Seeley, said: "Well done, thanks very much, but I'd have a word with your engineer if I were you – that development engine wasn't half as good as the one I had in practice …"

*Military-style support from Duckhams for the British Army team in the Lombard Esso Scottish Rally of 1977. (Colin Taylor)*

While running mainly in the lower formulas of motor racing, Duckhams was also involved with the Unipart Formula 3 team, one of whose drivers was a certain Nigel Mansell. Ron Carnell remembers him mainly through his father: 'We were at Silverstone one day and there was a tap on the door; in came this young man with his father, who said, "Can I talk to you about oil?", and I didn't know them from Adam. It was the way his father asked about oil temperatures, when it should be changed, etc – I could see they were keen to do the thing properly and I said, "Fine, let's have a deal, I'll give you some oil and you can put some stickers on." That was it – I hadn't taken any notice of him or his driving ability up to then.

'Once he got the Duckhams stickers on, I watched him start to do well and move up; to be honest, that's all we did for Nigel that season. Later, though, when he was starting a little high-performance tuning and servicing garage with a friend in Birmingham, he came back to me. "I've got this thing going, servicing Porsches and Ferraris and the like. You helped me when I was starting, so I'm not going to any other company – I want Duckhams in the lubrication bay." That was nice, but he didn't need that business for long!'

Another famous name briefly associated with Duckhams is that of Ayrton Senna. In his early racing days he was supplied with oil, decals and perhaps a small bonus; like Nigel Mansell, he had yet to achieve fame. That was in Formula Ford, and among competitors in that formula who also received Duckhams backing were Eddie Irvine and David Coulthard.

Coulthard in particular is remembered by Ron Carnell. 'I sponsored him in Formula Ford before he even sat in a car. A friend asked me to come and watch this lad David who was driving in a kart race at Silverstone. I did, and he was fantastic. I met his father, who obviously wanted to set things up properly and we agreed a deal in Formula Ford without more ado.'

The last major motor racing involvement was in Formula 3000. The early days were entertaining, with Duckhams-backed cars winning the championship for the first two years. Soon, though, as it became more of a training ground for Formula 1, the big-bucks sponsorship hit this as well and, mindful of the lesson learnt in F1, Duckhams decided to get out. 'After all,' says Ron Carnell, looking back over his colourful competition days, 'Our natural home has always been with the enthusiast, the broader band of competitor.'

Another sentiment with which Alexander Duckham would undoubtedly have agreed.

# Chapter 6

# TOWARDS THE MILLENNIUM

In an interview for the house magazine in January 1970, Neill Foster told staff that BP had been considered an 'attractive' suitor compared with the original bidder. Chairman Sir Richard Manktelow agreed, while expressing the regrets felt by many of the staff over the unavoidable change in Duckhams' status:

'We were the only remaining company of any size in the lubricating field, and we all had every reason to be proud of the results of our

*A Range Rover of the British Trans-Americas Expedition negotiates a ladder bridge built by the Royal Engineers. (Rover Group)*

*Duckhams was involved in the foundation of the National Motor Museum at Beaulieu, and has maintained links since. The picture shows the sponsored motorcycle gallery in the 1980s.* (National Motor Museum)

efforts, especially in the last few years. However, we realised that we really had not the financial resources to meet the substantial competition from the integrated petroleum companies. We felt that a takeover was inevitable and we count ourselves fortunate that events have taken us into the BP Group.'

In what was becoming an age of environmental concern it was fitting that, during 1970, the company conducted a trial run of an alternative and traditional form of transport for bulk deliveries to Aldridge works. Having no direct rail access, and given its large annual throughput, deliveries of bulk raw materials, and the associated containers etc, were increasing road congestion in the site and its surrounding area. Most raw materials already

arrived at Hammersmith by Thames lighter, so consideration was given to waterborne deliveries to Aldridge via the adjacent Wyrley & Essington Canal.

After some logistical experimenting, the solution was reckoned to be to deliver bulk oil by coastal tankers of 700–800 tons, via the Mersey and the Manchester Ship Canal, to storage contractors Berry Wiggins & Co at Ellesmere Port. From here it would travel by road tanker for three-quarters of a mile to a wharf on the Shropshire Union Canal and be unloaded directly into canal boats.

Two narrowboats, 70 feet long by 7 feet wide, were each equipped with four rectangular tanks; working together, a motor boat towing a 'butty boat', between them they carried some 38 tons of oil, equivalent to almost three full-size road tankers. A pipeline manhole was installed on the towpath at Aldridge, connected via a pump to bulk storage tanks, enabling direct transfer of the raw material.

It was proposed to run four pairs of boats on the 180-mile round trip, giving an estimated capability of about 6,000 tons per annum. Unfortunately unforeseen snags, including longer than anticipated transit times, meant that the pilot scheme was not extended.

The kind of happy arrangement that had so often been struck by Duckhams was repeated in September 1970 when an agreement was signed with the Royal National Lifeboat Institution for the company to supply the lubrication needs of the whole of the UK fleet of lifeboats. These also included (yes, really) special oil to pour on troubled waters; the new Heath Government could perhaps have used some of this as the upbeat mood of the 1960s fast disappeared in the growing industrial unrest.

Following on the heels of Duckhams (New

Zealand) Ltd, another associated company, Duckhams (Sweden) AB, was set up. At the end of 1970 sales volume exceeded 70 million litres and turnover was up by some 10 per cent, but with competition hotting up, trading profits had fallen back below the million-pound mark when Sir Richard Manktelow retired in December, Neill Foster taking over as sole managing director.

It was with the inevitable wind of change already blowing through Duckhams that its president Jack Duckham died while on

*'New Formula Q' was an upgraded version of Q20-50 introduced in 1973. Here test bed operator Robert Fowler fills a BRM V12 engine with the new oil, watched by Duckhams competitions manager Ron Carnell. (Colin Taylor)*

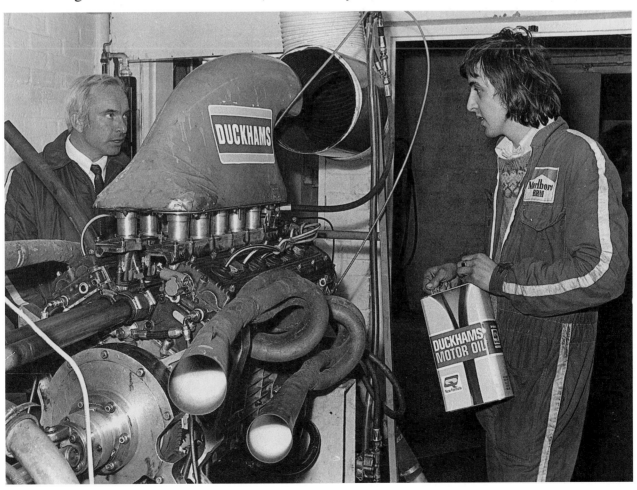

*Clay Regazzoni (Marlboro-BRM) running on New Formula Q in the 1973 British Grand Prix at Silverstone.* (Colin Taylor)

holiday in Tunisia in January 1971, after serving the company for 43 years. In his will he had, typically, provided for a party for all staff with more than 15 years' service with the company. So it was, in October of that year, a total of 224 employees and spouses attended an all-expenses-paid luncheon and tea-party at Armoury House, in London's City Road. Some staff had served considerably longer, like Ernie Cox who, retiring with 50 years to his credit, was joining only two others – W. H. Palmer (1903–1954) and G. T. Joyce (1907–1962) to have achieved the half-century.

The sales battle was now being fought to a large extent in the High Street outlets like Woolworths, where other recognised oil companies like BP, Shell and Castrol also offered their brands. However, the concept of 'own branding' of oils, produced by other major companies, initially for well-known dealer groups, was growing too.

Q20-50, still of course by far the company's best-selling line, was from time to time updated to the latest technical specifications. Improved engine cleanliness, reduced thickening and better protection against wear were among the claims made when the product was upgraded to meet API/SE and the latest Mercedes-Benz diesel car specifications early in 1972.

Publicity was now being gained from the involvement in motorsport already described, the testing for the F1 collaboration with Team Surtees being used in advertising. In April

*A view of the new central laboratory opened at Hammersmith in 1974. Duckhams scientists continually monitored production quality as well as pursuing new research projects.*

*The new wax pastillator installed at Hammersmith in 1974, with (l to r) Duckhams staff Ted Atkins, Steve Jacobs, Eddie Munroe, Frank Tranfield and Roger Dinning.*

1972 Q20-50 featured in a Land's End–John O'Groats run by a 1934 Austin Seven; oil consumption over the three-day trip was just one pint. A couple of months after this came Duckhams' successful participation in the Le Mans 24-hour event.

Later in 1972 the company supported 'the most ambitious expedition ever': a north–south crossing of the American continent from Alaska to Cape Horn, led by Major John Blashford-Snell. The 14,000-mile trek involved negotiating the Darien Gap, one of the last barriers in Central America to the opening of a Trans-American Highway and consisting of a daunting 250-mile mix of impenetrable jungle, swamps, mud, ravines and mountains. That the expedition eventually won through was all the more amazing when it was revealed that it took the 90-strong party almost three months to get its two specially equipped, Duckhams-lubricated Range Rovers through the Gap.

The year 1972 also saw the opening of the National Motor Museum in Beaulieu, Hampshire, with Duckhams among the list of subscribers to the trust through which it was financed.

Further changes were taking place within the company. As capacity was fully met by the new Aldridge plant, the Manchester works ceased to blend lubricants. More departments transferred to the company's HQ at Summit House, West Wickham, leaving only the technical and production staff at Hammersmith.

The competitive atmosphere in the field meant that the servicing of Duckhams outlets had to be a constant priority, and by now the number of PSMs (Publicity Service Men) responsible for this had reached 22. Their job was to ensure that the Duckhams signs, forecourt cabinets, etc, were in top condition, and that service bays received the necessary back-up.

In 1973 the company held its corporate breath as another crucial product launch saw the foundation of its current success, Q20-50, superseded by 'New Formula' Q. Accompanied by a press and TV advertising campaign, this was basically a relaunched Q20-50 with improved characteristics and packaging. All-round performance was enhanced, with much better viscosity and shear stability, while the pack design simulated the green oil flowing down the can.

The new oil was trialed by the Marlboro-BRM F1 team in the International Trophy meeting at Silverstone, the cars finishing 3rd, 5th and 9th. New Formula Q was now taken up officially by the Team Ensign, Hesketh Racing and LEC Formula 1 teams, with others also testing it in preference to the vegetable and synthetic alternative 'racing oils' traditionally used.

Internal reorganisation continued, with the closure of Duckhams' own printing department and the modernisation of the Manchester factory, which, with the purchase of adjacent buildings, became home to various operational staff, the industrial sales department and the publicity stores. Soon after this Works No 2 closed and a new central laboratory opened at Hammersmith. A new, more powerful computer was installed at head office to assist the still expanding business, as profits showed a substantial increase on the previous year to break through £1m again.

However, the Middle East crisis of 1973 brought huge rises in the price of crude oil and, as rumbling industrial unrest eventually erupted, chaos for the country. With striking mining unions lined up against the Heath Government, enforced power cuts and shortages of raw materials soon meant a three-day working week for most of industry. Road fuel, while never officially rationed, was restricted by availability. The election forced

upon Edward Heath in February brought Labour back, but without a majority, while a second election in October gave Harold Wilson a majority of just three.

In spite of the recent restrictions, three million motorists were by now reckoned to use Duckhams Q, while on the track it was in the engines of more than 1,000 contracted drivers, including no fewer than six Formula 1 teams. James Hunt had recorded his first F1 win in April with the Duckhams Q-lubricated Hesketh, and the following month Ronnie Peterson won at Monaco for John Player Team Lotus. In the lead-up to the British Grand Prix, the newly sealed association with the John Player team was being exploited through car stickers and the marketing of Q/JPS T-shirts and other linked merchandise, with the mail-order 'Duckhams Motor Sport Shop' doing great business.

August 1974 had seen the severing of Duckhams' final link with its founding family, when Neill Foster left after 14 years' service, to be succeeded as MD by Ray Strettell.

That year, the 75th anniversary of the company, was marked by a series of parties. Regional staffs held their own celebrations, while in London some 900 guests attended a dinner-dance at Grosvenor House. There was an extra cause to celebrate for, despite continuing difficult market conditions, trading profits for the year were on course for a new record at more than £1.5m.

This also being the 150th anniversary of the Royal National Lifeboat Institution, on 31 December at the Earl's Court Boat Show the RNLI was presented with a cheque for the purchase of an inshore lifeboat, to be named the *Alexander Duckham*. Without doubt the philanthropic gentleman after whom it was named would have thoroughly approved!

As Margaret Thatcher ousted Ted Heath in 1975 to become Tory leader, the 1970s continued to bring changes. Fulham works was sold, while expansion was announced at Aldridge on the purchase of extra land

# THE LIFEBOAT *ALEXANDER DUCKHAM*

The inshore lifeboat *Alexander Duckham* was funded through a donation by the company to the Royal National Lifeboat Institution in 1974, the 150th anniversary of the RNLI and the 70th anniversary of Alexander Duckham & Co Ltd. During her time at station the *Alexander Duckham* spent a total of 1,647 hours at sea, was launched on 618 occasions (including 475 to the aid of pleasure craft) and saved 207 lives.

Her station record is:

| | |
|---|---|
| 1976–1987 | West Mersea |
| 1988–1990 | Mudeford |
| 1991 | Poole |
| 1992–1993 | Falmouth |
| 1993 | Poole |
| 1995 | Port Erin |

Since 1995 the *Alexander Duckham* has been available as a relief lifeboat and is currently based at the Inshore Lifeboat Centre, Cowes, Isle of Wight, awaiting station allocation if necessary.

In celebration of the dual anniversary in 1999 – Duckhams 100th and the RNLI's 175th – the company is donating a replacement for the *Alexander Duckham*.

*The inshore lifeboat* Alexander Duckham *at sea and with its crew at West Mersea.*

opposite the existing works. On the packaging side, the 1-gallon can was phased out in favour of the 5-litre version as metrication progressed.

Rally ace Paddy Hopkirk was contracted to feature in a five-week television campaign, plus associated press advertising promoting Q, with a 'save money on motoring' theme, backed by a 16-page giveaway magazine. As a mobile promotional gimmick, a Mini was used as the basis for a giant Q can: the first airing for the Duckhams 'Q Car' was a promotion at Woolco.

Competition from 'own brands' was still

*A 'Q'-liveried AEC Mercury 2,000-gallon tanker of 1973.*

growing. The Ford Motor Company had introduced its own oil in 1972 and, among others, Woolworth and Tesco were shortly to join it. It was predicted within the industry that 'own brands' would capture some 14 per cent of the market by the end of the 1970s.

Against strong international competition, a major new contract was won in May 1975 under which Duckhams was to supply London Transport with all lubricants for its London buses. This was calculated at around 2.5 million litres annually.

It was a year when Duckhams-lubricated vehicles excelled in competition at all levels, with James Hunt's all-British Hesketh-Ford 308 winning the Dutch GP and coming second in the French event. The only disappointment

*Rally star Paddy Hopkirk was enlisted for a TV ad campaign in the 1970s.* (*The Ullage* magazine)

was a singular lack of success for the John Player Lotus team; its outdated cars were being replaced for the next season and, although the direct sponsorship arrangement was now ending, the team continued to use Duckhams lubricants. The year closed on a sad note with the death in an air crash of double World Champion racing driver Graham Hill, together with five members of the Lotus Grand Prix team.

Internal reorganisation continued at Duckhams. The existing joint venture company Shell-Mex & BP Ltd was now to be wound up and it was suggested that as a result there may be closer links with BP on the manufacturing side.

January 1976 brought the grand opening of Birmingham's National Exhibition Centre by HM The Queen. Thanks probably to the company's prominence in the city's Festival of Motoring over the previous few years, Duckhams was invited to be one of the few commercial concerns to exhibit, mounting a 20-metre stand with a motorsport theme at the special opening show, which was attended by

an estimated 150,000 people.

In March, when James Callaghan took over as PM from Wilson, an announcement was made to staff concerning the probable closure of Hammersmith works (scheduled to become a residential and recreational area under the Greater London Development Plan) and a £3m expansion of the Aldridge plant.

Under constant pressure from the budget-priced, own-brand oils, Duckhams' continuing assertion that 'quality is economy' received some vindication when it was arranged for the AA to take 13 oils from the shelves of UK supermarkets and have them independently tested. More than 50 per cent failed to meet the very basic Leyland low-temperature requirement, while 10 did not comply with published requirements in one way or another. Duckhams used this information in advertising, which, while it received a mixed reception, achieved its objective of making consumers think.

With no formal sponsorship now in operation as the company concentrated on the grass roots, Duckhams-lubricated cars never-

*London Transport's entire bus fleet went over to Duckhams following a contract signed in 1975. (Quest magazine)*

theless continued to win in the big events. The Italian GP was won by Ronnie Peterson in a March 761, while the JPS 77 of Mario Andretti won the Japanese GP at Fuji, with 29-year-old James Hunt clinching the World Championship in the same race in his McLaren.

For the Queen's Silver Jubilee in May 1977, Duckhams produced a 5-litre container of Q in a special carton carrying the Union Flag, together with a free Silver Jubilee medallion, half a million of which were affixed to cans at Aldridge and Hounslow. In a separate exercise, a special limited edition of 2,000 hallmarked and individually numbered solid

silver medallions was struck at the Birmingham Mint, for presentation to key customers and as prizes in competitions. The entire promotion was supported by radio and press advertising, and by the 'Q Car' which, complete with medallion, embarked on a nationwide tour.

With sales of non-motor oil products still providing valuable turnover, the diversification programme had borne fruit. Jenolite and the Jenolizing process, taken over eight years earlier, provided a service to industry for corrosion protection through both mobile and factory-based systems.

In a new venture, Duckhams launched Q on the West Coast of the USA through strategi-

*Duckhams was the major sponsor of the 1975 Birmingham Festival of Motoring.*

*Duckhams was one of the few companies privileged to exhibit at the opening of the National Exhibition Centre in January 1976. (Gareth Lewis)*

cally placed distributors. Blended locally to the company's specification, the oil would be packaged in US quart containers exported from Britain. For the UK 5-litre oil cans, the former metal screw caps were replaced by a new plastic 'Clipper' cap, which removed the risk of cut fingers. In this as in other matters, Duckhams led the industry, with others following soon afterwards.

In a motor oil market dogged by over-capacity, Duckhams was clinging to its substantial share, but only by joining the heavy discounting that was rife, to the conse-quent detriment of profitability. Competition support was maintained at the important grass-

roots level during 1977, with 175 events covered by the conspicuous Duckhams caravans, but the budget was slashed for the new year.

That year marked a major attempt at boosting the company's image, extending even to kitting out the industrial staff in new modern workwear. The biggest advertising campaign ever mounted, embracing TV, press and 1,000 hoardings around the country, including sports ground locations, was aimed at convincing 12 million motorists that Q was best. With the theme of 'The Utmost Care', it depicted an engine cocooned in a green oil droplet.

In further reorganisation the Hounslow plant moved into the control of BP, while the Hammersmith plant began to run down. The Aldridge extension, which incorporated a pipe bridge carrying blended oil from the stock

tanks across the road to a new warehouse and filling lines, was officially opened in May.

Despite margins squeezed by multinational and own-brand competition, the half-year loss already forecast by the pundits was prevented from being disastrous by the contribution from overseas and industrial sales. By the year end, however, the still shrinking margins led to the posting of a £750,000 deficit.

With further diversification still a sensible option, early in 1979 Duckhams increased its stake in the wax sector by acquiring a 49 per cent stake in wax producer Kerax. Other small-scale, non-lubricant activities were developed, such as water filtration and treatment, and new product launches included DPP, a multi-purpose de-watering and penetrating aerosol spray.

In March 1979 the Labour Government lost a crucial 'no confidence' vote and the ensuing election brought the installation of Margaret Thatcher as Britain's first woman Prime Minister. Duckhams backed the Transglobe Expedition (led by Sir Ranulph Fiennes and of which the Patron was HRH Prince Charles), which aimed to circumnavigate the globe by ice, sea and land.

A new, updated and more aggressive TV ad campaign was launched, and a fleet of 13 new, versatile delivery trucks was introduced for drops in remote areas where a bulk tanker was not cost-effective. The fully-liveried vehicles delivered bulk oil from lift-on 250-gallon tanks and also carried prepacked product.

Half-year results for 1979 showed a remarkable turnaround as prices were made to 'stick', and despite the Aldridge plant's production surpassing 50 million litres, the company struggled to satisfy demand. This at least provided encouragement for the launch of

'The Utmost Care for Bikes', a programme to bring new market-specific packs to motorcyclists, backed up by Duckhams participation in the Superbike Championship.

Year-end results appeared to confirm the reversal of fortunes with a trading profit of £1.4m. This was, however, to some extent enhanced by increasing stock prices, and profits soon slumped again. As Britain waged war with Argentina over the Falklands in 1982, Duckhams was fighting its own major battle against overheads, eventually involving the disposal of part of the West Wickham premises and the Westgate works, and the folding of both the house magazine *The Ullage* and the consumer title *Quest*.

The Manchester operation was reduced to a depot only, and Gateshead depot was closed, as was the loss-making Jenolite Corrosion Services operation. The Duckhams South Africa plant was sold and marketing responsibility handed over to BP South Africa; and the 40 per cent stake in Duckhams Sweden was sold to BP Sweden. Hammersmith's barge and former canteen-cum-social club *Aphrodite* was also sold.

Great efforts were made to turn the business round. New UK Industrial and Retail divisions were formed, the former becoming so successful that it managed to halt the slide, thanks largely to the setting up of an increasing network of UK distributors.

The product-led marketing strategy had never been forgotten, and March 1982 saw the launch at London's Mayfair Hotel of Duckhams Hypergrade. The result of three years' intensive development work, this was a 15W/50 engine oil developed to meet the needs of all cars, including diesels and turbocharged models. Completely replacing Q motor oil, it was approved by every motor manufacturer and surpassed the industry's highest specifications.

While international markets retained the Q brand, and some regrets were expressed within the company at its disappearance in the

UK, the Hypergrade launch was accompanied by a massive marketing exercise, with all signage at outlets being changed and a national TV campaign supporting the product, which was presented in new-image 5-litre metal cans and a newly introduced small plastic pack. This major commitment of resources was reported to have built a strong foundation for improving future sales and profits.

Industrial Division's success continued as new product lines, like a new range of industrial aerosols, new soluble oils and the revolutionary long-life cutting oil Endura, gained significant ground. With industry's new computer-controlled equipment geared to minimum downtime, Duckhams' traditional philosophy of working closely with customers and machinery suppliers was paying off, and relationships were cemented through regional distributor conferences and a nationwide 'meet the customer' programme.

It was in 1983 that another major restructuring wrought real changes to the previously largely autonomous Duckhams. On the sale of Hammersmith, BP assumed responsibility for all production and distribution activity and a study team was set up to review Duckhams' internal structure. In the autumn of that year Duckhams' industrial operations were taken over by BP's Industrial Division, and all remaining Duckhams industrial product lines were rebranded BP. The changes were not confined to industrial operations, the Aldridge blending plant being transferred to BP in December together with the London and Manchester depots.

The reorganisation showed in improved financial results, but by now just 160 staff remained to attend the conference held in January 1984 to discuss concerns.

*Built on Mini underpinnings, the Duckhams 'Q Car' proved a big attraction wherever it went. The livery was updated from time to time to match the current packaging.*

With brand awareness paramount, motor-sport backing continued, major support being provided to Team Toyota Europe and the Van Diemen Formula Ford team, the latter relationship remaining strong today. Excellent results in 1985 included wins for the Toyota team in the Ivory Coast and Safari rallies, and championship wins in European Formula 3000 (Christian Danner), European Formula Ford (Paulo Carcaste) and World Hot Rod Championship (Ormond Christie).

The Japanese motor industry established itself in Britain for the first time in 1986 with the opening of Nissan's Sunderland plant. That year, following a TV ad campaign featuring the catchline 'The Engine's Choice', Duckhams broke from its traditional one-product approach to the retail oil market with

*'Composite' trucks, used for deliveries in outlying areas, carried lift-on tanks as well as small packs of product. Note the built-in delivery hose.*

*The 1982 successor to Q was Hypergrade, a superior quality mineral-based oil that equalled the new synthetics in performance.*

the launch of QXR as an additional line, aimed particularly at the increasingly popular 'hot hatch' sector of the car market. A 10W/40 performance-enhanced oil developed through co-operation between the Duckhams/BP Oil technical support staff and BP Oil International, this was successful in its aim of converting many motorists currently using an inferior 'own label' oil to a premium type.

Presented for the retail market in an expensive blue plastic 5-litre pack complete with explanatory booklet, and supported by eye-catching advertising and through motor-sport exposure, QXR gained acceptance relatively quickly. Hypergrade too continued to be promoted, and it was also transferred from the traditional tinplate to plastic packaging.

AFTER MULTIGRADE DUCKHAMS THINK YOU'RE READY FOR AN OIL CHANGE

DUCKHAMS

15W/50 HYPERGRADE™

MOTOR OIL

*The first plastic retail packs were introduced for Hypergrade in 1987, replacing the customary tinplate ones.*

Duckhams was now building once more on its image as an independent lubricants brand both at home and abroad, and it is pleasing to record that in 1987 the company funded the renovation of the memorial to the Blériot cross-Channel flight at Dover, originally commissioned by Alexander Duckham himself. The freedom symbolised by that historic flight was beginning to be reflected behind the Iron Curtain, where Soviet leader Mikhail Gorbachev was calling for *perestroika* (reforms) and *glasnost* (open government).

With the lease on the company's offices at West Wickham due to expire, a new head office location was earmarked in Bromley and officially opened in February 1987 by HRH Prince Michael of Kent.

The following year Jenolite, now outside Duckhams' core business, was sold, leaving the company to concentrate 100 per cent on motor oil. A new Toyota Team Europe sponsorship deal was confirmed for 1988, and the same year an agreement was signed with motoring publishers Haynes for Duckhams products to be featured in their best-selling range of service manuals. Regular national promotions continued, the most successful being the purchase-related special offers on overalls and a used oil collector.

In what might appear an odd move, Duckhams reintroduced to the UK market during 1988 that old favourite, Q20-50, previously superseded by Hypergrade. As Q20-50 was now two generations older than the state-of-the-art QXR, the intention was not to place it in the premium sector, but rather to provide a direct and well-known competitor to the ever-increasing number of own-brand oils. The theory was that, faced with the choice of Bloggs or Duckhams oil at a similar budget price, the motorist would opt for the well-

known name every time; and it was largely borne out in practice.

In 1989 responsibility for Duckhams' international business passed to BP Oil International, leaving Duckhams to concentrate on its UK sales and marketing, including BP retail activities, while providing the international operations with brand expertise. An international brand manager was appointed, to co-ordinate brand development 'worldwide' – an expression that was beginning to have a whole new potential as the Berlin Wall crumbled that November, followed closely by the collapse of Communism itself.

As the peoples of the former Soviet Union celebrated, many Britons were rioting, or at least protesting, against the Poll Tax, culminating in the removal of Mrs Thatcher, to be succeeded as Prime Minister by John Major.

While the UK economic downturn at the beginning of the 1990s, reinforced by the effects of the 1991 Gulf War, influenced sales of motor oils, Duckhams' branded sales held up well, with QXR making further advances in an otherwise stagnant market. A difficult

*The Blériot memorial at Dover was restored at Duckhams' expense in 1987, prior to celebrations for the 80th anniversary of the historic flight it commemorates.*

*The Padgetts Racing teams were another highly successful Duckhams partnership, both in solo and sidecar events. Pictured is Darren Dixon, winner of the European Sidecar Championship in 1990. (Colin Taylor)*

year for the parent company in 1991 saw further restructuring of the UK lubricants business, the main result of which was that Duckhams would once again become more or less independent from BP.

Meanwhile the company launched a new five-strong range of engine oils in new plastic packs. Included were the fully synthetic oil QS, an improved-specification QXR, and new products Duckhams Diesel and Hypergrade Plus. In another 'first' for Duckhams, this range brought the latest API SH specification to the UK market.

Introduced in 1993, QS was Duckhams' first fully synthetic engine oil for the UK, although such oils had been made available previously to distributors in cold regions. The company had traditionally argued that the premium grade QXR would meet all the requirements of a fully synthetic oil 'more cost-effectively', but had never ruled out producing synthetics should motor manufacturers start to recommend them. After months of testing and comparison with other synthetics on the market, the company was confident that QS was at the top of its class.

The launch of Duckhams Diesel, already successfully test-marketed in Ireland, was ideally timed to meet the increasing numbers

*The Bromley head office was opened by HRH Prince Michael of Kent in 1987.*

*Duckhams launched its first fully synthetic engine oil in 1993, together with Duckhams Diesel and Hypergrade Plus, meeting the latest API SH specification – another first for Duckhams in the UK market.*

of diesels in the UK. Sales quickly accelerated to unexpectedly high levels, with plenty of evidence of buyers switching brands to this new diesel-specific lubricant.

That year the Duckhams-lubricated Van Diemen team won the Formula Ford Championship, while in the British Rally Championship Steve Bennett and Duncan McMath, running a Peugeot 205 on the new QS oil, bagged the BBC Top Gear Award.

With the product range now being tested in a number of new markets including the Middle East, international activity generally was increasing as expertise and ideas were shared. Continuing strict control of budgets meant that brand awareness had to be maintained in a cost-effective manner and,

following a redesign of packaging, the new format was introduced across the range. In a series of developments, this was followed soon after by multi-lingual labelling, which reduced plant complexity and helped service developing markets; this was replaced again on 5-litre cans by peel-off, multi-layer side labels that gave even more countries the opportunity to have own-language information on the product.

In 1995 a marketing agreement with British Motor Heritage paved the way for the launch of the new Heritage range of products aimed at classic and older vehicles, with packs and support material designed to represent earlier versions. A special older formulation of Q20-50 was used as the main launch grade.

As an international sales conference in Portugal in early 1996 confirmed the export progress being made (Duckhams was now marketed in more than 60 countries), another major announcement concerning the future of the company was about to be made. The setting up of a joint venture between BP and Mobil would involve the transfer of Duckhams' UK and European activities to Mobil, with non-European operations moving to BP.

As these decisions took formal effect, planned product introductions continued with the launch of upgraded QXR and QS meeting the latest API SJ specification. With assurances in place concerning the maintenance of Duckhams as a stand-alone brand, it was well presented at the start-up meeting of the new joint venture in Rome. A sales conference announced major new marketing initiatives and confirmed Duckhams' co-operation with the Ford Mondeo team in the British Touring Car Championship.

In the run-up to the Millennium, history continues to be written. Shortly after the landslide Labour victory under Tony Blair in May 1997, the country was plunged into mourning for the Princess of Wales, killed in a car crash in Paris. More recently, the launch of the Euro has brought uncertainties over Britain's position on monetary union and its relationship with Europe.

After a century at the forefront of oil technology, Duckhams is still taking the lead. It decided in the spring of 1998 that the time had come to do away with the complicated technical jargon surrounding the marketing of a diverse range of motor oils.

Recognising that the majority of today's drivers want 'fill-and-forget' reliability, it

*Ian Simpson, 1994 HEAT British Supercup Superbike Champion with QXR, on his Duckhams Norton.* (Turn One)

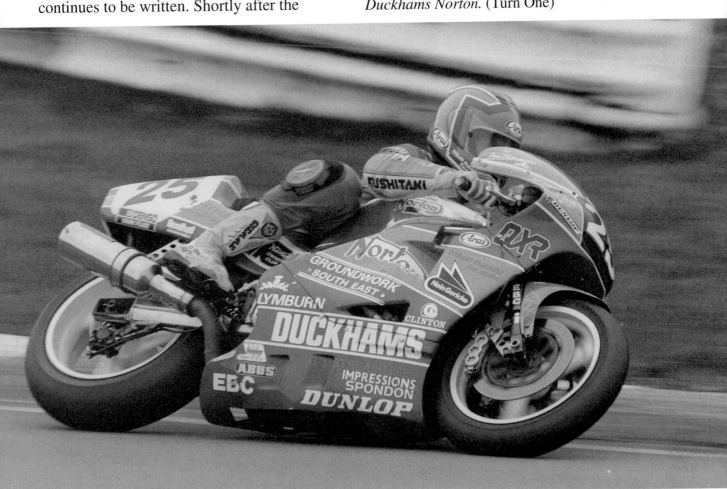

relaunched Duckhams brand motor oil as a simplified range, accompanied by straightforward product descriptions, that nevertheless brings the best quality and performance ever available to motorists. The relaunch was marked by major investment that included a return to television advertising for the brand after a 10-year absence.

Upmarket silver plastic packs, with colour-coded caps and labels, now offer the simple four-way choice of Hypergrade in petrol and diesel engine versions, or QXR Premium in petrol and diesel engine versions. All technical specs (apart from the key information concerning viscosity) are confined to a small panel on the back of each pack, beneath an easy-to-follow guide to checking the car's oil.

While all are made to a high quality, the QXR Premium oils offer additional protection that makes them particularly suited to cars that have longer service intervals, as well as aiding starting in cold conditions.

Reinforcing its grass-roots appeal, Duckhams in recent years has turned its sights on football, and sponsorship of Sky Television's coverage of the Nationwide League is continuing for a third season in 1999/2000. This is backed by promotions and competitions giving fans the chance to win VIP trips to see their favourite team and meet Sky's football commentators.

Accompanied by a restyled form of the familiar blue and yellow logo, the relaunched range takes the brand forward into a new century that will bring further technical advances of which we can only dream today. Duckhams' investment in its valuable brand is testimony to the confidence with which it approaches the Millennium and the start of its

*While maintaining its support for grass-roots motorsport, Duckhams has recently signed a football sponsorship agreement with Sky Television for its coverage of the Nationwide League, to continue for the 1999/2000 season.*

*With its simple, user-friendly range of oils, Duckhams is ready to serve the motorist of the 21st century.*

second hundred years. Its story is a unique one, founded as it was by a man of exceptional skill and vision, and nurtured through the past century by a loyal and dedicated staff, together with representatives around the world, all of whom believed that the customer was there to be served, and problems were meant to be solved.

Alexander Duckham had a great sense of occasion. The centenary of the company in 1999 is one celebration in which his spirit will be participating with special enthusiasm.

# INDEX

*(brackets indicate illustrations)*

# UNION J
## THE STORY

Tina Campanella is a former tabloid and magazine journalist. You can tweet her at @littlebell1982

# TINA CAMPANELLA

# UNION J
## THE STORY

JOHN BLAKE

Published by John Blake Publishing Ltd,
3 Bramber Court, 2 Bramber Road,
London W14 9PB, England

www.johnblakepublishing.co.uk

www.facebook.com/Johnblakepub facebook
twitter.com/johnblakepub twitter

Part of this book was first published as *Union J v District 3:*
*Battle of the Bands*
This updated edition published in paperback in 2013

ISBN: 978 1 78219 744 7

British Library Cataloguing-in-Publication Data:

A catalogue record for this book is available from the British Library.

Design by www.envydesign.co.uk

Printed in Great Britain by CPI Group (UK) Ltd

1 3 5 7 9 10 8 6 4 2

Papers used by John Blake Publishing are natural, recyclable
products made from wood grown in sustainable forests.
The manufacturing processes conform to the environmental
regulations of the country of origin.

Every attempt has been made to contact the relevant copyright-holders,
but some were unobtainable. We would be grateful if the appropriate
people could contact us.

# CONTENTS

## CHAPTER ONE

# 'TRIPLE J' AND GEORGE – SEPARATE PATHS

Louis Walsh definitely took notice as he watched the three earnest young boys bound onto the stage and yell: 'Hello, London!' Already he could already see the potential in this new group.

Met by girlish screams from the 8,000-strong audience in the capital's O2 Arena, they were a refreshing change from the hundreds of hopefuls the judges had seen that day. Shy and nervous, overconfident and bizarrely talentless, weird and wacky – the four-strong team of judges must have been tearing their hair out in frustration at what they'd had to sit through already.

With two of the lads casually dressed in white T-shirts and the other one in blue, they all shared broad smiles when Louis asked: 'So who have we got here?'

'We're Triple J,' said the confident boy in the centre to more screams of support.

The camera panned around the audience to show just a few of the giggling girls in the crowd, all whispering and pointing. It was clear that their first impression had been a good one.

Attempting to calm the growing atmosphere, Louis asked: 'Have you got people with you here today?'

'Yeah, all our mums are backstage,' laughed a very cute second band member, setting off another round of clapping – this time from the boys' families, who were anxiously waiting with presenter Dermot O'Leary.

'They're more nervous than us, I think,' added the third and final boy in the act.

'Off you go then,' Louis said abruptly, giving them the cue for their one chance to begin.

The crowd was suddenly silent. Would these three young boys have the talent to match their looks? Might this be the last time Triple J would grace a stage before disappearing into obscurity?

From the moment they launched into song, the boys' powerful voices echoed throughout the arena as they gave the Rihanna and Calvin Harris classic 'We Found Love' everything they had. Moving effortlessly around the stage, their voices harmonised and soared, brimming with emotion.

Judge Gary Barlow instantly sat back in his chair – it was as if he had been metaphorically punched in the face by the wall of sound! Guest judge Rita Ora bobbed her head in time to the beat as the rumbling cheers from the audience grew and grew.

'Shine a light through an open door...'

The lyrics were spookily appropriate because everyone listening to them suddenly knew that this performance had definitely opened the door for three talented boys. Finally they finished, throwing their heads down with the effort of the last few notes. Then the trio anxiously stood back up, to be greeted by thousands of instant, screaming fans. One by one they had risen to give the boys a standing ovation.

The crowd loved them. Now all they could hope was that the judges felt the same way...

Judge and solo artist Tulisa Contostavlos was quick to voice her praise. 'This is what a boyband's about – good-looking lads,' she announced.

Louis had the excited sparkle that said 'definite potential' in his eyes, while Rita Ora enthusiastically agreed, saying: 'I think the girls will love you.'

But it was Gary Barlow who fated the boys to stardom. 'In a good boy band it's not just about looking good, you've got to sound great, too – and you really do sound great,' he told them.

Brimming with excitement, the three boys could barely believe what they were about to hear.

Tulisa: 'Yes.'

Louis: 'Yes.'

Rita: 'Yes.'

Gary: 'That's four yeses, well done!'

The arena exploded as the boys patted each other on the back in disbelief before running backstage. Throwing their arms around their mums, all three were nearly toppled over by the force of their families' affection.

And that was how the world was introduced to singing sensations Jamie Hamblett, 23, Jaymi Hensley, 22, and 19-year-old Josh Cuthbert.

Within days of the boys' audition being aired, their Twitter account, @triplejofficial, had gathered more than 60,000 followers. It was obvious that they had been a staggering success, and the boys could hardly keep up with the constant stream of tweets from fans – all wishing them luck and declaring undying love for the instant heartthrobs.

But that was just the beginning. No one could anticipate the transformation that these three boys would undergo.

By contrast, Bristol teen George Shelley was alone when he took to the stage for his *X Factor* audition. He had no one to share a nervous smile with, or to sneak him a comforting wink if the judges were a little harsh on him. Prompted to audition by his good friend Emily Tollner, he didn't even tell his mum that he was going until the last possible moment. And so it was probably a shock to everyone who knew him when he casually walked out to take his spot in front of the judges.

Wearing a hoodie and jeans, with a guitar slung across his front, the first thing anyone noticed was his mop of perfectly constructed, immaculately messed up curls. Then he flashed his killer smile at the audience and got himself an instant fan base. With his peachy skin and fresh-faced good looks it was obvious he was going to be a firm favourite with the girls.

His grin was definitely verging on cheeky as he stood in front of the judges. Tulisa looked stern as she asked his name.

'I'm George Shelley,' he replied, without a hint of nerves.

The audience cheered and made a mental note to themselves to remember that name. If he could actually play the guitar he was clutching, and even half hold a tune, then surely this gorgeous boy was going to go far.

'How old are you?' Tulisa continued, still refusing to smile.

'I'm 18,' he said, prompting a wave of 'Awww's.

And the questions kept coming.

'What are you doing with yourself at the moment?' asked another judge.

George explained that he worked in a coffee shop, before he began chuckling to himself – making a few hundred more audience members fall hopelessly in love with him in the process. 'I'm going to sing 'Toxic' by Britney Spears,' he added.

It was a brilliant song choice – so different to what everyone was expecting from the teen dream standing in front of them. Tulisa suddenly took notice and cracked a smile.

'Hmm... Interesting choice,' she said. 'Go for it...'

Both guitar and voice sprang to life, surprising everyone in the room. The girls in the audience were transfixed by his sweet voice and Louis looked totally overjoyed at the package of talent in front of him. Especially as he sure could play the guitar!

'I'm addicted to you...' he sang, and surely half the audience was already starting to think the same thing.

When he finished the audience moved as one to stand up and applaud the talented teen in front of them.

Louis could hardly contain his excitement as he managed: 'Great look, great vocal!'

Gary instantly agreed. 'It's a yes from me.'

'And a massive yes from me,' said Tulisa, who by now had definitely been won over.

George put his hands to his face in shock. He couldn't believe the reaction he had got. He gave the audience one last smile, along with a casual wave, before walking off stage.

All four boys had never felt so excited in all their lives. It takes guts to stand up on stage and sing in front of famous and talented stars, but for them the bold gamble had paid off. They all went back to their respective homes, buzzing with excitement. They told family and friends, and even their local newspapers about their experience. Then they had to wait for Bootcamp to begin.

Triple J member Jamie – known as 'JJ' – excitedly told his local paper, the *Newmarket Journal*: 'I have always loved singing but never had the bottle. Singing is something I've always wanted to do and I'm grateful that I'm doing something I've always wanted to do.'

It was a sentiment that all four boys shared. Triple J and George Shelley were off to Bootcamp to begin their musical journey. There would be heartache ahead before their rebirth as the band we all love today – Union J.

But we're getting ahead of ourselves. So let's go back, before we go forward...

**DID YOU KNOW?**
Glamour model Bianca Gascoigne and former *Popstars* and *Pop Idol* contestant, Hayley Evetts, auditioned for the judges this season, too. Hayley made it as far as Bootcamp, but Bianca didn't get past the auditions.

## CHAPTER TWO

# THE UNION J BOYS – HUMBLE BEGINNINGS

## JAMIE 'JJ' HAMBLETT

**QUICK FACTS**
**DATE OF BIRTH:** 25/3/88
**BORN:** Newmarket, Cambridgeshire
**PARENTS:** Paul and Karin Hamblett
**SIBLINGS:** Ashley, 26; Otea, 7
**GREW UP:** Newmarket, Suffolk
**SCHOOLS:** Scaltback Middle School, Soham Village College

For someone so clearly at home in one of the biggest boybands in Britain, Jamie Hamblett had an unusual start to his singing career. But when you look at the family he comes from, it was hardly surprising that his first line of work would be working as a jockey – riding racehorses. Maybe he should be called 'GG' instead of 'JJ'!

Jamie comes from a place called Newmarket, which is at the very centre of the British horseracing world and many people in the town rely on the sport for work. His father Paul was a jockey, who later moved into training horses – work that requires getting up early every single day to muck out the horses' stables and take them for their exercise.

Not long before he himself started racing professionally, Jamie's brother Ashley had worked at one of the top stables in the family's hometown and had won a series of races. As well as Ashley and JJ's father, Paul, his uncle Martin also trained horses in Germany. And another distant cousin, Liam Heard, was a rider who helped improve horses' fitness. Horses were very much a part of JJ's life from the moment he was born, so it was no surprise when at the age of 14, he followed his father and brother into the horseracing industry.

With his dad's help he was apprenticed to the world-famous racehorse trainer, Sir Michael Stoute. Soon after that, he started competing as a jockey. It wasn't long before he had won his first race, and by early in his second racing season – at the age of only 16 – he had won four races.

It seems that winning is something JJ is very good at. Despite being nearly four years younger than Ashley, by 2006 he was winning just as many races as his brother and had made a big impression on the horseracing world. During his four-year career in the saddle, he took part in

270 races and won 24 of them. Part of his success may have been down to having a dad who was ambitious. It was this ambition that would later propel him to *X Factor* fame.

Jamie said his dad was strict about the need to work hard when he was young. Whenever Jamie looked like he didn't have anything to do, his dad would say: 'Why haven't you got a ride today? Phone your agent and ask why you don't have a ride.'

Paul would tell his sons to go for a run or something, to get them out of the house. He liked the boys to be busy, and this work ethic was great preparation for the *X Factor* competition – which is toughgoing!

It wasn't only his dad who used to offer him advice, though. Both Jamie and his brother would receive help and words of encouragement from racing stars like Kieren Fallon and Frankie Dettori.

By the age of 16 Jamie was putting a lot of pressure on himself to do as well as he could. He told the *Racing Post* in 2006: 'The worst thing is when I don't live up to my expectations.'

Sir Michael Stoute described him as being a very promising young rider. 'He's getting plenty of exposure on the racetrack now and he's developed a nice position in the saddle,' he said. 'He needs to work on his strength, but he's got talent and is certainly on an upward curve. I can see the progress he's making and he's the kind of rider who could end up doing well for himself.'

It sounds just like the kind of thing that Gary or Louis might say on the *X Factor* panel, so JJ obviously had a lot of experience in being judged and taking both praise and criticism.

While racing for Sir Michael, he was given the chance to ride one of the horses owned by Her Majesty the Queen. The Queen owns several horses and many of them take part in races around the country, ridden by jockeys like JJ. About two or three times a year, Her Majesty would call in at the stables to check on her animals.

Jamie said it was a daunting experience, meeting the ruler of the country. He told the *Daily Express*: 'Once or twice a year, she would pop into the yard to check on her horses – it was so weird, seeing her.

'She sauntered in, wearing Wellington boots as if it was normal – and she walked into the horses' box that I was in at that time. She said 'hello', fed the horses some grass and left. Apart from *The X Factor*, it was the most surreal moment of my life.'

As his career progressed, though he found it harder and harder to keep his weight down. If a rider is too heavy it makes it more difficult for the horses to go fast. Although Jamie wasn't overweight, he was heavier than most jockeys, many of whom are tiny compared to most people. The ones who are successful often weigh below 8 stone (51 kilos). In 2006 he weighed 7st 12lb – about two or three stone lighter than most boys in their late teens. Although his mum fed him a special diet designed to keep his weight low but his energy up, it became difficult to prevent him from becoming too heavy to make sure his horses kept on winning races.

In October 2009, he took part in his last competitive

horse race. It might have been difficult for the young boy to see a different future after he was no longer able to pursue his career as a jockey, especially as this exciting job had been the sole focus of his life up until that point.

When asked in 2006 what he did in his spare time, Jamie just laughed and shrugged off the question. He didn't have time to relax – it was all about the horses.

He continued to be involved with horses by helping out at a stables run by another trainer called John Gosden. Until the day he entered the *X Factor* competition, he helped train the horses by taking them out on practice runs every morning. The riding has kept him very fit, as so many girls around the country now appreciate.

With looks that most men would die for, it was inevitable that with a body honed by such hard work and the kind of chiselled features that are made for the camera, he would try modelling and acting. But, according to his family, he has sung at home all his life. They used to hear him sing along to the radio the whole time and often thought he had more than just the ability to carry a tune. After he started carving a career in the entertainment industry, he came across the other two 'J's', Jaymi and Josh, and leapt headlong as fast as one of the horses he used to ride towards the chance to form Triple J.

# JAYMI HENSLEY

**QUICK FACTS**
**DATE OF BIRTH:** 23/2/90
**BORN:** Luton, Bedfordshire
**PARENTS:** Jackie and David Hensley
**SIBLINGS:** Aaron, 17
**GREW UP:** Luton
**SCHOOLS:** Putteridge High School

As a dance teacher and choreographer for her local theatre group, Jaymi's mum Jackie had always hoped her oldest son would take up a career in the performing arts. From an early age Jaymi often joined his mum on stage with the Phoenix Players, Luton's amateur dramatics group.

The first time he took to the stage with adults was in 2001, aged 11, when he took on one of the lead roles in the production of *Blitz!* – a musical by Lionel Bart, writer of the hit musical *Oliver!* In the same year he began attending Luton's Putteridge High School, but despite homework and studying, he continued appearing in productions with the Phoenix Players.

At 14, he decided to do something incredibly brave for someone so young. He had been torn by feelings for others around him that many other people of the same age did not share. Taking them to one side one day, he gathered his family and other people close to him around him and summoned up all his courage.

'I'm gay,' he told them. It wasn't as if those who knew him best hadn't guessed, but sometimes people can react badly when so many people still find it hard to understand how anyone can be attracted to someone of the same sex. Jaymi had been worried those close to him wouldn't understand. Fortunately his family took the news really well. This allowed him to move on and concentrate on what really mattered to him – his singing career.

He later told *Heat* magazine: 'It is not a big thing for me – I came out when I was 14 to my family and friends and never had one piece of negativity.'

After leaving school at 16, he put his heart and soul into his plan to work in the entertainment industry and tried out for a new band called Code 5. Not only did he win a place, but the band were quickly snapped up as an exciting new boyband and were given the chance to support Irish act Westlife on one of their last series of arena gigs, called 'The Love Tour'.

As the youngest member of the five-piece act, Jaymi had only been with the four other band members for two months when he travelled up and down the country, playing some of Britain's biggest venues including Brighton, Wembley, Newcastle, Dublin and Belfast.

His bandmates included 'Ash', cousin of Antony Costa from the boyband Blue, and 'Jossy', who had both had previous stabs at boyband fame. Code 5 were brought together as a manufactured vocal harmony boyband to sing a mix of material written specially for them, as well as versions of songs by other artists, some as diverse as Lionel Ritchie.

Louis Walsh, Westlife's manager, was said to have personally chosen Code 5 as one of the support bands for the tour, but who knows if he remembered Jaymi when he performed in front of him at the auditions, five years later?

After the Westlife tour, the band continued touring before featuring in a BBC3 programme fronted by top rock record producer Tommy D, called *Singing with the Enemy*. The programme saw Code 5 having to work alongside their musical opposite, anarchic performance artists called K-Tron and The Exploding Triangles. They all had to put aside their differences and work together. The bands had just one week to dream up and record a brand new track and then perform a surprise gig in front of their die-hard fans.

Viewers watched as they struggled to live together in an intense pressure cooker of creativity and reconcile their musical differences. Despite all the attention, Code 5 didn't achieve the success they had hoped for, which left Jaymi looking for a new challenge.

After a spell at a holiday camp on the entertainment team, he returned to Luton, where the talented vocalist was able to make ends meet by teaching singing and dancing – just like his mum. At every opportunity, he did what he could to return to the stage and perform in front of a wider audience, though.

In 2010, he performed at the Maspalomas Gay Pride festival in Gran Canaria, Spain, in front of an audience of thousands. Before that he had been working as a singer, touring the clubs and bars of Britain and the resorts like those found on the beaches of Spain.

Also in 2010, he entered a competition to find singers

called the Open Mic Competition. After sailing through the regional heats, he made it to the final at London's indigO2, where he sang a slowed-down version of Michael Jackson's 'Billie Jean'. It was a close-run competition and he narrowly missed out on winning by being beaten by another competitor.

Jaymi tried out for BBC1's *The Voice*, but didn't make it through to the final stages. Then in 2011, he thought his time had come when he nearly made it through to the last acts in *The X Factor*. On this occasion he was part of a band called Brooklyn, who were all from his hometown of Luton.

When the four-piece group tried out in front of Gary Barlow, Louis Walsh, Tulisa Contostavlos and Kelly Rowland, it was the first time they had performed together on stage. They had formed in January of that year and just five days later, travelled to Cardiff to audition for the ITV show. Despite hardly knowing each other and having only a few hours to rehearse, they made it through the first rounds to audition in front of a live audience of 4,000 people.

They were allowed to perform two songs: 'Forget You' by Cee Lo Green and 'In My Head' by Jason Derulo. Their audition caused some disagreements between the judges but despite this, the boys still made it through to Bootcamp. At the time, Jaymi said: 'The whole experience was just surreal. We spent 24 hours a day with cameras following us round. The press were everywhere and we were being driven round in big *X Factor* buses that had to go on huge detours because we were being followed by paparazzi.'

But that was as far as Jaymi and his new pals went – they were booted out before they could get to the Judges' Houses stage. The group managed to sing on a tour of schools before yet another of Jaymi's shots at the big time came to an end and he found himself looking for yet another route to success. But he certainly wasn't about to give up: this time he had got so close. He knew that fame and fortune must only be round the corner.

Within just a few months, Jaymi had met up with the other boys from Triple J and finally, he was on his way to the superstardom he was destined to achieve.

# JOSHUA CUTHBERT

**QUICK FACTS**
**BORN:** 28/7/92
**PARENTS:** Kathryn and Graeme Browne
**SIBLINGS:** Callum, 13, and Victoria, 10
**GREW UP:** Winkfield, Berkshire
**SCHOOLS:** Cranbourne Primary, Charters Secondary School, Farnborough 6th Form College

The self-appointed frontman of the band, Joshua ('Josh') Cuthbert first found his voice when he auditioned for the part of Scrooge at Cranbourne Primary School in Winkfield, aged just 11.

Mum Kathryn later recalled the event for the *Bracknell News*, saying: 'I had no idea he had a voice – we were blown away by him singing. We got him straight into

Stagecoach in Bracknell, who told him to audition for *Chitty Chitty Bang Bang*.'

Less than a year later he was performing in the magical car musical at the London Palladium as 'George', alongside Jason Donovan, Christopher Biggins and the late Stephen Gately of Boyzone, who played the child catcher. He had the role for an exhausting nine months!

Between 2003 and 2008, he attended Charters School in Ascot, Berkshire, near the Windsor home of HM the Queen. The school has a track record for producing some great entertainers, despite being a specialist sports and science college. Among those who have been a student is Chesney Hawkes, known for his number one hit, 'The One And Only'.

As well as being a great singer and performer, Josh was also a fab footballer and played for Ascot United's junior team. Martyn Parker, co-headteacher of Charters School, remembers him as someone who would liven up a classroom with his sense of humour.

Mr Parker has since told the *Bracknell Forest Standard*: 'Josh is well remembered by staff and some pupils at Charters as a real character, who brought a smile to the face, could be a bit cheeky, but had a sparkle about him.'

In 2006, he joined his first band, Westend Boys – a five-piece that included his eventual manager, Blair Dreelan. (Blair also tried out as an *X Factor* contestant but wasn't so successful.)

Eagle-eyed *X Factor* fans might have recognised Josh when he appeared in Triple J because as part of Westend Boys, he attempted to get into the 2007 *X Factor* finals.

The group made it to Bootcamp, where they were sadly axed. Josh admits it may have cramped his style, having his mum chaperone him everywhere because he was still so young. He was only 15! The following year the band split up and went their separate ways.

Between 2008 and 2010, he attended Farnborough Sixth Form College but after tasting musical success he was determined to keep trying to break into the notoriously tough industry. In the year before he finished college, Josh was hard at work trying to find his next musical project.

He got together with another group of friends to form new band Boulevard. With him in the Ireland-based band were singers Ryan Davis and Andy Rice, along with Alistar Jay, who eventually joined Eli Prime – a band that later impressed the judges at the Manchester auditions of *X Factor* 2012.

By March 2011, Josh was supporting Boyzone on tour with Boulevard at a small series of gigs in Ireland, including the INEC, Kilarney, The Royal Theatre, Castlebar, and Belfast's Odyssey. They also supported *X Factor* legends Jedward in Dundalk and at the time were being tipped as Boyzone's replacements.

Singer Andy Rice told the *Dundalk Argus* at the time: 'The band are currently working on an album. We've already recorded a few tracks so far and over the next couple of months, we hope to finish it off and then finalise a deal with a label.'

But things didn't quite work out quite the way they'd all hoped, and Josh ended up spending five months selling mobile phones in Wokingham for the telecoms giant '3'. Later, he got a job as a new business executive for a computer firm called Tectrade. On his LinkedIn page, Josh described his skills as: 'Communicational skills, Confidence, Customer Interaction, Building Relationships'.

Eventually though, he got back in touch with his old bandmate Blair Dreelan, who in the meantime had himself appeared on *The X Factor*, hitting the headlines when his girlfriend left him for 2010 winner Matt Cardle.

It was Blair who took Josh, JJ and Jaymi to *The X Factor* as Triple J, before they were disbanded and reformed as the band we now know and love: Union J.

# GEORGE PAUL SHELLEY

**QUICK FACTS**
**DATE OF BIRTH:** 27/07/93
**BORN:** Bristol
**PARENTS:** Toni Harris and Dominic Shelley
**SIBLINGS:** Tom, 29; Will, 23; Harriet, 16
**GREW UP:** Clevedon, Somerset
**SCHOOLS:** Yeo Moor Primary, King Alfred Comprehensive, Weston College

George Shelley comes from a very musical family. His mum Toni plays the guitar and used to perform in pubs near their home in North Somerset. When he was younger, his granddad Dave was in a rock and roll band. These days the retired policeman, now 75, is keeping up the family's musical tradition by entertaining the residents with his accordion in retirement homes! George's brother Tom is a drummer whose band has just recorded their first single in Australia and his uncle John is also a singer and songwriter.

Coming from such a talented family, George was destined to follow in their footsteps. When he was just a toddler, his mum encouraged George's budding musical ability by giving him empty washing-up bottles filled with a small amount of rice – a maraca! George was fascinated and was quickly shaking the maracas along in time to his favourite songs, while his family sang along. They must have been like the modern equivalent of music legends The Osmond Family or The Jackson Five.

Toni took pictures of her son pretending to play the drums, with a huge grin on his face. George would use a wooden spoon to bang pots and pans, copying the stars he saw on TV. His talented mum was also a nurse and named George after an elderly patient she used to care for when she was working.

When he was three, George's parents split up and George, his two brothers Tom and William and his sister Harriet went to live with his mum. He continued to be fascinated by music and soon after he became a teenager his granddad Dave 'busker' Harris bought him his first guitar. Almost immediately, he had mastered the instrument and at just 14, took to the stage at the Priddy Folk Festival, in a village near to his family's home.

His mum Toni, who has also taught aerobics, told his college website: 'George sang as soon as he could talk and is able to harmonise perfectly. He's never had a guitar lesson in his life but he's got a natural ability.'

And speaking to the *Weston-Super-Mare People*, she said: 'We have a musical family and his granddad Dave was a real rock and roller.

'George, even as a young boy, always wanted to join in and used to pretend he was playing on the drums, using a saucepan and a wooden spoon. We also used to make instruments by filling up washing up bottles with rice. He has always loved singing, dancing and playing instruments and enjoyed drama and being in plays.'

She added: 'He has always been the sort of person who could pick up an instrument and play it – a talent he got from his granddad.'

While at school, George wasn't sure if he could make it as a full-time musician. He was wise enough to know that it was difficult to make a living out of music when there are so many wannabe stars out there to compete with. So although he kept his musical dreams alive, he sensibly worked hard on his schoolwork, too. As well as music, he had always had a passion for art. He decided that he would study graphic design, so he could become a designer and travel abroad.

At Weston College he was considered an outstanding student and won distinctions in all his subjects, completing an Extended BTEC in Graphic Design. As part of the course, he got to travel to New York. He loved it so much out there that he ended up wondering if a career in graphic design in America was what he really wanted to do. He applied to study at a higher level and ended up winning a place on a foundation course at the prestigious Bath University.

Concerned as to whether he could live up to the musical standard set by so many members of his family, he kept his bid for stardom quiet while growing up. But his musical past kept nagging away at him and he could never dismiss the lingering desire to sing on stage. He confided in his friend Emily Tollner, who suggested that he should audition for *X Factor*.

Having made it through to the later stages of the auditions, George felt he had no choice but to consider taking a year out between school and college to see how far he could get. If this was his one chance, then he would give it all he had but it hadn't been easy for him at home in the run-up to entering the competition.

His mum Toni also had to fight her own battle after she suffered a stroke in March 2011. George and the family lived through a terrifying few hours after she was rushed to hospital, where she was initially diagnosed with a severe migraine and sent home. Despite being released, her symptoms continued and the normally fit and active mum knew something wasn't right.

Toni actually experienced a bleed in her brain, which continued when she was sent home and left her with loss of feeling on her left side. She has also had recent extensive surgery on both wrists for a condition known as carpal tunnel syndrome and has been unable to find work since. She said: 'It isn't very easy given my medical history, but I am feeling much better and it's wonderful to be part of this experience with George.'

With his mum unable to work, George has also needed to make ends meet to help in his goal to achieve fame. So he found a part-time job as a barista at Costa Coffee.

Despite the scares at home and his fears over whether it was the right thing to do, George listened to his friend Emily and went after his goal of achieving singing success. Unlike his bandmates, he turned up at the *X Factor* auditions on his own and immediately impressed the judges with his good looks, boyish charm and striking voice. With a clear musical talent too, it was not long before he was singled out and added to the lineup of one of the UK's hottest new young acts.

## CHAPTER THREE

# BOOTCAMP – FATE LENDS A HAND

Both Triple J and George Shelley had made it through to Bootcamp, but they had a long way to go yet. They'd had time to calm down from the initial excitement of their successful audition, and all their friends and family had told them over and over that they were so talented – they really believed they could do it. This was their big chance...

But as they travelled to Liverpool for the intense three days of Bootcamp, their nerves had all started up again. Only 25 acts would go through to the Judges' Houses and when they arrived at the Echo Arena, the boys could see that it would be an epic competition.

The room was full – with 211 acts, to be exact, and the judges would have to be super-harsh when they made their final cuts. One small slip-up and they would be out.

The tension was unbelievable. Hardly anyone ate or drank anything; they were all so nervous. The waiting room was a cacophony of voices, all singing different songs at the same time.

The boys were all relieved when they survived the shocking first cut, which saw 70 acts eliminated from the competition in a new twist for the *X Factor* contestants. Those acts weren't even given the chance to sing again before they were axed. For them, their dreams were over – for that year, anyway. Plenty of people audition for the show year after year, hoping they will have improved enough to finally make it.

The rest of the singers were put into groups and had to take part in a nerve-wracking sing-off.

As the three days passed, the number of acts slowly dwindled. Many went home and had to be comforted by their friends and family.

George Shelley had met Triple J during these exciting days and had instantly liked Josh, JJ and Jaymi. They were all of a similar age, and bonded over their shared nerves. But Triple J were sad when they found out that George didn't make it through Bootcamp.

He left Liverpool and went home, wishing his new friends in Triple J all the best and trying to figure out how he would ever get used to normal life again. Meanwhile, Triple J were still going strong, but now the judges had a problem. They'd found it really difficult to whittle down the acts, and now they were well and truly stuck: there was one spot left and two bands who desperately wanted to fill it.

Both were talented and good-looking groups of guys and it would be hard to choose between them.

They were GMD3 and Triple J.

The two hopeful bands would have to go head to head in front of the judges and they needed to sing their hearts out for the final spot.

Standing on stage, Triple J looked over at their rivals. They were handsome lads and they could certainly sing – they'd heard them practising so they knew they would be stiff competition.

Gary looked at them all and explained the situation.

'Okay, guys, the only way of settling this is to battle it out,' he said. 'We want to hear you sing again.'

Each band took a minute to decide what they would perform. They all huddled together, whispering secretively. Sipping water, Josh told the other Triple J boys: 'We've just got to not make a mistake.'

It was true, but the boys were so nervous, it would be difficult not to let everything overwhelm them.

'Triple J, can you go first?' asked Gary, kindly. Nodding in reply, the boys took a few deep breaths and began.

Their words echoed hauntingly around the stage. Harmonising to 'Yeah' by Chris Brown, the GMD3 boys bobbed their heads to the sound of their rivals' voices. It was clean and in time, and the boys had done themselves proud.

The judges watched intently as they performed with no backing track. Even GMD3 looked nervous, which the Triple J boys took to be a good sign.

'Okay, guys,' Gary said to GMD3. 'Are you ready?'

This was it – this was what it had come down to. The

next few minutes would decide whether Triple J would go on to be mentored at the Judges' Houses – or whether they would be going home. They just had to hope that whatever the GMD3 boys sang, it wasn't as good as what they'd just offered up to the judges. But sadly, it was…

Singing 'Bless the Broken Road', the performance was almost faultless. They sounded much less nervous than Triple J, and the boys wished that they'd had the chance to go second. It had given Greg, Mickey and Dan time to compose themselves, with the result being a beautiful performance.

Triple J looked devastated but the judges hadn't immediately made up their minds, and instead they whispered to each other, deep in concentration.

All the boys could do now was wait.

'It's very close, there's not much between them,' said Gary, knitting his brow in concentration.

'This is tough, they both did so good,' said former Pussycat Doll and fellow judge Nicole Scherzinger.

On stage, Triple J looked close to tears, desperately hoping for the wait to end. It was torture for all the boys, who had worked so hard to get to that stage. Finally, Gary spoke. It was time to put everyone out of their misery.

'Okay, guys, you've been neck and neck throughout this competition and I'm sorry it's come down to this,' he said, 'but we've got to pick one of you right now.'

He paused while both the bands made silent prayers.

'The act taking the last place at the Judges' Houses is… GMD3.'

It was all over for Triple J.

The boys were gutted.

JJ courageously said thank you to the judges, before throwing his arms around Mickey from GMD3.

Backstage, the boys wiped the tears from their eyes and once more embraced.

'We're not going to walk away downhearted,' they said after composing themselves. 'We've got this far, we've got to keep our heads high and carry on.'

Then they went home, where their families tried their best to console them.

Soon after, Louis' bands were all set to fly to Las Vegas for the next stage of the competition – the Judges' Houses. Rough Copy, MK1, GMD3, Mitsotu, Poisonous Twins and Duke all had their bags packed and were ready to go. But before they could leave, Rough Copy received some devastating news: one of the band members had a visa application being considered by the UK Border Agency and so he couldn't leave the country in case he wasn't allowed back in.

The producers were so excited about them as a band, but they found out about the potentially difficult situation just as they were organising flights for everyone. The judges had no choice but to axe Rough Copy from the competition. And that left space for one act to be recalled to *The X Factor* but who would it be?

Louis had a lot of thinking to do. There were two bands that he was considering taking to the next stage in their place – Times Red and Triple J. But there wasn't enough time to decide between them so they were both invited along to the Judges' Houses round.

Triple J couldn't believe their ears when they heard the news. They had gone back to their old lives and old jobs, and were trying hard to move on, but now they were back in *The X Factor*! With one more chance to show they were worthy of the public's adoration, they packed their suitcases in a hurry to leave.

But Louis had one more surprise up his sleeve: he hadn't been able to stop thinking about another of the acts that the judges had axed. And he had an idea that wouldn't go away.

He picked up the phone and dialled one more number…

George Shelley was at home in Bristol when the phone rang. As the caller started to speak he couldn't believe who he was talking to. Louis Walsh. *X Factor* Judge. Boyband King.

'Yes, yes, of course,' he mumbled. And then put the phone down. Had that conversation been real? Did Louis Walsh really just say what he thought he'd said?

George was back in *The X Factor*! He was going to join his new friends, Triple J, to make the band a fab foursome. And they would have a new name.

Union J was born.

## DID YOU KNOW?
Josh's nan spent over £800 on tickets to see him in *Chitty Chitty Bang Bang* – she went every week!

Let's take a look at who made it through Bootcamp…

# MENTOR: NICOLE SCHERZINGER (BOYS)

### JAHMENE DOUGLAS

Fact: Schoolfriends of the shy Swindon supermarket worker used to pay him in sweets to sing.

### NATHAN FAGAN-GAYLE

Fact: Nathan had two top 40 singles before joining *The X Factor* – under the guise of 'StarBoy Nathan'.

### JAKE QUICKENDEN

Fact: A lifeguard from Scunthorpe, Jake hoped to win so that he could pay his mum back the cash he owed her.

### ADAM BURRIDGE

Fact: An admin worker from Middlesex, Adam dreamt of playing at Glastonbury.

### JAMES ARTHUR

Fact: James ran away from home when he was young and has always said music is his coping mechanism.

### RYLAN CLARK

Fact: An Essex model, Rylan's dream is to release a dance album.

# MENTOR: TULISA CONTOSTAVLOS (GIRLS)

### JADE ELLIS
Fact: A London bike mechanic, this single mum hoped to win to provide a good life for her daughter.

### AMY MOTTRAM
Fact: Student Amy has been nicknamed the 'Essex Adele' because of her big voice.

### LUCY SPRAGGAN
Fact: The Sheffield portrait-seller bravely performed her own song at the first audition.

### LEANNE ROBINSON
Fact: A sales assistant in London, Leanne prided herself on having no gimmick about her – just a fab voice.

### ELLA HENDERSON
Fact: Ella overwhelmed the judges, but couldn't believe she'd got through Bootcamp.

### JADE COLLINS
Fact: The Belfast student enlisted her mum's help to make her stage outfits.

# MENTOR: LOUIS WALSH (GROUPS)

### MITSOTU (HOLLY COOPER, JAMES COLLINS AND JIMMY ESSEX)

Fact: The North London trio said they were shocked at how emotional it was on the show – and by the lack of sleep!

### DUKE (MARKO PANDAZIS, EDWARD TRAVERS AND FLYNN STRONACH)

Fact: The beatboxers from Gloucestershire got a massive 2,000 new Twitter followers in the two hours after their first audition.

### MK1 (CHARLIE, REAL NAME, LOTTE RUNDLE AND SIMEON DIXON)

Fact: The London dubstep group dropped their third member after the judges said he looked like an accountant!

### POISONOUS TWINS (STEPHANIE MCMICHAEL AND SOPHIE HOUGHTON)

Fact: This was Liverpool born Steph's second try at fame – after being first out of 2008's *Big Brother*.

### TIMES RED (STAZ NAIR, SCOTT RITCHIE, LUKE WHITE)

Fact: Geri Halliwell was particularly taken by the sexy Times Red trio.

### DISTRICT 3 (DAN FERRARI-LANE, MICKY PARSONS, GREG WEST)

Fact: District 3 were originally called GMD3.

And of course, our boys: Union J.

# MENTOR: GARY BARLOW (OVER 28S)

### BRAD SHACKLETON
Fact: A London motivational speaker, Brad's dream was to work with Gary Barlow.

### MELANIE MASSON
Fact: The Glaswegian full-time mum-of-two belted out Janis Joplin's 'Cry Baby' at her audition.

### CHRISTOPHER MALONEY
Fact: The Liverpool customer services adviser deliberated for five years before entering *The X Factor*.

### CAROLYNNE POOLE
Fact: A casino singer from Huddersfield, Carolynne got as far as the *X Factor* Judges' Houses in the previous year.

### KYE SONES
Fact: A London chimney sweep, Kye used to be in electro-pop band, Diagram Of The Heart.

### NICOLA-MARIE BLOOR
Fact: The Derbyshire lass had been an Amy Winehouse and Lady Gaga tribute act before she went to auditions.

## CHAPTER FOUR

# JUDGES' HOUSES – WHAT HAPPENS IN VEGAS

Landing in Las Vegas, it must have seemed like a whole new world for the Union J boys. The acts that perform here are mega-stars – singers who pack out casino stages, night after night. Mariah Carey, Elvis Presley, Elton John, Barbra Streisand... The echo of every music legend's voice has reverberated around this very city.

Tulisa had taken the girls to St Lucia with Tinie Tempah, while Nicole jetted the boys to Dubai with R&B star Ne-Yo. Gary and the over-28s remained in England, travelling to Boughton House in Northamptonshire, where they were joined by a surprise guest: Cheryl Cole. Her appearance was so top-secret that she had to hide under a tablecloth while the acts performed!

But our two favourite bands were in Vegas for one reason only – to prove to Louis Walsh and his sidekick

Sharon Osbourne that they should go through to the live stages. It was a dramatic backdrop for the next stage of the battle.

Sitting in a plush hotel, more decadently decorated than their wildest dreams, Union J spoke from the heart about their experience so far.

'We weren't even meant to be here, originally,'mused Jaymi. 'We've been given such a lifeline.'

Josh was keen to include George in their new band, and said: 'George has only been with us for three or four days so it's been a bit of a rollercoaster, to say the least.'

George certainly looked at ease with the boys, who could hardly keep still with excitement.

Reclining in his leather seat, JJ said: 'We feel like brothers, he fits like a missing puzzle piece. We feel ten times stronger than ever we were as a three.'

Having been together for such a short period of time, the boys must have been nervous about singing for Louis and Sharon. But as night fell over Vegas, it was time for the foursome's first performance together. They walked down a huge cast-iron staircase onto an amazing roof deck, which overlooked the famous Vegas strip. Millions of coloured lights twinkled and flickered behind them.

The walk must have felt as if it took hours, but in just a few seconds they were sat facing the judges.

Breaking the tense silence, Louis spoke first. 'What would it mean to you guys to get through to the live shows?' he asked.

'It would mean everything, it's what we want so much,'

said Josh. 'Going back to our normal jobs after Bootcamp was horrible because reality hit us and it's something we've dreamed of.'

Nervously shuffling their feet, they tried to keep the fear from their faces as Louis said, simply: 'Off you go...'

George started strumming on his guitar and Josh began to sing 'Call Me Maybe', the song they'd performed as Triple J at the auditions. One by one George, Jaymi and JJ joined in and together their confidence grew. On their own they could sing, there was no doubt about that, but together they were transformed into a professional slick group, brimming with talent.

They may have been a little rough around the edges, but this was the real start of their journey and it had a huge impact on their growing fan base.

Sharon, wearing a white jacket, grinned at Louis. She nodded her head as Union J finished their song.

Waiting for their reaction, the boys must have been disappointed when Louis signalled for them to leave, saying: 'Thank you very much.'

Silently they trooped back to where Dermot O'Leary was waiting for them. 'How did it go?' he asked, gently.

It was, they agreed, very emotional.

Under the stars, Louis and Sharon discussed their performance. 'A couple of them have picked up really novice bad habits,' said Sharon, gravely. However, Louis came to their defence, saying: 'But with a bit of work they could be fantastic.'

There was nothing the boys could do now but wait for the verdict.

**DID YOU KNOW?**
**Jaymi has a whopping 17 tattoos and claims that**
**some of them are very tricky to find...**

The next day the sky was a brilliant blue. The sun shone on the handsome boys as they stood on the same deck on which they had performed the night before. They were dressed casually, but there was nothing casual about what was about to happen. At last they would find out if all the heartache had been worth it – would they be in the final 12? Would they grace the X Factor stage in the live shows?

Josh clutched his hands together as if he was praying, as Jaymi said: 'We've already had one no and we don't want to go home devastated again – we've waited so long for this. Louis brought us back because he saw a spark in us and then to come here and blow it – we'd be devastated.'

Josh tried to say that he didn't want to let his family and friends down, but the tears falling down his cheeks were so heartfelt that no one was listening to the words coming out of his mouth – those tears spoke volumes enough.

Seeing his bandmate cry affected JJ deeply, and the pair of them broke down and had a little weep together. They're such a close bunch that it was bound to happen. George tried to comfort them so that everyone could compose themselves for the verdict, which was merely moments away.

Biting their nails, they listened as Louis, sporting sunglasses, began to reveal his decision.

'Guys, we loved your first audition, we saw great potential and in the sing-off that's when you showed a little bit of spark.'

The boys nodded and tried to take deep breaths to calm themselves down.

'George, putting you in, it was a bit of a gamble. I think you fitted in very well with the band but there's an awful lot of work to be done and we haven't got months, guys.'

It wasn't sounding very positive and Josh, who had just finished wiping his tears away, began to sob once more.

'The problem is, boys, there are other boybands in this competition who have the edge on this group because they've been together longer. I thought long and hard about it, guys. We're in Vegas and I'm not a gambling man...'

The moment was coming and it was all too much for the boys. They'd been through such an emotional time; they didn't know what to think or feel anymore. As they all began to weep, they could hardly hear Louis.

'...until today. You're through!'

The boys were stunned and for a split second they let it all sink in. They were in! They would sing live on the *X Factor* stage, seen and heard by millions of potential fans. All they could do was jump up and down and hug each other, yelling: 'We're going to the finals!'

'Don't let me down,' warned Louis.

**DID YOU KNOW?**

**When Union J were announced as one of Louis' final three, One Direction's Louis Tomlinson went crazy with excitement, tweeting: 'Yeyyyyy I really like Union J!!'**

Here are the final 13 lucky acts who made it through to the first live show:

James Arthur
Rylan Clark
Jahmene Douglas
Jade Ellis
Ella Henderson
Lucy Spraggan
Christopher Maloney (wildcard)
Melanie Masson
Carolynne Poole
Kye Sones
District 3
MK1
Union J

# CHAPTER FIVE

# UNION J GO LIVE!

## WEEK ONE – HEROES
6/7 October 2012

What Union J sang: 'Don't Stop Me Now' – Queen

What the judges said:
Tulisa: 'What was important was missing – if you get through this week, I need to hear vocals.'
Gary: 'You're a good band, but Louis, you've destroyed their night.'
Nicole: 'Well done for performing for the first time as a group.'
Louis: 'We'll get it right next week.'

The sun was shining on a beautiful October day as the black cab drew up at the Corinthia Hotel in London – a

294-room palace of a hotel, just minutes away from Trafalgar Square.

As the now four members of Union J got out and looked at the grand entrance, their faces lit up. If they were lucky, this could be their home for the next few months.

'This is a lot nicer than my house at home,' said Josh, staring in amazement.

'I bet the Queen lives here,' added JJ, walking up the huge steps to where a smartly dressed doorman was waiting to let them in.

'Welcome to the Corinthia Hotel,' said a smiling receptionist as she handed over the keys to the suite. She and the rest of the smart hotel's staff would have a huge job on their hands – keeping out the hordes of *X Factor* fans who would surely soon arrive, hoping to catch a glimpse of their latest idols.

'This is still like a dream,' said Josh, as they stepped into the swanky lift. Opening the door to their suite, the boys' eyes widened still further: it was huge! Plush purple and gold cushions lay across the enormous bed – there was a giant TV screen and even a lounge. It must have felt like being given the keys to their own brand new flat, complete with maid service and room service.

'Shotgun!' yelled George, leaping onto the bed and claiming it as his own.

'Oh no!' the others groaned, 'You're not shotgunning the bed!'

But there was plenty of room for everyone in the beautiful suite. And anyway, once they'd unpacked they had little time for exploring.

They were taken for vocal coaching before heading off to have choreography lessons with legendary dancer and choreographer Brian Friedman. He has worked with stars like Britney Spears and Salt-n-Pepa, and even organised the moves in the film *Charlie's Angels*.

In the huge dance studio, Brian took them through some steps before giving the boys some advice. 'You have to be the heartbeat of the party,' he told them. 'You have to sell that this is a united group. Union is part of your name, so what I need more of from you is interaction with each other.'

He would be responsible for taking the boys' raw talent and honing them into stars.

With their singing and dancing being taken care of, it was then time for the stylists and hairdressers to work on their look. The boys couldn't believe how much pampering and preening they had to go through. They had their eyebrows plucked, their hair cut and styled and they even went for facials.

'It was literally like a star treatment, that we're not really used to,' said George.

Next they were whisked to the famous *This Morning* studios, to reveal their feelings on their new band to the nation. George told the presenter that he'd always hoped to be put into a band, so he had got his wish!

'I came into *X Factor* hoping to be put into a group scenario,' he said. 'Especially after my first audition, I felt like I need something around me.'

Sitting beside him on the sofa, JJ, Josh and Jaymi grinned, showing how happy they were to have George on board.

Jaymi admitted that it had been a rollercoaster of a journey so far, and he was just happy to be back with a second chance. 'We auditioned as a three-piece and we didn't make it through Bootcamp,' he said. 'Then Louis rang the house and said, "Guys, I've had a problem with one of the groups' visas so we're going to offer you a place at Judges' Houses – plus we're going to add George".'

The boys were obviously happy with their new line-up. They were now one step close to becoming a superband...

Union J had just over a month to get to know each other properly and rehearse for the live shows. They had to make their acts as slick as their fellow groups, MK1 and GMD3, who had both been together for years and knew each other like brothers.

Speaking about George, Jaymi told the *This Morning* viewers: 'We met at Bootcamp and bonded really, really strongly and when we came out of the competition we stayed in contact. He has just fitted in straight away and we love having him.'

**DID YOU KNOW?**
**When Triple J met George at the auditions, they had been thinking of asking him to join their band anyway so it was perfect when Louis became their musical matchmaker!**

That week they also spilled the beans about some of the difficulties they faced in Vegas – with one of the other bands. According to the boys, one group were using some dirty tactics in Sin City. And surprisingly, it was the only girl band in the group – Poisonous Twin – who they described as an absolute nightmare.

'They would just speculate,' George explained to Heatworld.com. 'They were just poisonous. All the way through the Judges' Houses they were speculating about what was going on.'

At first, they had got on with the two girls – before their gossiping began to drive them nuts. 'When we got there they were saying, "Oh, we just overhead someone saying that they're going to split the boybands up and stuff".'

Josh said it was a dirty tactic, while sensitive Jaymi seemed upset by it all. 'It's sad because we thought they were quite close with us. When we got there, they were really nice to us.'

Apparently the duo even told Union J that they'd heard rumours that the show's producers were going to kick George out of the group – after he'd only just joined them.

'They were saying this just before we were about to go on and sing,' said Jaymi.

Luckily for the confused boys, Poisonous Twin didn't make it through to the first live show. And the rest of the contestants were getting on so well they felt like one big happy family.

All week they worked hard on their performance, getting themselves ready for the first live show. But they did take time out to eat together, where they constantly messed around, throwing bits of food at one another and teasing each other.

They stopped practising one night to head over to the

famous celebrity club Whisky Mist, where they were showered with female attention. Joined by Jade Ellis and Lucy Spraggan, MK1, Carolynne Poole, Kye Sones and Rylan Clark, the boys soaked up the celebrity lifestyle before the live shows had even begun. But though they had a few drinks, they didn't overdo it. It was just a chance for the boys to have one final night off before the fight of their lives began.

On the day of the live show, the boys filmed a short segment to be aired that night, where they spoke about how they were coping, spending so much time together. 'We're even bathing together,' joked JJ, much to the amusement of the others.

It was clear the boys were really looking forward to the first live show. 'We're really excited to get the chance to sing in front of Olympic stars,' said Josh. But there was one particular athlete they couldn't wait to meet.

'Laura Trott's going to be in the audience,' said JJ.

'She's really hot,' said Josh. 'Hot to Trott!'

'Nooo!' cringed the others, putting their heads in their hands and groaning at the bad pun.

'That's really cringy,' said George, giggling.

**DID YOU KNOW?**
**Louis Walsh had a hair transplant before the latest *X Factor* series. No wonder his barnet was looking so lustrous!**

That night, hearing their own voices on the pre-recorded snippet from backstage, the boys prepared to take their first steps onto the *X Factor*'s live stage. And they had a surprise before the show: One Direction were there to give them some advice.

The boys were definitely starstruck to see their heroes, and when they were all mingling, it was hard to tell them apart. They looked like one big superband!

'Just have fun,' the established singing sensations told the next big things. 'Literally, just go out there and have fun.'

One Direction had been in their shoes at that first *X Factor* live show two years before and they knew what it was like so Union J were very appreciative of anything they could say to make the experience a little easier.

'You know you can sing the song – you've been practising all week, so just get out there,' said Niall. 'Just be yourselves the whole time.'

And shaggy-haired heartthrob Harry Styles had some important words for baby-faced George. He told him: 'Never cut your curls.'

The pep talk had really given the boys the confidence boost they needed to go out on stage and fight for their place in the competition. They'd practised for hours, but would that be enough?

Standing on a huge plinth, with their new name emblazoned on it, the pressure was on. This was it. This was finally their moment. This was where they would prove to their mentor Louis that he had made the right decision. This was where they would prove to the other judges that they deserved to be in the competition. And this was where they would win the hearts of the eight million viewers at home.

'Tonight, I'm gonna have myself a real good time...'

George was the first to sing, to the appreciation of the audience, before he was joined one by one by Josh, JJ and Jaymi, all singing the Queen classic.

'If you wanna have a good time, just give me a call...' they sang and if any of the girls watching at home knew their numbers, they would certainly have been dialling.

After they'd sung a few lines, the stage was swarming with brightly dressed backing dancers and pyrotechnics and you could hardly see the boys against all that was going on. With so many scantily clad dancers gyrating in front of them, it was a wonder they could concentrate.

Tulisa looked stony faced as the boys belted out the tune but Union J were oblivious, lost in the excitement of the moment – their first ever, live, on-stage performance. When they finished, they jumped energetically down from their plinth and walked towards the judges, the cheers deafening them.

Tulisa began to speak, signalling for the audience to quieten down. It was time to hear what the judges had to say.

'Guys, it pains me to say this and I know the audience are going to disagree with me, but I just wasn't feeling that tonight. I don't think you're at your full potential.'

At this the mood in the arena changed and the cheers instantly turned to boos. The boys' hearts began to race – this wasn't sounding good.

'I didn't agree with that song choice, Louis – I really didn't,' Tulisa continued, focusing her attention on the boys' mentor.

'There was so much going on and what was important, which was the vocals, was missing,' she added, ignoring the angry fans behind her. Then she said the words that the boys' had been dreading: 'If you get through to next week, I need to hear vocals.'

*If...?* It was a shocking start to the competition for the new foursome and somewhere deep down they must have started to worry that their dreams would be over as quickly as they'd begun.

'Louis, what were you thinking?' Tulisa went on, getting more and more angry at her fellow judge. 'They're young and they're fresh, and you've made them feel so dated.'

It was a damning appraisal of all their hard work and Union J looked devastated.

Louis sounded unconvinced as he tried to defend himself.

'I gave them a big task with Queen, okay, but listen – it's fun, like something out of *Glee*...'

But Tulisa couldn't bear to hear anymore.

'Boys,' she said kindly, 'all the faults as far as I'm concerned aren't yours, it's down to Louis.'

It was small comfort to Union J, who knew that it didn't matter whose fault it was: if nobody voted for them, they were done for.

Gary decided to step in, but it wasn't good news from him either.

'I have to agree, Tulisa. And guys, I want to say this – you're a good band and I thought, Louis, that putting George in was a genius move, but you have to smooth them out. That was a catastrophic song choice and an awful version. It was so dated with the dancers.'

Then he turned to the Irish judge and said harshly: 'Since you worked in the business, boybands have changed.'

In the face of this verbal onslaught, Louis gave up defending himself and the boys and eventually had to agree with Tulisa and Gary.

'You know what,' he said quietly, 'I think the song choice wasn't great, it was too big for you.' Then he whined: 'But it's only Week One!'

Back and forth the arguments went. Tulisa was quite clearly angry with Louis and felt as their mentor, he'd let the boys down. Meanwhile, Louis tried to calm the raging fury directed at him by promising to do better the next week. But by now the boys must have been seriously wondering if there would even be a next week.

'I didn't want to play it safe,' Louis sulked. 'You're all playing it too safe.'

'I didn't play it safe,' said an indignant Tulisa, 'I had someone singing their own song!' she almost yelled.

She was referring to Lucy Spraggan, who had impressed the judges earlier in the show by singing her own composition, 'Mountains'.

It was as if the judges didn't even realise that the poor boys were standing on stage, where they must have been feeling very exposed. Surely they were praying it would end soon, so they could run away and hide!

Finally, Nicole put an end to the fighting. 'Well done boys for performing as a group for the very first time, live on television,' she said, hearing the booing instantly turn to cheers behind her. She went on to say that she agreed with Gary and Tulisa, though – which meant not one of the judges had really liked their first ever performance.

Louis tried to salvage the night for the boys as he could see that it was probably very lonely and scary up on stage, listening to such a landslide of criticism.

'Guys, you know what, let's hope everybody at home votes for you and we will do better next week. We're prepared to work hard...'

But it wasn't the most confident of pep talks, and the boys must have felt that their mentor had badly let them down.

'To be fair, we did the best we could with the song choice,' said JJ, the first of the boys to speak since their disastrous song.

Huddled together, George put his arm around his new bandmate for moral support as he continued: 'Like Louis says, maybe next time we'll try a different song. We're just praying that everyone votes for us.'

George tried to speak next, his face the picture of sorrow. But before he'd got one single word out, the previously silent audience began to scream their love for him. Blushing, he smiled for the first time since the awful judges' comments had begun and his beautiful face lit up. It was the boost he needed to continue.

'We're going to take on board what you've said to us and hopefully if we get through to next week we're going to do better,' he said in a determined voice.

But they had to get through first, and after being slated by the judges, it was going to be very difficult.

As they listened to Dermot O'Leary call out the number to vote for Union J, the boys waved and left the stage, their heads bowed and their hearts heavy.

**DID YOU KNOW?**
**Union J's Josh says his main influences are Chris Brown, Tinie Tempah, Bruno Mars... and Michael Bublé!**

After everyone had sung, George, Jaymi, Josh and JJ reflected on the evening. MK1 had picked up the pace and did a cool mash-up of Chipmunk and Hot Chocolate, strutting confidently around the stage, but their vocals weren't perfect.

Jade Ellis had put her sultry tones to good use, singing the Enrique Iglesias' ballad 'Hero', while Ella Henderson, who was fast becoming one of the boys' best friends, had sung Gary Barlow's 'Rule the World' to high praise.

Gary had even said: 'I've got to be honest, there's nothing I hate more than someone singing my song ten times better than me.'

The Union J boys were facing some stiff competition.

After a sleepless night and a restless day, they were back at the studio for the live results show. Thirteen acts would be cut down to twelve and the boys were praying that they wouldn't be the first to leave.

'Backstage, the nerves are jingling and jangling,' said Dermot O'Leary, opening the show – and he was spot on.

After joining with the other contestants to sing Emeli Sandé's 'Read All About It', the audience was treated to performances from former *X Factor* winner Leona Lewis and R&B star Ne-Yo. It was a bit of light relief, but the waiting was torture.

Finally, it was time to face the music.

The two acts with the fewest votes would be singing for their survival; one of them would be going home. The boys could only hope it wouldn't be them.

All the acts stood on the stage, trying to stop themselves from shaking. Standing next to Louis, Union J looked nervous.

Dermot O'Leary started speaking.

'In no particular order, the first act going through to next week is…'

There was a tense pause.

'…Kye.'

'Also through is James,' he said next.

'And District 3…'

The Union J boys hadn't heard their names being called and the odds were getting slimmer. But then…

'The next act through to next week is Union J!'

The audience exploded into cheers and the boys began jumping up and down with uncontrollable excitement. Jumping on Louis, who looked mightily relieved, they hugged him tight.

In the end, Rylan and Carolynne found themselves in the bottom two, and they both had to sing again for the judges.

Rylan sang 'One Night Only' from the musical *Dreamgirls*, and Carolynne sang 'There You'll Be' by country star Faith Hill.

But tensions were simmering between the judges.

Gary had taken an instant dislike to Rylan the night before, telling him: 'I really was having fun till you started singing.'

Nicole had made everyone laugh by telling Gary: 'Don't be an old grumpy fart now…'

But when Louis chose not to save Carolynne, which took the vote to deadlock, Gary was enraged. He couldn't understand why Louis wouldn't save the talented songstress over fun performer Rylan.

It wasn't Carolynne's night. At the mercy of the public vote she was sent home, prompting Gary to storm off the stage, angrily telling the camera crew: 'Get the camera out of my face!'

Even Rylan was in tears over Gary's impromptu rage. 'Get me somewhere else,' he wept, walking backstage to where his stunned fellow contestants were waiting.

Union J were first to comfort him. 'I just want to walk out!' sobbed Rylan. 'No, you don't,' soothed George sympathetically. 'You deserve to be here, they saved you.'

Everyone agreed.

Later that night the mood was lifted as all the remaining acts laughed and joked with Caroline Flack and Olly Murs on *The Xtra Factor*.

Jade Ellis revealed she was terrified of spiders and Lucy Spraggan said she hated chewing gum. While James Arthur told everyone how much he hated cricket, joking: 'How hard is it to hit a ball with a stick?' – before being handed a bat and failing miserably to hit a ball at least five times, much to the audience's amusement.

But all eyes were on Ella Henderson when a fan called

the show and said to her: 'You're living with a lot of really hot boys at the moment – out of all of them which one do you fancy the most?'

Ella went red and struggled to think of the right answer.

She wasn't helped when Caroline Flack and the other contestants all started mumbling and coughing 'George!' under their breath.

'I get along with all the guys, right,' she said, diplomatically, trying to avoid answering the question.

'Come on,' teased Caroline. 'If you *had* to fancy one, who would it be?'

'This is going to spiral into something, isn't it?' she said, sighing. 'Right, my best friend is George...' she admitted, to delighted whoops and some teasing laughter.

'I'll never hear the end of this now, never,' she added, prophetically.

**DID YOU KNOW?**
**Lucy Spraggan's self-released single 'Last Night' entered the UK Singles Chart at number 11 following her *X Factor* audition.**

## CHAPTER SIX

# LOVE BLOSSOMS

## WEEK TWO – LOVE AND HEARTBREAK
13/14 October 2012

What Union J sang: 'Bleeding Love' – Leona Lewis/'Broken Strings' – James Morrison

What the judges said:
Tulisa: 'Guys, much better than last week.'
Nicole: 'You did everything right.'
Gary: 'What a total transformation!'
Louis: 'You can be the next big boyband in the UK if you work hard.'

Waking up on Monday morning, the boys reflected on the weekend and their first live show. It hadn't gone as well as they had hoped and it made them realise that anything could happen – they just had to be prepared for it.

They also felt they hadn't worked quite as hard as they could have done. Maybe they shouldn't have had that night out at top celeb haunt Whisky Mist. They had been acting like rock stars, but they weren't quite there yet.

This week's theme would be 'Love and Heartbreak'. It seemed so appropriate – especially since the boys were feeling pretty broken-hearted about the ear bashing they'd received the week before.

'Unfortunately, things didn't really go to plan when we got on stage,' Josh recalled. 'We genuinely, when we were up on that stage, thought we were going home.'

It was time to take stock and move on. If they let it affect this week's performance then they would be out for sure.

At the rehearsal studios, the boys sat down with their mentor Louis for a heart-to-heart. The mood was sombre.

'Boys, you're lucky to be here,' he told them. 'You've got to work twice as hard now.'

Everyone nodded in total agreement. Union J were now the underdogs of the competition and this wasn't where they wanted to be.

'We didn't put enough work into it,' George admitted. 'It's really made us realise how much we want to be in this competition and we've got a lot of work to do this week.'

Gently, Louis tried to lift their sagging spirits.

'I want you to do three things this week,' he told them. 'Rehearse, rehearse, rehearse!'

The boys got to work. First, they watched their

performance and took notes on where they had gone wrong, vowing not to make the same mistakes again. They could see that it had been lifeless and old-fashioned but now they could work on turning things around.

Every single moment they practised their singing. On the stairs, in their room, in taxis – their life must have been like something out of *Glee*!

The country was clamouring for the boys' attention and they obviously had a lot to do besides rehearse. But even when they were attending interviews with magazines and newspapers, or cool photoshoots with top photographers, they used every spare second to sing together.

It was all work, work, work; the boys knew they couldn't have tried any harder. Each night they went to bed exhausted, lyrics and harmonies swimming round their heads. They also knew they had to do a lot better with their choreography, so they spent hours at the studio with choreographer Brian Friedman. It was tough going and the boys struggled.

'No, no, *no*!' Brian yelled. 'It's not good enough, we've got to do it again!'

It was Louis' battle too. After all, his reputation was at stake. He was backing the four boys and was worried he'd look past his prime if they couldn't win over the judges in their second week.

Even older fellow contestant Kye stepped in to help the boys with their song. How sweet!

'We're not going to let Louis down,' the boys agreed.

Slowly, their efforts began to pay off. After one stage rehearsal, Louis took them to one side and finally smiled.

'Guys, that was good! You're starting to look like a real pop group...'

**DID YOU KNOW?**
**Union J's Josh says his favourite food is pizza and his favourite place to go on holiday is St Lucia – where Tulisa took her acts in the Judges' Houses stage. Unlucky!**

In his rare moments without the other boys, George managed to find time to spend with 16-year-old starlet Ella Henderson. Rumours had been flying about the couple being in an *X Factor* romance and the national newspapers and magazines were filled with gossip.

And the duo didn't do much to make those rumours go away. They played thumb wars in the hotel bar, their hands locked together as they dissolved in fits of giggles. And they chatted in their jim-jams on George's bed, totally engrossed in each other.

Ella flatly denied anything was going on, though. 'Let's clear something up,' she said to the *X Factor* cameras. 'George and I, we've got so much in common with each other, we do spend a lot of time with each other, but I don't get why it has to be the *X Factor* romance, because it's really not.'

But her face was bright red and she kept laughing as she spoke, so it wasn't the most convincing speech.

She visited her mentor Tulisa on the set of the music video she was shooting and asked for some advice.

'Every single guy that I'm seen with, I'm automatically

having a relationship with,' Tulisa confided to the teen. 'It drives me mad!'

'I'll just laugh it off,' Ella decided.

But it wasn't just George she was supposed to be cosying up to – according to some newspapers, it was District 3's Dan, too!

Perhaps the boybands' musical battle would spill over into their personal lives as well...

But if love was blossoming anywhere in the *X Factor* Hotel it would only help them with that week's songs. They would surely be emotional and heartfelt tracks and tender-aged Ella – who said she'd never been in love – was worried that she wouldn't be able to really feel the emotion needed to do her song justice. Maybe a bit of harmless flirting with the other boys would give her the inspiration she needed on stage.

Finally, the live show began, with Dermot O'Leary bouncing onto the stage to the sound of 'Firework'.

'The boys have been rehearsing all week and I'm going to show Gary Barlow that I know a lot more about boybands than he thinks,' said Louis.

Clearly the tension between the two judges after their bust-up over Carolynne Poole hadn't disappeared completely.

So, what would the judges be like towards each other this week?

'Let's show Gary 'Borelow' what he's been waiting for!' Nicole told a nervous Rylan before the show.

'When two tribes go to war...' went the opening song, as the stage doors opened and Gary, Nicole, Tulisa and

Louis walked out. Gary was certainly standing a step further away than the other judges and the audience was nervous.

Time to clear the air, and peacemaker Dermot O'Leary, well accustomed to the judges' tantrums, made it happen by asking what had happened the week before.

'I just couldn't make up my mind,' admitted a distressed-looking Louis. 'Carolynne was the better singer, but Rylan's such an entertainer.'

'Gary, have you forgiven Louis?' Dermot asked.

There was a pause. 'Absolutely,' he said, standing up. 'This is a new day, let's shake hands.'

Everyone was visibly relieved. It was all about the acts, after all, not the judges. Sometimes they seemed to forget that.

Making up out of the way, it was time for the show to go on...

**DID YOU KNOW?**
Gary's mum told him off for rowing with fellow judge Louis Walsh. Gary told *The People* newspaper that he'd got a dressing down from Marge, who said: 'You shouldn't do that – he's older than you and you should show him some respect.' Too right!

Backstage, the boys were nervous. It was a big moment for them: they had to shine this week or it might mean the end of their X Factor journey.

As Louis introduced them, their backing music began. Dressed in cute winter coats and scarves, and standing against a stunning backdrop of bare winter trees, the boys sounded instantly better than the week before.

They sang Leona Lewis's 'Bleeding Love' so well that it sounded like it was their own composition. A few minutes later they moved seamlessly into 'Broken Strings', and the crowd screamed themselves hoarse. As they walked over to the audience and sang the words directly to their fans, it was clear the boys had listened to Nicole the week before when she told them to interact with the crowds more.

As the song ended, they knew in their hearts that it had been a much better performance than last week's disaster. But it wasn't their own opinion that mattered – now it was down to the judges...

Tulisa's grin was the first sign that things would be okay. 'Guys, much better than last week,' she said. 'Much better song choice and most importantly, I can hear your vocals and that's what I wanted.'

As she took a breath to continue, she found herself struggling to speak over the cheers from behind her. 'I know you guys have a really strong female following,' she added, 'so you've got a lot of potential to do well in this competition.'

George visibly breathed a huge sigh of relief and JJ, Jaymi and Josh all broke out into smiles.

Gary smiled too. 'Okay, what a transformation from last week,' he said kindly, before taking another verbal swipe at his fellow judge. 'I thought Louis really let you down with the song choice last week – am I right in thinking that Kye helped you with the song tonight?'

The boys nodded gratefully.

'Okay good,' Gary continued. 'In future don't listen to Louis, listen to Kye. Well done, boys, congratulations!'

Louis chose to rise above the snipe, and all his face revealed was the pride he was obviously feeling.

Nicole wasn't smiling as she began: 'Boys, I hate to be the one to break it to you, but...

'...you got everything right this week!'

In shock at their resounding success, the boys started punching the air with happiness. 'You stripped everything back, it was beautiful, it was simple. If you keep growing and performing like that you're going to be selling out the O2 one day.'

JJ couldn't stay silent and a loud 'Wow!' escaped his lips.

It was left to Louis to sum up the judges' feelings on Union J's second live performance.

'Guys, you worked so hard this week and it so paid off! You're like a new group, and you bring something to this show that no one else is bringing – excitement. I can feel it in the studio.'

And he was right. The air was positively crackling with it.

'Guys, you know what? You can be the next big boyband in the UK if you work hard.'

The boys were dumbstruck at all the praise they were getting. For a few moments all they could say was thank you. Then they realised they were on live television and that millions of people were waiting for them to speak.

'This week the judges' comments have put a massive smile on all of our faces,' said Josh.

As George opened his mouth to agree, the audience

went bananas, screaming out his name and making him blush – just as the week before.

'These comments are going to push us even harder,' he finally managed.

Dermot started to laugh. 'I do get the impression,' he said. 'That George, you could pretty much say anything and girls would scream in this audience!'

It was a nice note to end on, and with that the boys walked off stage, buzzing with their newfound confidence. Last week, the boyband battle had been won by District 3. Would this week belong to Union J?

**DID YOU KNOW?**
**Carolynne Poole, who was the first to leave in Season Nine after losing the sing-off to Rylan Clark, has auditioned for *X Factor* before. She reached the Judges' House stage in Season Eight.**

Ella Henderson sang next and once again blew the judges away with a stunning rendition of 'Loving You' by Minnie Ripperton. It was jazzy and fresh, while being soulful and full of power.

When it was time for Rylan to sing, even the audience was nervous. Gary and Louis had made up after last week's fighting over him, but what would Gary think of him this week?

The stage darkened and as a familiar and simple piano tune started up, all the acts, including the Union J boys, wondered what Rylan would sing – and whether Gary would soften towards the former model.

'I guess now it's time for me to give up...' he began soulfully.

Gary's jaw dropped.

Rylan was singing a Take That song!

In homes all over the UK, people gasped at his bravery. But then the music stopped abruptly.

'I ain't singing it, really,' the cheeky singer said in his loveable Essex drawl. 'That was just for you, Gary', he added, grinning.

Gary couldn't help himself. Rylan had pranked him good and he chuckled away, along with the audience. Before he could say anything, Rylan's real music started and as the beat on which he thrived kicked in, he put on a show that had everyone dancing in the aisles.

It was an energetic performance of 'Groove Is In The Heart' and summer club anthem 'Gangnam Style' and the audience enjoyed watching him prance around the stage surrounded by his dancers. 'Let's have some fun, *X Factor*!' he yelled halfway through, and Nicole obliged him by getting up and dancing, too.

Rylan may not have had the best voice – a fact he himself would admit – but there was no denying he was popular. He knew just how to liven up a crowd.

Pink balloons rained down as he finished and Louis described his performance as 'entertainment with a capital 'E".

But there was silence from Gary, who was met by a wall of boos before he even spoke – he was definitely turning into the pantomime villain of the *X Factor* season.

'Rylan, if this was a competition for how many songs

you could kill in two minutes, you would win hands down,' he said.

Thick-skinned Rylan laughed it off – he had seen this coming.

'Interestingly,' Gary continued, 'when you started off, actually the best bit was my song. After that it became this musical dirge to cover up the fact that you can't sing.' Ouch!

Time to get real. 'Look, I'm never gonna like this, okay? I hear from everyone backstage that you're a lovely guy and I'm sure if we sat and had a drink together I may well enjoy it – for about thirty seconds,' he said.

Everyone felt sorry for the poor lad but Rylan recovered quickly and quipped: 'Gary, I was a little bit worried, actually. I booked you a cab, just in case you, er, walked out!'

Everyone laughed at Gary's expense.

'That's funny,' Gary shot back. 'I've had yours on hold for two weeks now...'

Clearly there was no love lost between them. And if Gary would just admit it to himself, maybe one reason why he struggled to like Rylan was because with his stage presence, he reminded Gary an awful lot of someone he used to work with. Someone he had also spectacularly fallen out with...

But in any case, Rylan's act had cheered all the contestants up. It was the light relief that everyone, including Union J, had needed.

Backstage, all the acts were doing a great job of pretending they weren't a bag of nerves but District 3 were more nervous than most. After the success of the week before, they'd had an awful five days' rehearsing. They weren't very confident at all and when they took to the stage it showed.

**DID YOU KNOW?**
**George Shelley was born a blonde! Early pics show he had the cutest pudding-bowl haircut.**

The judges weren't impressed with their rendition of 'I Swear', by All4One. And the next night it was their turn to be in the bottom two, along with Melanie Masson.

Although they survived to go through to Week Three, this particular round of the battle of the boybands had definitely gone to Union J.

## CHAPTER SEVEN

# STARDOM BECKONS

## WEEK THREE – CLUB CLASSICS
20/21 October 2012

What Union J sang: 'When Love Takes Over' – David Guetta

What the judges said:
Tulisa: 'I knew I saw that potential in you.'
Gary: 'I think we are witnessing the birth of a new boyband.'
Nicole: 'You're very cool and effortless.'
Louis: 'This band has got a massive future.'

This week, loyal Union J fans were dealt a huge blow when they found out that the only member of the band who was still single was lovely George.

'I'm sort of early stage seeing someone,' Josh told *Star Magazine*. JJ said he was in the same situation. Jaymi spoke about his long-term relationship, before George happily announced: 'I'm single,' completely ignoring the rumours about himself and Ella Henderson.

George also said he was loving the attention all the boys were getting. 'It's great,' he admitted. 'It's crazy to think how we've gone from being normal to having fans following us everywhere.'

And JJ – who George, Josh and Jaymi once pushed onto their hotel balcony naked, to the delight of their fans – agreed. 'We had fans waiting outside our hotel for nine hours the other day. They're constantly tweeting us, saying: "When are you coming down again?"'

As often as they could, the boys made sure they'd go down and say hi – and even helped take pictures of themselves for the hundreds of patient JCats. They had to, really, because huge steeled gates and fences had been put up to keep the acts separate from the thousands of fans.

Everywhere they went, the boys were asked for photographs and autographs – even while they were once out shopping in Topshop. A posse of excited girls followed them around the store before throwing their arms around the boys for hugs.

George tried on some silly glasses and posed, asking: 'What do you think?'

But even in funny specs he still looked gorgeous.

Teddy bears and love notes were being delivered to their hotel daily, and while the boys thought it was great, Louis was becoming increasingly concerned that all the female attention would distract the boys. As their mentor, he sat them down for a heartfelt chat.

'Who gets the most girls?' he asked them one morning in the rehearsal studio. He understood that it wasn't their fault that they were so adored – they couldn't help being handsome and talented.

'Josh and George,' replied JJ, immediately.

'I know there's hundreds of girls screaming for you outside but don't get distracted,' Louis told them, wisely. 'You've got a long way to go yet and an awful lot of hard work.'

'It was really hard last week,' said Jaymi, in a serious voice. 'We can't rest on that, because if we slip slightly people might not believe in us. We've got to work ten times harder.'

George looked sincere as he added: 'With the support we've been getting, it's really important for us to go out there and not let anyone down.'

Everyone agreed. Louis had said his piece and the boys appreciated it. They all high-fived and went off to rehearse.

But not everyone was taking the competition so seriously. Rylan Clark and Lucy Spraggan found themselves in big trouble after they went out following Sunday's results show and got staggeringly drunk.

They were so excited to discover that they were still in the competition that they'd gone to the famous London club G-A-Y and drank far too much. When they got back to the hotel, they made such a racket that the show's bosses were not at all impressed. Especially since the paparazzi had been waiting for them and had caught the whole thing on camera.

They were screaming and shouting, swearing and smoking – which is bad for your voice, let alone your health – and the pair had totally embarrassed themselves. Rylan nearly got naked and Lucy was videoed picking him up and carrying him around. They were obviously so drunk they had no idea what they were doing. It was an awful example to set the younger contestants – and their fans.

The pair of them got an almighty telling-off, and as punishment they were moved from the swanky Corinthia Hotel to a Hilton in Wembley – to get them away from the other acts. Oops!

They were now very far from the glitzy London nightlife they'd been enjoying. Instead they were much closer to the studio, so that their mentors could keep a closer eye on them.

Lucy was upset and tweeted that she'd had a miserable week. The *Mirror* reported that Tulisa had read her the riot act, accusing poor Lucy of not taking the competition seriously enough and throwing away a great opportunity.

But Rylan didn't seem bothered at all and tweeted: 'We've been naughty so we're going to the Attitude mag after party!!!'

The cheeky Essex boy wasn't taking any notice of the judges and was determined to have a good time.

**DID YOU KNOW?**
**Union J's Josh loves Nando's. He always orders a half peri-peri chicken and chips. Yum!**

After a lot of practising, the boys found themselves at the *X Factor* studios for yet another live show. It was amazing to them that they'd got this far – but it wasn't so amazing for everyone watching the show at home. They were naturals!

They began their performance by sitting quietly on stage, before Josh started singing: 'When Love Takes Over'. Then, with a quick key change, lights started flashing, the beat kicked in and all four boys got up and danced their socks off.

Tulisa absolutely loved it. 'Guys, I'm so happy! I knew I saw this potential in you – you are finally finding your feet in the competition,' she said.

'Each week you're getting better and better and better. And your female fanbase is getting stronger and stronger and stronger.'

The boys were so pleased they had to stop themselves from jumping up and down right there on the stage. But Tulisa wasn't finished. 'This is just the beginning for you guys. That was a wicked performance tonight – I can just see it getting better each week,' she concluded, leaving the boys buzzing with confidence.

Gary took a pause before he gave his verdict. 'I think we are witnessing the birth of a brand new boyband right here,' he said, looking very pleased with the lads. But then he added: 'Just a little bit of technical stuff – you sound great when you sing individually, I could just do with a little more harmony.'

But the boys could see that this was constructive criticism and were happy to take the seasoned singer's advice.

Nicole had some reservations, too. 'The reason why I like you guys and why we all like you so much is you're very cool and effortless when you perform,' she began, adding to everyone else's praise. 'But this is Club Classics... I need more energy, boys – you were still singing the song like you were singing the ballad last week. I need more energy and we need a harmony. We had four people singing in unison.'

More valuable advice. District 3 had their harmonies down to a fine art form. It would be tough to challenge them, but Union J would certainly try.

Louis gave his usual proud father face and said: 'Guys, it's working! The hard work is paying off. There's a great chemistry, there's great fun and the image – guys, it's coming together.'

It was only Week Three and the boys were doing so well, especially since they'd not been a band for very long at all. In such a short space of time, they were capturing the public's hearts – no easy feat.

The boys were pleased, but humble. Dermot O'Leary asked them what they thought and Josh said: 'Yeah, really happy, obviously we've got a lot to work on still, but we're new and we're hoping to develop.'

And with that they left the stage.

Next, Lucy Spraggan and Rylan Clark took to the stage one after another with their usual gusto. As usual, Rylan caused arguments between all the judges with his performance of club classics 'On The Floor', 'Don't Stop The Music' and 'I See You Baby'.

Earlier in the week, his mentor Nicole had given an exclusive interview to the *Mirror*, where she spoke about how she would defend Rylan until the bitter end and protect him from his harshest critic: Gary Barlow. She also spoke about the pressures of the show, which the contestants were doing a great job of hiding – or at least they had been, until last week.

Poor James Arthur had suffered a panic attack and thought he was seriously ill. An ambulance was called and he was treated at the scene, but it gave all the acts something to think about.

The Union J boys had each other to rely on and confide in, which must have helped, but the pressure was still very intense. Nicole told the *Mirror*: 'People watch it on TV but they don't realise what goes on behind the scenes and how much pressure they were under.'

She went on: 'This is what happens when you are thrown into an environment you're not used to. You are working every single day, non-stop. He is around new people... Getting your glasses taken away from you, spray-tanned, hair cut – it is a completely different world.'

James's experience was scary for everyone and a warning to work hard, but not overdo it.

On the results show 24 hours later, the acts all sang

Chaka Khan's 'Ain't Nobody' together and the stage vibrated with energy. Superstars Emeli Sandé and Labrinth performed next, before former *X Factor* contestants JLS sang their new single, 'Hottest Girl In The World'. It was inspirational for all the acts, but especially Union J and District 3. Both were aspiring to be just as successful as the top band, if not more.

Then Dermot O'Leary took to the stage and said: 'Okay, it's time for the results.'

Would their hard work pay off? Were they going through to the next live show? They couldn't wait to find out...

Dermot soon put them out of their misery.

'The first act returning is Union J!'

The boys screamed and jumped up and down, hugging each other tight. Then they threw their arms around Louis and the other groups before Dermot had the chance to continue announcing which of the acts was safe for another week.

One by one, everyone celebrated their survival – apart from MK1 and Kye Sones, who found themselves in the bottom two. And after a tense sing-off, it was time for MK1 to go home.

**DID YOU KNOW?**
**MK1's Sim turned down a football scholarship in America to study Music Industry Management at Buckinghamshire University. Now that's dedication!**

## CHAPTER EIGHT

# THE FAN MADNESS BEGINS

## WEEK FOUR – HALLOWEEN
27/28 October 2012

What Union J sang: 'Sweet Dreams' – Beyoncé/'Perfect'
– Pink

What the judges said:
Tulisa: 'Jaymi, you have a seriously powerful voice.'
Nicole: 'I thought that was absolute perfection.'
Gary: 'I've kind of seen this performance before.'
Louis: 'I know you can perform more.'

Safe in their cosy hotel room, the boys looked out of the
window and saw a familiar sight: girls camped outside in
the freezing cold, hoping to catch a glimpse of their new

heroes. They'd been there for weeks now, starting out as a small group, which had slowly grown as the weeks had passed. Some of them had even managed to break in, sneaking past the huge bodyguards on the doors and surprising the boys outside their bedrooms – while wearing their favourite onesies!

As much as the boys appreciated their fans, it was quite a shock to see them in the privacy of their hotel. Some of the girls had even been really clever and sent their CVs to the hotel, hoping to get jobs in the bar.

The boys felt a little bit like they were being chased. They could no longer leave the hotel through the front doors because they were always mobbed, so they had started to leave by the secret back exit.

Some girls were even sleeping outside the hotel. It was crazy and the boys were worried about them. 'Where are their mums?' they asked each other, shocked.

'We could see them trying to work out which room we were in,' Josh told the *Sun* newspaper. 'They were removed by two beefy security lads.'

George added: 'We're just normal guys doing our thing and it's crazy to think girls would chase us around and want to be near us all the time.'

They were quick to point out that they all thought it was lovely that everyone was supporting them, but show's bosses were still concerned. They decided to draft in extra security for the lads, just in case.

The boys took some time out from rehearsals to attend Rylan's Halloween-themed birthday party, dressing as scary surgeons. Poor Ella couldn't go because she was too young, so the boys went on a spooky bus tour of London too, so she wouldn't feel left out.

Ella was sitting next to Josh, and everyone was screaming as the bus tour guides told them spooky stories and kept making them jump. The boys all screamed like big girls!

George decided to speak to *Now* magazine about his newfound fame, and said that he was struggling with being described as such a ladies' man.

'I know the others would say I'm the womaniser of the group but I wouldn't describe myself as that,' the magazine reported.

George has often been compared to One Direction's Harry Styles. But in the interview he said that despite having the same floppy hair, beautiful lips and face of an angel, he was a bit upset when he came face to face with Harry and discovered that actually they look nothing alike!

'We were doing a photoshoot and I bumped into Harry Styles,' he said. 'I have to say I was gutted, as despite being compared to him, I look nothing like him!'

There's room in our lives for both of you, George.

Previously, the judges had told JJ, Jaymi, Josh and George that they wanted to hear more harmonies and see more energy. Union J knew that the District 3 boys had great harmonies and they needed to work on their own, so they practised and practised.

And they were exhausted after going over and over their dance steps. When the big night came, they were going to be ready...

**DID YOU KNOW?**
Ella Henderson took her GCSEs at almost the same time as singing at her *X Factor* audition but she still managed to get seven, including an A in music.

Sitting on a car in dark outfits, the boys looked sultry as they began to sing Beyoncé's 'Sweet Dreams' to the judges. Their voices were beautiful and when they leapt effortlessly down from the vehicle they looked really cool. Then suddenly they were leaping all over the place, confidently singing to a few very lucky girls in the audience, and storming the stage as if it was a massive stadium gig! But when they finished and the cheers died down, they were in for a shock.

Tulisa began.

'Guys, I think the vocals were really good tonight. Jaymi, you were particularly strong – you have a seriously powerful voice,' she said, praising the cutie. 'My only issue tonight was that in the past two weeks you've improved so much that I'm kind of waiting for you to get better. And I felt like you played it just a little bit safe tonight.'

Gary agreed. He called it 'overproduced' and said he could tell everyone loved the performance, but he thought it was 'safe'.

'Come back with something different next week and change it up,' he advised.

Nicole loved it, though, calling it absolute perfection. 'I love every single one of you,' she gushed. 'You stand there, you own it, you pay attention to the girls, you're honest... It was simple, it was beautiful – I don't know what all the fuss is about.'

But although the American judge-performer had loved their song, Louis gave the boys a shock when he said: 'Guys, it was great but I know you can perform more. I believe in this group so much, I don't want them in the bottom two.'

He looked worried as he appealed to everyone to vote for the act. It was a mixed group of comments and the boys didn't know what to think. They had no idea whether or not they were safe and had a sneaking suspicion that there would be tough times ahead.

'We took your comments on board about the harmonies,' said Josh. 'So we really tried to work on that and we sort of gave it our best.'

His fellow singers nodded in agreement when he added: 'And we're hopefully gonna develop week in, week out.'

One act was missing from the line-up in Week Four – Lucy Spraggan had fallen ill and couldn't sing. She was automatically put through to the next round, making lots of Union J and District 3 fans angry. They thought it was quite unfair, but it wasn't Lucy's fault.

Rylan had enjoyed the week of his life – not only did he have a birthday party, but Robbie Williams had lavished him with attention. Gary Barlow's bandmate spent lots of time helping Rylan with his act and even had a special message for Gary.

'Gaz, I don't know what this man has done to offend you so much. I am a big, big fan,' Robbie told the cameras. 'And I don't understand how you are missing the obvious brilliance and talent of Rylan, but I'm not. I'm team Rylan all the way,' he added, as Rylan looked chuffed behind him.

Rylan sang Britney Spears' 'Toxic', and it was brilliant.

Gary might have been a little offended by it all, though because he was quite mean to Tulisa that night.

She had blamed Gary for Christopher Maloney's dodgy song choices and after a brooding silence, Gary told her: 'Tulisa, I don't know what's offended me more tonight – what you've said or your fag-ash breath.'

He even wafted his hand in front of his face for effect.

Tulisa was shocked and stared with her mouth open at the camera. She stewed while Gary spoke to his act, but it wasn't long before she hit back at him, saying: 'Lay off the red wine, Gary, because I can really smell that as well.'

Miaow! At least all the acts were getting on, because the judges were acting like children.

The next night, Robbie Williams entertained all the acts at the live results show, singing his new song, 'Candy'. But the mood dropped when it was time to find out who would be singing for survival.

It was a disaster for the boys.

Everyone was safe apart from Jade Ellis – and Union J. The poor lads were in the bottom two...

Obviously nervous, they took to the stage to sing 'Perfect' by Pink. They sang their hearts out but then so did Jade, with a beautiful rendition of Dido's 'White Flag'.

No one had a clue who was going to leave and the boys looked terrified as they stood on stage with Dermot O'Leary and Jade, waiting for the verdict.

Louis went first and obviously sent Jade home, saying: 'I'm the mentor for Union J – I love them. I don't want to lose them.'

Tulisa was next and looked very sad. It was as if she knew what was coming.

'This is easy for me,' she said. 'That's my girl up there, she sang her heart out tonight. The act I'm sending home is Union J.'

It was one vote each – what would the other judges have to say?

'Jade, you are a beautiful, beautiful young woman – a strong young woman, who has been through so much,' said Nicole. 'I know that whatever happens you're gonna get a recording deal because you're a recording artist and a brilliant one.'

Jaymi's bottom lip started to quiver and George looked crushed as Nicole praised the talented female singer. Were they going home?

'Union J, you boys, through your performance and through your work have proven yourself to me, so the act I'm sending home, I'm sorry, is Jade.'

Relief flooded their faces – now it was all down to Gary, who hadn't always been their biggest fan.

'Guys, I have been tough on you,' he started. 'You know I'm a band member myself and every week you've come on this show, you know it's been good but it's not been exceptional...'

Jaymi, Josh, JJ and George tried to stay strong but they must have been feeling sick with worry at this point. They were loving being on the show and didn't want it to end.

'Jade, you are a phenomenal vocalist, you really are and you really sang your heart out. But I just wonder whether I want this for you more than you want it...'

Everyone was silent as he continued: 'The act I'm sending home is Jade.'

It was a mixture of happiness and sadness – Union J were through to the next week, but they would have to say goodbye to lovely Jade, something they really didn't want to do.

By now the acts were all so close there were always tears on Sunday evenings.

Tom Parker, from The Wanted, tweeted: 'Jade Ellis, you did yourself proud!'

After an emotional goodbye it was time for *The Xtra Factor* and Josh had cheered up enough to tell Caroline Flack his worst fear: wasps!

Jedward were guests on the show and they got up to their usual cheeky antics, while Ella got a surprise when Caroline and Olly Murs managed to get her beloved dog, Trixie, on Skype! The cute little doggie barked with joy when he saw Ella, who was missing him so much. But it showed that being apart from your family was one of the prices you had to pay for being in *The X Factor*.

**DID YOU KNOW?**
**Ella's fave shop is River Island, but she also scours vintage stores for exciting one-off finds.**

## CHAPTER NINE

# RISING FROM THE ASHES

## WEEK FIVE – NUMBER ONES
3/4 November 2012

What Union J sang: 'Love Story' – Taylor Swift

What the judges said:
Tulisa: 'Well done, you nailed it!'
Gary: 'I thought that was a brilliant performance.'
Nicole: 'They've knocked it out of the park every week!'
Louis: 'You definitely made the right decision, saving the boys last week.'

After their bottom two showdown, the boys were feeling a bit low when they woke up the next day. But they couldn't let it affect them and as usual, Louis was on hand to talk things through.

It had all got a bit overwhelming for JJ, Josh, George

and Jaymi. Their fans and the audience watching them on TV at home may have seen them as polished and professional singers, well on the road to success, but the boys just felt like normal lads with very normal backgrounds – this had been a whirlwind experience for them all.

Bright and early on Monday morning, the boys sat down with Louis in the rehearsal studios.

'I couldn't believe you were in the bottom two last week and I saw your faces,' he said, worried for his boys.

'It was a numb feeling, we didn't really know what to expect,' admitted George. 'We had to really fight to come back and sing,' said Jaymi, recalling the initial terror they'd felt before the sing-off. 'Your mouth goes dry, you're shaking, you want to be sick. You've got to use every little bit of you to come back and give a performance. Waiting to hear if you're through or not, your heart is just pounding.'

It was a very revealing conversation, and the words came straight from their hearts.

'So we've got to turn all the negativity into positive attitude,' continued Josh. 'You know – prove to the judges why we deserve to be in the competition.'

In rehearsals, Jaymi took the boys to one side and spoke to them. 'You need to take it seriously,' he told George, JJ and Josh. 'Do you want to end up where we were last week?'

They all agreed that was the last thing they wanted. This week the boys would be singing a love song and Jaymi was adamant they would make it a success.

'We just want to go out there and just have fun with it,' he told the cameras. 'Think about the first time we were in love and just go out there and let loose!'

At practise, George was seen strumming on his guitar, so everyone knew they'd be in for a treat when the boys performed. He is a great guitarist!

Louis was nervous about the next live show, too. He told the cameras: 'I want the people at home to see the real Union J this week – we've got four very different people in the group. I don't want to see them in the bottom two again.'

They certainly are very different people, and it's lovely how well they all get on. Josh is the funny guy – all the boys think he's hilarious. Jaymi is definitely the father figure of the group; he always gives them little pep talks and is the most organised. George is the cheeky one, with his gorgeous smile, and JJ is the one who gets teased the most.

One morning Josh and George decided to make the other acts laugh by wearing their beloved onesies around the hotel and saying: 'It's number onesies' week!' But James Arthur threw a pillow at them when they tried to record a video for *The Xtra Factor* in their favourite nightwear.

The boys love their all-in-one outfits and George never wears any boxers underneath his.

Meanwhile, Kye had been teasing Josh mercilessly about his hair – all the acts had noticed that he was constantly rearranging it, and the one thing he asked them the most was: 'Is my hair alright?'

We love your hair, Josh!

**DID YOU KNOW?**
**The first gig that George ever attended was to see Bon Jovi, Josh's was Chris Brown, and JJ has never been to a proper gig!**

Halfway through the week the boys took some time out to go to the *Mirror*'s Pride of Britain Awards, where ordinary people receive recognition for the amazing things they do. It's always an emotional event and for the boys, who are all ordinary boys really, it was particularly overwhelming.

And with emotions running high, onlookers watched as George and Ella cosied up together, fuelling the rumours about their blossoming love.

The *Mirror* reported that they were holding hands during the tear-jerking speeches, with their chairs moved away from the rest of their group's table, which included Jahmene, Kye Sones and James Arthur. And George was even seen gently stroking Ella's back and whispering to her.

They wouldn't be the first couple to get it on at The Pride of Britain Awards. Footballer Frank Lampard met Christine Bleakley there, Russell Brand and Geri Halliwell dated for a week after attending one year, and although much less successfully, former Beatle Paul McCartney met his second wife Heather Mills at the event.

Cupid obviously attends the Awards...

A source told the *Mirror*: 'They really connected when they first met, but they wanted to get to know each other before taking it up a notch. Now, after spending such an emotional evening together, they are taking things more seriously.'

Lucy Spraggan was supposed to be at rehearsals, after being off the week before, suffering from what X Factor officials were calling a 'severe bout of flu'. But the boys were shocked to see she wasn't there. It was looking as if she wouldn't make the live show this week, either – what would the producers do?

And there was more disaster when two days before the show, Josh woke up feeling dreadful.

The boys had eaten a Chinese takeaway the night before and Josh had scoffed his favourite prawn toast but now he was suffering with food poisoning.

While the other boys left the hotel to go and rehearse, Josh stayed in bed, tweeting: 'Haven't left my bed for the last 36 hours with food poisoning. Been so ill.'

Later, he added: 'Still feeling awful. Worrying about tomorrow.'

All their fans tweeted him their love and George, Jaymi and JJ all looked after him. But they were obviously worried that he wouldn't be okay for the live show. It would be a disaster if he couldn't perform and after being in the bottom two last week, this could easily mean the end of their X Factor dreams.

'We're just praying that he recovers in time for the show,' tweeted JJ.

By this time, both District 3 and Union J had suffered through a sing-off and apparently tensions were rising between the two groups. Both bands knew that this week they both had to wow the judges, and as much as they liked each other as people, the national newspapers were reporting that the bands weren't really talking to each other all that much.

**DID YOU KNOW?**
**Kye Sones is best mates with radio DJ Fearne Cotton. They met at an under-18s disco in Ruislip when they were both 11 and have been besties ever since.**

Finally, it was time for the live show, and the boys appeared on stage to sing. George stepped out first, holding his guitar, followed by Josh, JJ and Jaymi, all wearing jeans and suit jackets. They looked so good in their outfits – bet there was some serious swooning in the audience that night!

Singing Taylor Swift's 'Love Story', they were pitch-perfect and as usual, the audience loved them, nearly drowning out their powerful vocals with their cheers.

It was a definite improvement on last week and the boys knew it.

'First of all,' said Tulisa, when the boys had finished, 'I would like to congratulate Louis on making such a brilliant song choice.'

Louis looked so happy. 'Well, we picked the song together,' he said proudly. 'How much have they improved?'

On stage, the boys grinned.

'Do you know what?' Tulisa continued. 'It all goes to show song choice is key, and the one thing Louis knows about is boybands and he's trying to find your market and nail it. At the end of the day, your fans are loads of young screaming girls across the country and all they want is to see you up there, singing beautiful love songs, beautifully to them. You did that tonight. Well done, you nailed it.'

Gary was next to speak and the boys waited patiently to see what the usually strict judge had to say.

'Guys, I was concerned on Sunday that we might have made the wrong decision voting Jade off,' he began, 'but seeing how you've reacted tonight I don't think we have – I thought that was a brilliant performance.'

But he did have some criticism – about George, of all people!

'George, you fit wonderfully in the band but I think you could work on your blend just a little bit more.'

George nodded, respectfully. He wasn't going to have a tantrum when someone as knowledgeable as Gary Barlow gave him some advice.

Nicole was as pleased as everyone else to see that the boys had taken advantage of one of George's great talents. 'It's so nice to see you finally reunited with your guitar,' she told him. 'Boys, I thought that was a really solid performance. I've loved it every week. Like Tulisa said, they're singing to their fan base – good work, boys!'

On cue, the girls in the audience began screaming and the boys chuckled on stage. It was obvious that their fans really made a difference to their confidence.

'Guys, you definitely made the right decision saving the boys last week,' Louis told his fellow judges. 'Boys, you came back fighting – you've got a whole new energy.'

Dermot O'Leary asked Gary what he meant by his

comment to George, and Gary joked that he had far too much hair.

Leave his curls alone, Gary!

But he explained that he meant that he wanted them to work on blending their vocals. As the boys left the stage they were chuffed to bits.

But despite their happiness, the boys were sad about one thing that night – Lucy Spraggan had decided not to return to *The X Factor*.

'I'm gutted not to be able to continue on this journey,' she said in a statement that very morning. 'To accept another free pass, having missed last weekend would not be fair on the others in the competi

That night, on *The Xtra Factor*, Caroline Flack congratulated the boys on their amazing performance and asked what it was like being in the bottom two throughout the week.

'We were quite down and stuff,' said Jaymi. 'We really wanted to pick ourselves up. We went home to see our families, which really gave us a big boost. Hopefully we won't be in the bottom two tomorrow.'

Christopher Maloney revealed that JJ always eats with his mouth open and Caroline Flack asked Ella who she fancied more: Olly Murs or George Shelley?

'I don't fancy George!' she protested at the teasing.

'_____ right!' said Caroline.

population. I wish them all well.'

Close friend Rylan tweeted her: 'Gonna miss u being with me so much @lspraggan I love you x'.

She had been his partner-in-crime since the very beginning and he would now have to struggle on without her.

The mood was sombre, but lightened when footage showed Nicole visiting *TOWIE* star Amy Child's Essex salon with Rylan, so that he could get an eyebrow wax.

Nicole had never been to Essex before but learned some of the local lingo, and even practised it that night when she told Gary to 'Shuup', and that he was just 'wel jel' of Rylan.

Union J had mixed feelings when they saw District 3's performance. It wasn't their best and the judges were harsh. Would this be the week they won the battle of the boybands? Were District 3 going home?

They'd have to wait until the next day to find out...

**DID YOU KNOW?**
**The first single that JJ ever bought was Backstreet Boys' 'I Want It That Way', and Jaymi's was 'Genie In A Bottle' by Christina Aguilera.**

The next night the boys were relieved to find out they were first to be declared safe from the dreaded bottom two. And surprisingly, District 3 were saved too! Obviously everyone had realised that they were fab, really – it had just been a bad night.

But Rylan and Kye Sones had to battle it out, and the judges just couldn't decide who to send home. Gary and Nicole voted to keep their own acts, and Louis voted to keep Kye, so it was down to Tulisa. 'I've got to go with my heart,' she said and opted to save Rylan. This caused a deadlock, which meant it would come down to the public vote.

Dermot opened the envelope that revealed who would be going home.

It was Kye Sones. The public were loving Rylan's entertaining performances and talented as Kye was, he just didn't have enough votes.

Gary was fuming as he took to the stage. 'Good singers go home every week,' he declared.

But it's not always so black and white on *The X Factor*. And there would be a good deal more shocks in store for everyone before the competition was over.

## CHAPTER TEN

# THE BATTLE OF THE BOYBANDS

## WEEK SIX – BEST OF BRITISH
10/11 November 2012

What Union J sang: 'Fix You' – Coldplay/'Run' – Snow Patrol

What the judges said:
Tulisa: 'Let the battle of the boybands commence…'
Gary: 'I think something big is about to happen.'
Louis: 'Your families are so proud of you.'
Nicole: 'Beautiful song, boys – you did it justice.'

This week's performance was particularly important for Josh, JJ, Jaymi and George. Sunday would be Remembrance Day, the day when Britain takes time to honour those who have given their lives in war and conflict. All four of the boys had some kind of connection to the Armed Forces, so they really wanted to make this performance their best.

Jaymi comes from a long line of men who have served in the Royal Air Force – every male in his family has served in the RAF, going back to World War II!

Josh's dad was in the Navy for 15 years and he's always been exceptionally proud of him for it. Josh told the X Factor cameras: 'It would be nice to go on stage and do something that would hopefully make him proud.'

For George the connection was even closer to home. His big brother is a Royal Marine Commando, who has completed three tours in Afghanistan.

George was just 13 when Will first went to Afghanistan. He has said: 'It's really hard, knowing that your big brother is going out to fight for your country and he just might not come back.'

So when the boys sat down with Louis to discuss what song to sing, George told his mentor: 'It's Best of British Week – we want to dedicate our song to what we feel the best of British is, and that's the Armed Forces.'

Louis agreed, and everyone decided they would do a stripped-down version of Coldplay's 'Fix You'.

'To be honest, you need to just stand there and sing and enjoy yourselves,' said Louis. 'It works, it *really* works.'

He also wanted to praise the boys for last week's performance, which had blown all the judges away.

'You were amazing on Saturday night, that was the best performance so far,' he told them. 'I saw something brilliant, I saw a glimpse of what you could be.'

The boys were so amazed they'd made it so far in the competition. It had been so exciting and as young boys, dreaming of singing on stage, they never thought they would ever be on the *X Factor* stage with hundreds of girls screaming their names.

'We literally keep pinching ourselves,' said JJ. 'To be in this position, we couldn't ask for more.'

They began rehearsing and were determined to get the song perfect.

'George, I don't want to start off with you,' said Louis. 'I want to start off with Jaymi.' He added: 'And guys, the harmony is too loud but we're going to get it right.'

Everyone nodded. It was time for some serious hard work.

The boys were up early every day and went to bed really late. They were so tired, but hope was keeping them going. George tweeted that he had never been so tired in his entire life, while instead of going out partying, Josh snuggled up with his hot-water bottle.

They also had to do a very important photoshoot – for the winning *X Factor* single CD cover!

All of the acts had to have their pics taken, just in case they won, and Josh tweeted: 'Hopefully the next time we see the pictures it will be on that CD cover...'

And it was announced that Union J would definitely be on *The X Factor* 2012 tour, along with Ella Henderson, District 3, Christopher Maloney, Jahmene Douglas, Rylan Clark and James Arthur. It was so good to know that whoever won, everyone would be together again for a super-exciting stadium tour, just a few months away.

Things were getting very real: the four boys were actually making it in the music world.

On Saturday, the boys made their way to the studio and that was when the nerves really started to kick in. Josh tweeted: 'Dress rehearsal is minutes away!! This is when I'm always dying for a wee haha!!'

And finally, it was time for them to perform.

Louis told them: 'Guys, don't forget who you're singing this to – you're singing this to your families. You're going to be great tonight.'

George replied: 'We've just got to go out there tonight and smash our performance and sing our hearts out.'

District 3 had already sung their song and received some amazing comments from the judges. How would Union J compare?

A curtain fell to reveal the boys on stage, all in black jackets and dark jeans. George strummed on his guitar while Jaymi started singing. It was very moving and their vocals were totally perfect. Their families must have been very proud – they certainly did them justice. And when it was over there must have surely been quite a few people weeping over their tea and biscuits at home.

'Louis,' began Tulisa, 'I have to confess you're on a roll tonight – you've nailed it again. Brilliant song choice, brilliant performance, what you've done tonight is you've found your market and you're very much appealing to them, so great job tonight.'

But she did have some concerns, which she went on to voice next.

'My only worry is, being honest, it's now battle of the

boybands and both bands did amazingly,' she said. 'I can't call it. My only worry is – is it going to split the votes? I don't know. Let the battle of the boybands commence!'

The boys looked really pleased, but Tulisa was right and they knew it. There was a showdown coming, and neither band was looking forward to it.

'Good job tonight,' said Gary, 'one of my favourite songs. I thought that you all sang it really well. There's often just a little bit of pitching problems when you're blending together, just work a little bit more on that because it's all about rehearsal.'

It was advice they'd been given before and they were all trying their hardest to improve technically but unless you're an *X Factor* judge you never would have picked up on anything being wrong – the boys had sounded amazing and Gary knew it, despite his small criticisms.

'I think something big is about to happen,' he told them. 'I feel really good about you guys.'

George looked very emotional when Nicole spoke next.

'Beautiful song, boys – you did it justice. I just want to say thank you for recognising and honouring the men and women, the heroes of our Armed Forces.'

She told Jaymi his voice had shone that evening, describing it as delicate and controlled, with so much soul. It was such great praise!

'Guys, it's such a pleasure to work with four guys who work so hard. You're young, you're relevant, your families are so proud of you,' Louis told them. 'Jaymi, I know what this means for you, you've waited your whole life for this – this is your moment.'

The boys were philosophical when Dermot O'Leary asked them about their competition with District 3.

'Obviously, we're the two boybands in the competition so obviously people are going to say there is rivalry,' said Josh. 'But everyone is in competition with each other, there's no more competition with us two than there is anyone else, so we love them to bits.'

It was very nicely said and the District 3 boys must have been glad to hear it. It's not great, being in competition with your friends.

George gave Dermot a hug and the boys left the stage.

That night, the boys went on Twitter and found that the judges weren't the only ones who loved their version of the Coldplay classic.

*TOWIE*'s Lauren Goodger tweeted: 'I really like Union J's voices!!xx', while Katie Price wrote: 'union j are awesome defo top 3', which the boys retweeted proudly.

After the performance, the boys spent some time with their families and later that night Josh tweeted: 'I'm finally back home after a wicked night with the family :)'.

It can get lonely, staying in a hotel, even if you are with your best friends in the world. Sometimes only your family can make you feel better and having them there had made it a great night for the boys.

When they woke up the next morning, there was more than just *The X Factor* on their minds. They held a two-minute silence along with the rest of the country and tweeted: 'Love and thoughts go out to everyone who lost their lives to make the world a better place. Thank you. #RemembranceSunday'. But after that, they started to get nervous again – one more act would be leaving that evening and Union J were wishing and hoping that it wouldn't be them.

They'd received some great comments the night before, but as always, you just never knew what was going to happen.

The boys spent their time playing their favourite Pokemon game. They love it, especially Josh, who wouldn't put his Nintendo DS down! But eventually it was time to head back to the studio for the results show. And this would be the night when the Battle of the Bands would be well and truly over.

The acts were treated to Ed Sheeran singing 'Give Me Love' and Little Mix performing their new single, 'DNA'.

It was great to see how far another former *X Factor* group had come, and as the girls stormed the stage, the boys could only hope that they themselves would be there in a year's time. The night flew by and finally it was time for Dermot O'Leary to reveal the results.

It was so tense and everyone's faces showed it.

'In no particular order,' began Dermot. 'The first act through is James, then Rylan…'

Union J looked very nervous.

'…then Jahmene, then Ella…'

It was down to three acts: District 3, Union J and Christopher Maloney.

'Only one is certain of a place,' said Dermot. 'The final act returning next week is… Christopher!'

George looked close to tears and Josh, JJ and Jaymi all seemed utterly crushed.

It had come down to the moment they had all been dreading. They would have to go head to head with their friends and rivals, District 3. Only one band would survive and go through to the next live show.

The boys waited while Greg, Dan and Mickey went first. They could hear the boys singing and could also hear how nervous they were. They took the time to compose themselves, taking deep breaths and going over the lyrics in their heads. Then it was their turn to sing.

Louis introduced them, trying his hardest not to look sad. He knew what was coming – he'd have to make a decision that he'd hoped he would never have to make. 'Okay, guys, this is it, sing your hearts out – get ready for Union J!'

The boys began singing Adele's 'Set Fire To The Rain' and it was a confident performance. Despite this, Jaymi's face clearly showed the inner turmoil he was feeling. He couldn't stop now, this had been his dream his whole life. With every note he sang, he would fight.

And when it was over the boys hugged each other. Their work was done. All they could do now was listen to what the judges had to say.

Louis refused to vote – they were both his acts and he didn't want to send either of his beloved bands home. So Gary went first and when he turned to District 3, all the boys listened intently.

First, he told them that he'd thought it was going to be a simple decision, because he believed District 3 had always been better vocally. But then he told the poor lads that it had been the worst performance Greg, Dan and

Mickey had done so far, and at that moment, the Union J boys knew they were in with a chance.

'Guys,' he said, turning to JJ, Josh, George and Jaymi. 'Although there were less harmonies in your performance I felt like you wanted it so much more.'

The boys were relieved when he revealed that he was sending District 3 home, but they were sad, too. They didn't like to see their friends suffering.

Nicole told District 3 that they should be proud of themselves and praised their harmonies, but then she said: 'The group that I think is a more mature group and a little bit more ready for this right now is...'

Josh put his hand to his mouth, waiting for her answer. It was the tensest moment of all their lives. If Nicole sent their rivals home too, they would automatically be through to the next round.

'...Union J! The act I'm sending home is District 3.'

They couldn't believe it. Jumping up and down and hugging each other, their nerves disappeared completely, replaced by a huge feeling of happiness. Even if they were voted out next week – which they hoped wouldn't happen – they had won the battle of the boybands. But when District 3 trudged over to give them all hugs, suddenly they felt sad again. Their friends were going home because of them.

That night, on *The Xtra Factor*, a caller asked Nicole whether she thought Union J would make the final – after all, they'd now been in the bottom two twice.

'Anything is possible,' she said, brightly. 'Imagine where Union J started and how far they've come already, they've grown so much! Lord knows they've got a lot of fans.'

The audience cheered when she added: 'I can barely get my car in every day because there's so many Union J fans waiting outside. All it takes is believers and they have a lot of believers.'

Dermot O'Leary had also seen the thousands of fans outside the *X Factor* studios. 'Whenever I turn up to soundcheck there's always hundreds of fans outside and I ask who they're voting for, and every single one says District 3 or Union J.'

He'd been astonished that they were both in the bottom two that night – both their Saturday night performances had been amazing.

The Union J boys spoke to Caroline Flack and Olly Murs about what it had felt like to sing off against District 3.

'We kind of knew it was coming,' said Josh. 'We spoke to District 3 and we said, "Can you imagine?" Perhaps we shouldn't have said anything.'

Jaymi was very emotional. 'It was gutting, getting through and we were like, breaking down, 'cause that's like our best mates. It's such mixed emotions.'

And he chatted about the rivalry between the two bands, saying: 'There's a healthy rivalry but we've become best of mates. It was hard enough singing against Jade and seeing her go out, but this was a million times harder because they want it just as much as us and you've got a bond 'cause you're both in groups, so you both know what it feels like.'

Then the presenters decided to lighten the mood. It had been a sad day and everyone needed a bit of cheering up. And nothing cheers people up better than an embarrassing revelation!

'We've heard that you, Josh, are wearing boxer shorts that say 'Believe The Hype' on them. Is this true?' asked Caroline Flack, giggling.

Everyone laughed and of course Josh had to pull his jeans down to show everyone. He went bright red!

Little Mix said neither of the bands deserved to be in the bottom two – and then admitted to fancying the Union J boys!

On the weekly segment, 'Fighting Talk', George and Ella battled it out in a fake boxing ring, starting more rumours that they were secretly dating.

'Ella's going down!' said George playfully, as they got ready to start the war of words.

Question one: How many relationships have you had?

Ella admitted she'd had none, while George bragged that he had ten!

'He's never even had a girlfriend,' joked Ella.

Question two: How many schools have you attended?

Ella said two, while George said seven.

'Did you get kicked out of loads?' asked Ella.

'No,' replied George, giving her his cheekiest smile. 'I'm an international jet-setter.' It wasn't true at all!

Clearly the pair had great chemistry as they joked around, answering the silly questions.

Question three: how many animals have you had?

Ella said she'd had about seventeen pets and listed

them all – bunnies, parrots, ducks, geese, fish – the list was endless.

George was obviously feeling very left out.

'I've had a giraffe, an elephant and a lion,' he lied. But this was all in good humour and everyone found it very funny.

That night, the boys went back to their hotel for a well-earned rest. Union J were safe for another week but it had been an epic night, one they would never forget. And with their main rivals out of the competition they were in a strong position to go far. But first they had to say goodbye to Greg, Dan and Mickey and that can't have been easy, especially when they knew they were the reason the trio were leaving.

The boys went to bed feeling a mixture of happiness and sadness but as Dermot O'Leary had said: 'District 3 have sung their last song in this competition, but the other acts must go on.'

## CHAPTER ELEVEN

# PERFORMANCE IN PARIS

## WEEK SEVEN – GUILTY PLEASURES
17/18 November 2012

What Union J sang: 'Call Me Baby' – Carly Rae Jepsen

What the judges said:
Tulisa: 'I'm not a fan of that song.'
Gary: 'I think you've definitely bounced back from last week.'
Nicole: 'You sounded really, really good.'
Louis: 'You can't be in the bottom two again.'

It was dark and the night had a chill to it, as a young couple took a midnight stroll in November, hand in hand through the West End of London. She was dressed in a cosy coat, her long hair flowing, while he was covering his curly locks with a wooly hat. Holding hands, they looked like any other young couple as they walked back to the hotel they were staying in.

But onlookers were stunned to see that it was Ella Henderson and George Shelley – were all the rumours true? Were they an item?

It was just a few days before that Ella had protested they were not boyfriend and girlfriend and had spoken about how they were just friends. She told *Fabulous* magazine: 'We've got a lot in common, we're in synch with one another. You don't come into this competition or this kind of show to make a friend for life and stuff, but with certain people I think I've found that.'

But clutching each other's hands on the cold evening, passers-by saw a completely different story.

Wrapping up warm, all the boys were remarkably bright-eyed as they arrived the next day at King's Cross St Pancras station. After finishing in the bottom two the week before, they knew they had a lot of work to do to get their confidence back up. Plus, it had been a sad time for the foursome. Saying goodbye to their friends in District 3 had been tough, especially since they were the ones who were chosen to continue in the competition – over their mates Greg, Dan and Mickey. But they were grinning ear to ear when they were handed a glass of champagne, before stepping onto the Eurostar train.

The boys and the remaining finalists were all off to Disneyland, Paris!

'You'll be performing for their 20th Anniversary,' Louis

had told them, watching their eyes light up. It was to be their first performance away from the *X Factor* stage and naturally it was a very big deal.

For the boys it was their first real step on the road to being a proper band. They would be entertaining thousands of people and not all of them would even have heard of Union J. Their job was to convert them into fans!

Unable to contain his excitement, Josh tweeted: 'WE ARE OFF TO DISNEYLAND PARIS!!!!!! Ah...soooo exciting!! I can't wait to go on the flying dumbo ride!!'

They were so excited, in fact, that according to the *Daily Mirror* they spent the whole of the journey drawing moustaches on Christopher Maloney's face as he slept.

But before their stage time, the boys got to enjoy the theme park. Greeted by Disney royalty Mickey and Minnie, all the finalists swarmed around the famous mice. But Ella was definitely Mickey's favourite – he threw his arms around her as soon as he saw her. Wearing a fun blue spotty skirt with some Minnie ears, they looked like the perfect couple – we hope George wasn't jealous!

But in fact George had the biggest grin of everyone as the finalists took in the sights, munched on French treats and were completely mobbed by autograph hunters.

The guys were so surprised. Being far away from England, they didn't think they'd be recognised but it made them realise just how much of a stir they were making all over the world.

Ella and George posed for photos wearing matching Mickey and Minnie Mouse ears and huge grins – before sharing them on Twitter for their delighted fans.

Disneyland is always exciting and the boys were totally swept away by the lights, the costumes and of course the rides. Ella joined them on the log flume and screamed with laughter as it whisked the finalists around the park.

Excitable George went on rollercoaster after rollercoaster, including one he tried out with presenter Caroline Flack. He went on the Space Mountain ride with her too, along with fellow finalist Jahmene. But after a few hours, he began to look pale.

It was soon obvious something was wrong – he wasn't his usual self at all. Eventually he gave his bandmates some distressing news: he'd overdone it and needed to lie down!

So while Jaymi, Josh and JJ continued to enjoy themselves with the rest of the finalists, poor George went back to his hotel and tried to sleep his nausea off. All that up and down and round and round will do that to you, George!

It was obvious he'd learnt his lesson, but would he be okay for their first ever, proper performance that evening?

The boys were a bit worried as they wandered around, enjoying everything the park had to offer.

George stayed in bed, missing out on the fun. He must have been feeling very sorry for himself; he was desperate to be well enough for his first ever live performance outside of *X Factor*. All he could do was hope.

But while George was laid low, the other finalists were surprised to see his rumoured love, Ella, getting very close to his bandmate Josh Cuthbert.

It was him she sat next to on the rides, laughing and

screaming with joy. Onlookers were left to wonder if maybe Ella had stayed tight-lipped about her romance with George because her feelings were shifting towards his friend and co-singer.

One eagle-eyed fan even told the *Daily Mirror* that they had seen Ella and Josh walking back to the *X Factor* hotel earlier in the week, with their arms around each other. Another source told the paper that George was so devastated that he was on the verge of tears when he found out about the walk – and that Rylan had to calm him down.

George had only just revealed to *The X Factor* online that he would consider dating the songstress once the show was over.

So, would the boys battle over Ella?

Only time would tell.

**DID YOU KNOW?**
**Melanie Masson runs a music class for under-fives called Fairy Flutterby's Little Rockabyes – so Melanie is known as 'Fairy Flutterby'!**

At the eleventh hour, George declared that he was well enough to perform, much to everyone's relief.

As day turned to night, the Disneyland stage was set for a magical show. A huge glittering white Christmas tree nestled on huge blocks of snow, providing the backdrop for the impending performances. Placed directly in front of the famous Disney castle, which was lit up in purple, it looked like something out of a fairytale.

In the contestants' rooms the mood was frantic but everyone was in high spirits. Outfits were chosen and put on, hair styled and re-styled, make-up carefully applied. The excitement was palpable – just a few months before they were at school or stacking shelves. They must have felt as if they were living in their own Disney movie – a rags-to-riches tale every bit as romantic as *Cinderella*.

First onto the winter-themed stage was Rylan Clark, dressed for once in a smart outfit of tight black jeans, white open T-shirt and black blazer. He even seemed a little stage-struck as he belted out a Spice Girls' medley in front of the 1,200 people in the audience. But he energetically stormed the stage, screaming: 'Alright, Disney, I think we need to have a bit of fun tonight. I love the Spice Girls! Cheers, Disney – see you later!'

Next up were our favourite boys, Union J, in coordinated brown jackets and dark jeans. Waving to the hordes of fans they put their heart and soul into singing Leona Lewis' 'Bleeding Love'. The audience was over-whelmed by the foursome, who were now experiencing the adulation of a top-selling stadium band. And the feeling was reciprocated, with George telling them: 'Thank you so much, that's the first time we have performed outside *The X Factor* so it's such an amazing feeling!'

Next to experience the excitement of the lucky crowds was Ella Henderson, who had kept her Minnie Mouse ears on, teaming them with matching gloves. Much to everyone's delight, she chose to sing the Katy Perry classic, 'Firework'. It must have been an amazing feeling to hear so many people singing along to the well-known tune with her.

'Baby you're a firework, come on let your colours burst...'

It was a perfect song. As the stage lights flickered and changed through a rainbow of colours, Ella looked right at home in Disneyland. She told the crowds: 'It has been amazing! I have loved it here. It's like being in a fairytale!'

**DID YOU KNOW?**
**Ella has always been a huge Minnie Mouse fan and was so excited to meet her – along with her other Disney favourites, Cinderella and Ariel.**

Somewhat surprisingly, Christopher Maloney was the only finalist to sing a Disney song, choosing 'A Whole New World' from *Aladdin*. 'Can I just say, ladies and gentlemen, boys and girls,' he said humbly, 'giving me this opportunity to sing today has been amazing. If you had told me 10 months ago that I would be singing at Disney, in front of the castle, to celebrate their 20th Anniversary, I really wouldn't have believed it. Thank you so much for all your amazing support.'

As the final contestant left the stage, the crowds must have been feeling a little deflated but then Caroline Flack appeared and told them: 'We've had the most amazing day here, so thank you so much.'

They began to cheer with delight as the *X Factor* stars trooped back on stage – accompanied by their favourite Disney stars!

Jahmene was with Donald Duck and James Arthur was

with Goofy – although Rylan, whose actual companion was Pluto – stole him away for a huge hug. Christopher Maloney had main star Mickey by his side, while Ella obviously was holding hands with her beloved Minnie. Union J had the cheeky Chipmunks to contend with, all dressed in Santa outfits.

After their exciting time in Paris, the contestants flew back and began to prepare for Saturday night's show – Guilty Pleasures.

The singers had to pick their own embarrassing guilty song pleasure, and reinvent it to make it cool again. But our favourite bandmates found the time to support one of their favourite charities first – by trying to get all their fans to support them, too. They tweeted: 'Everyone please check out an amazing charity for children with brain tumours. They are amazing and so lovely @JossSearchlight RT RT josh xxx'.

It just proved how lovely all the boys are. They were thinking of other people even when they had so much work to do.

With fewer and fewer girls left in the competition, the *X Factor* styling team may have been feeling disappointed that they didn't have as much make-up to apply to the contestants' faces but in a series of photos on Facebook, it was revealed that the make-up team were still being kept busy – because the boys from Union J also wear eyeliner and foundation to go on stage!

Josh was photographed having mascara added to his eyelashes, while George was being primped and preened by the hairdressing team. And George had some explaining to do when he was seen with a bright red lipstick mark on his cheek... care of an over-enthusiastic fan outside the studio!

**DID YOU KNOW?**
**District 3 is also the name of one of the fictional colonies in *The Hunger Games*.**

With three weeks to go, the mood backstage at the *X Factor* arena was tense. As the seats began to fill up, it was clear that this would be another packed live show.

'Six acts remain but none of them can take anything for granted,' announced Dermot O'Leary, as the live show began. Trying to relax the nervous crowd, he asked the judges about their own guilty pleasure songs.

Nicole replied: "Push It' by Salt-n-Pepa.'

Gary said: 'Anything by Rick Astley.'

Tulisa revealed: 'The Backstreet Boys.'

And Louis really showed his age when he said: 'Engelbert Humperdinck', before changing his mind to 'Take That' after seeing Dermot's embarrassed face.

Earlier on in the week, Louis had given the boys a pep talk to try and give them a much-needed boost.

'Guys, it was really tough,' he told them. 'It was the battle of the boybands. You're going to have to work really hard.'

The boys nodded enthusiastically in reply, and Josh said: 'Last week was really devastating for us to be in the bottom two. It was really hard going up against some of our best mates in the competition.'

After the devastating showdown, Ella had run up to them and said that she was worried she was going to lose her four big brothers!

After their mentor had given them his vote of confidence, the boys felt much better. 'We're coming back fighting! Kerpow!' they yelled.

When they bounced onto the stage, it was with a renewed enthusiasm. They had the audience clapping as they sang the hit song 'Call Me Maybe' to cheers of excitement. Smiling and obviously enjoying themselves, the song went down a storm with both fans at home and in the crowd. But it was the judges' verdict that mattered, and that must have been all they could think about when they finished singing.

The cheers hadn't even died down when Tulisa began to speak. 'Guys,' she began sadly, 'I'm going to be really honest…' It was obvious that she wasn't happy, and the crowd began to boo. 'This is a really hard performance for me to judge and I'll tell you why: I'm not a big fan of that song.'

As the booing got louder, Tulisa was quick to say, 'I think you sounded great – it had good energy. But it's still too cheesy for me and the whole point of guilty pleasures is to take a cheesy song and make it cool – maybe there wasn't enough of that for me.'

The boys looked crestfallen, and even Gary appeared shocked by Tulisa's comments but he came to the boys' defence immediately, saying, 'If it's guilty to like that song, then I love it! It's been one of the best songs of the year and I think you've never looked better.'

Shadow Chancellor Ed Balls was watching at home and tweeted his disagreement, too! 'Sorry Tulisa,' it read. 'But Carly Rae Jepsen's 'Call Me Maybe' was THE song of 2012'!

Their spirits definitely began to soar as Gary continued: 'I think so far for you guys you've always been competing with the other band – and now you've won the battle of the boybands, it's about winning for you guys.'

The icing on the cake was when he finished with: 'You know what? That was a pretty good performance from you tonight, I think you've definitely bounced back from last week.'

And things only got better when Nicole told them that she thought the boys had done the song justice. She'd spotted the audience drooling over the good-looking guys and had some advice for the group.

'Engage with the audience more,' she said, wisely. 'What I would like to see from you is to get a little bit more creative with your staging. Enjoy it, love it – and you look expensive and that counts, too!'

The boys had certainly come a long way since they'd arrived wearing nothing but their fresh faces and high street clothes to the London audition. And to have Nicole recognise this was amazing.

Dermot spoke about the hordes of swooning fans that had begun to follow them everywhere. The boys chuckled as he said: 'You turn up for rehearsals there are loads of girls outside, all chanting your name. The girls down the front, they all love Union J. You've been in the bottom two twice – what is it, Louis?'

Louis looked just as puzzled as Dermot as he tried to think what could possibly have led to the sing-off. Totally stumped, all he could say was that he still truly believed Union J would be the next big boyband.

George had obviously thought long and hard about what could have been letting them down. The whole band knew they had something special, they believed in themselves, just as the thousands of fans they had accumulated since that first moment when they appeared on TV at the auditions.

'I think it was quite difficult to have the two boybands and the rivalry, and maybe votes were being split between the two,' he mused. 'But we just wanted to come back fighting this week and we tried really, really hard.'

It was the kind of observation that showed a wisdom far beyond his years and in homes all over the country, people were nodding in agreement.

### DID YOU KNOW?
**Josh's favourite dessert is apple pie, while George likes to get his caffeine fix from Costa Coffee and he also loves home-cooked roast dinners. Get your aprons on, girls!**

It was an evening of outstanding talent and all the contestants who followed Union J's opening performance really sang their hearts out.

After an anxious night's sleep, the six final acts returned to the *X Factor* studios to hear their fate, but they were about to receive what has been described as the biggest shock in the show's history. That night, the contestants all performed Tulisa's song, 'Young', before *X Factor* alumni Olly Murs and R&B superstar Alicia Keys each took to the stage to entertain the crowds. They certainly showed the finalists how to perform like pros! As the live camera watched their every move, it was then time for the quarter-finalists to be announced.

Chris Maloney mouthed to his family: 'I'm going home,' before the jaw-dropping results were revealed. It was a relief when Union J quickly learnt that they were safe for another week. But the sing-off would be between James Arthur and Ella Henderson!

The boys' hearts must have skipped a few beats. They were through to the quarterfinals of *X Factor* 2012! But the moment was bittersweet – their beloved Ella wasn't safe from elimination. She could be going home.

Dermot O'Leary couldn't hide his surprise. To him, as to people all around the UK, it was unbelievable that one of those two acts would be going home.

Leona Lewis tweeted: 'No way should Ella and James be singing against each other.'

A wave of anger swept the nation – but the worst was yet to come. Union J nervously went backstage to wait for the result. Whatever happened, it would be a sad night in the *X Factor* hotel.

After walking out together, arm in arm, both Ella and James took to the stage once more. James performed an acoustic version of Alicia Keys' 'Fallin' on his guitar, while Ella sang Daniel Bedingfield's 'If You're Not The One'.

It was all down to the judges…

Nicole chose to save her singer, James, while Tulisa did the same with her girl, Ella. It was only natural that the judges would save their own acts.

'I shouldn't have to make this decision,' Tulisa lamented, while Nicole tried to ease her guilt by saying that she had no worries about Ella's career, but she had to stick with 'her boy'. Now it was down to Gary and Louis – what would they decide?

Louis went first, saying: 'I'm in shock – I thought they were two finalists. Nicole and Tulisa are broken-hearted. Ella, you have so much potential. You've got so much more to give in this competition. James, you are amazing. You're a readymade act for a record deal…'

Then he made his decision: 'But the act I'm sending home is James.'

Gary was quiet for a moment before he announced his decision. 'It's about the vocals,' he finally said. 'It's a singing competition. The act I'm sending home is Ella.'

Everyone was stunned.

It was a deadlock, which meant it would all come down to the public vote. And when it was revealed that James Arthur had more votes than Ella Henderson, the audience went into a stunned silence before erupting with anger.

Ella – the nation's newest sweetheart – was going home!

Being the sweet and talented teen she is, Ella graciously accepted her fate. Standing beside a visibly pained Tulisa, she took her last moments on stage to thank and praise her fellow contestants.

'I've grown so much as a person,' she said, full of emotion, 'and that's what I'm taking with me.'

Meanwhile, on Twitter and Facebook angry fans vented their rage. *TOWIE*'s Arg wrote: 'Can't believe @Ella_Henderson gone! She deserved to be in the final and more.' While fellow reality star Millie Mackintosh asked: 'How did @Ella_Henderson just get voted out?' And teen starlet Chloë Grace Moretz, of *Kick Ass* fame, was so upset she decided to boycott the show, saying: 'Not watching #XFactorUK anymore. Such a rig.'

It's a wonder the *X Factor* judges weren't a teensy bit afraid – after all, Chloë knows a lot about martial arts!

But Union J were the most devastated at the loss of the pretty teen. Whatever the rumours of romance that had been flying around, there was no denying how close the boys were to their fellow contestant. And if there was any bad feeling between George and Josh, it was put to one side while they shared their sorrow at her loss.

Tears rolled down their cheeks as Ella left the stage to thunderous applause for the last time. And it was to the Union J boys that she went first, where she was cocooned in hugs.

'We've lost one of the most amazing people in the world,' Josh told Caroline Flack, after the showdown.

Selflessly, the boys refused to wallow in their own misery. Instead they decided to cheer Ella up by taking her back to the hotel they all shared and plying her with sweet treats.

'I was with them at the hotel last night,' Ella told the *Metro* the following day. 'It's a horrible feeling but I'll be seeing them soon and hopefully I'll be seeing them there, singing at the final.'

Naming her the band's unofficial fifth member, Union J tweeted: 'Gutted for @ella_henderson but she will be massive anyway!! She's amazing!!'

Although they'd already said that *X Factor* hairdresser Jamie Stevens should be their fifth member, who knows how big the band will grow? It's nice to know they've got such huge hearts.

**DID YOU KNOW?**
**Lucy Spraggan has 'Olly Murs' tattooed on her right foot. She asked the presenter/singer to perform with her on *The Xtra Factor* and in exchange she said she'd have his name inked – she kept her word!**

The following morning Ella was up bright and early. She had an interview to give with Phillip Schofield and Holly Willoughby on ITV's *This Morning* and she took the opportunity to show her support for her favourite finalists, Union J.

'I'm definitely going to be supporting Union J,' she said, confidently. 'They're like my big brothers.'

She also revealed she had a gut feeling that she was going to be eliminated, even though she said that she felt more in control of her performance that night than ever.

'Everyone assumed that I'd go through to the final but so much good stuff is going to come off the back of this for me,' she told the presenters.

No one doubted it.

## CHAPTER TWELVE

# KNUCKLING DOWN

## WEEK EIGHT – ABBA VS MOTOWN
24/25 November 2012

What Union J sang: 'The Winner Takes It All'–
ABBA/'I'll Be There' – Jackson Five

What the judges said:
Tulisa: 'What a night for you guys!'
Gary: 'I think you're on a roll now.'
Nicole: 'I felt like I was watching your concert.'
Louis: 'I think the next big boyband is on stage.'

Emotions were already high in the *X Factor* hotel. The
final was drawing near and everyone was fretting over
what they could do to make their act the winning one.
But one contestant was struggling more than most, and

his worries had nothing to do with the weekend's drama.

A young fan had asked him a question and he didn't know how to answer it.

Jaymi Hensley went to his mentor, Louis Walsh, to talk it through. And with his help he came to a decision: it was time to tell the world he was gay.

The heartthrob wasn't the only gay finalist in the show – Rylan Clark, Lucy Spraggan and Jade Ellis had all proudly admitted their sexuality. And he didn't want to hide it to gain votes, because Jaymi is very proud of who he is but for one reason or another, he had decided to keep it to himself.

Now it was time to tell the world.

His bandmates had always known the truth: that he had been in a relationship with his boyfriend, a hairdresser, for three years. Totally loved-up, the couple planned to marry and have children.

'I didn't want to do it in five years' time when I have a career,' he told the *Sun On Sunday*. 'I don't think anyone should have to hide who they are.'

The *X Factor* bosses and of course, Jaymi's mentor Louis (who is also gay) were a real help in his decision. 'If I can help just one kid out, that's enough for me,' said Louis. He even laughed and added: 'Every boyband has got to have a gay one!'

Jaymi's bandmates publicly rallied round in support of his bold move. 'It's been a tough week but we're so proud of Jaymi. He's so brave,' they told the *Metro*. 'It will help out other people having a tough time and give them courage.'

Jaymi and the band were really thrilled with the support

they received from their fans who overwhelmed them with positive tweets.

A few days later they all wrapped up warm and attended the opening night party of 'Winter Wonderland' in London's Hyde Park. With fake snow, fun rides and lots of Christmassy music it was a great night but they couldn't enjoy themselves too much because this week they had to sing two songs at the live show, which would be the quarterfinals.

They would have to learn one ABBA song and one Motown classic. It was twice as much work and with the final just around the corner, they didn't want to let themselves or Louis down, especially now they were so close to winning.

Gary Barlow managed to take some time out that week, too – to collect his OBE! He was invited to Buckingham Palace to meet HM the Queen, who thanked him for his Services to Charity and the Entertainment Industry and pinned the award on his chest. Such an honour!

**DID YOU KNOW?**
**Rylan Clark was once mugged by a fox! After coming face to face with the creature one evening, he was so surprised that he dropped his wallet – which Foxy picked up and ran away with.**

That week the boys were very excited about their performance. Rehearsals had gone well and they knew every note of their songs. They also thought they sounded really good and couldn't wait to show off on stage!

At the live show, it was finally their turn to sing. The stage was empty except for the four boys, as they began their first performance of the night.

Josh began to sing 'The Winner Takes It All' and the boys must have been hoping that the lyrics would come true! Of course they wanted to be the winners and to take it all – 'all' being a recording contract and a long career as a band. They moved over to the audience and took the hands of a few lucky fans as they sang.

And Tulisa was grinning as they finished their first song of the night. 'You know what, guys? I've got to give it to you – the vocals were on point tonight, with Jaymi really taking the lead there,' she began. 'The staging was simple, no gimmicks, just you and the voice. Good job, Louis – I really loved that!'

It had started well, but what would grumpy Gary say?

'Guys, I feel so good about this band, it just feels right,' he said, heaping more praise onto the happy boys. 'Like Tulisa said, you sounded great tonight and you look great tonight.'

No one was going to argue with that – the boys looked hotter than ever. 'Josh, your voice is coming through as well – I thought that was particularly good from you,' he added, singling Josh out. 'I think you're on a roll now, guys, I really do.'

Wow! It was high praise indeed from the normally serious judge.

Then it was Nicole's turn to speak and the boys were hoping she'd agree with Gary and Tulisa – to get great comments from all the judges on one night would be just amazing.

'Boys,' she said in her sexiest voice. 'I love the way you addressed the girls this week – get used to it, get comfortable with it 'cause that's what your future looks like, right up on that stage. I felt like I was watching your concert.'

She was totally right. It had felt like a real concert for the boys and for the first time they must have felt this week was almost in the bag.

Nicole also commented on Josh's great voice, saying: 'Josh, you have such a beautiful voice and whenever you sing, you sing with such ease.'

All they could do was thank the stunning brunette.

As usual, Louis was brimming with pride: 'Yes, Josh and Jaymi did the lead vocals, but the four guys sing, everybody sings in this band and they work so hard.'

It was obvious how far they'd all come from that first week when they'd been told off for not working hard enough. The boys had really knuckled down and their efforts were definitely paying off. They looked as if they couldn't wait to get off stage and jump around, screaming for joy.

But Louis took a moment to beg the public to vote for his boys. Ella's recent shock departure had made it very clear that however much everyone might like an act, they would leave the stage if people didn't pick up the phone.

No one wanted that to happen.

On stage, George was so happy he couldn't speak. But even as they walked off the boys knew that tonight wasn't over – they had one more song to sing and it had to be good for them to reach the grand final, now just two weeks away.

They couldn't relax, but they waited patiently for the other five acts to sing their songs before it was once more their turn. This time Jaymi kicked off proceedings with the Jackson Five classic 'I'll Be There' – and he sounded brilliant! It sounded so polished and George looked particularly fit. He was really turning into a hunk on stage and the girls all loved him. That kind of adoration is a lot for a teenager to take, but George looked perfectly at ease with it, and wasn't distracted when he heard his name being shouted out from the audience, over and over.

All they could do now was listen as the judges said what they thought of their second song.

'Wow, guys, what a night for you!' said Tulisa, blown away by the band. 'Two amazing song choices, two amazing vocal performances! For me this is your best night in the competition.'

It was just what they wanted to hear – they'd nailed it!

But Gary had returned to his former grumpy self. Obviously one heap of praise was enough for one night. 'What you had tonight with Motown was a massive opportunity. Boybands were essentially born in the Motown era – The Drifters, The Temptations, The Four Tops…'

Already people were yawning as Gary droned on.

'I thought that was an open door for you guys to do something really one-off tonight and you didn't really take that opportunity.'

No one agreed with him. Anywhere. But still he kept going.

'It was a good performance,' he admitted, 'but I thought you could have gone the extra mile there and you didn't.'

What was he expecting? Fireworks? Gymnastics?

The judges began to argue among themselves. 'It was a great performance,' insisted Tulisa, backed up by Louis. And Nicole added: 'I think all the little girls will beg to differ right now. Because they will pretty much be playing it on repeat.'

All the little girls – and all the big ones! Everyone loved the boys and no one could understand why Gary was being so negative.

'Guys, that was your best performance yet,' pronounced Louis, after asking if Gary had recently gone deaf. 'That was amazing! We didn't want to play it safe; we took a chance. These boys are a vocal harmony band and they've got something special.'

And with that, the audience erupted into cheers again.

Jaymi leapt to the defence of his bandmates: 'The reason we've kept it safe is that we've really found out who we are as a band on this show. We've learnt every week who we are and where our market is, and we just wanted to show that we could take a song and make it a Union J song.'

All the boys nodded because that was exactly what they had done. But was it enough to get them through to the semi-finals?

Thousands of their fans certainly thought so – including Little Mix, who tweeted: 'Union j's best performance last night smashed it make sure you vote for them guys nobody is safe.' And Niall Horan from One Direction was pretty impressed, too, tweeting: '@UnionJworld congrats lads! Smashed it tonight! Great job! Proud!'

Before they went to sleep, the boys took some time to say goodnight to their fans: 'Off to bed now sooo tired had a wicked night tho thanks so much for your support and if you have already voted. We love you all nite JJx.'

**DID YOU KNOW?**
**James Arthur once wet the bed on a family holiday – after drinking too many ginger beers. Aw!**

The next day, the boys were a bag of nerves but they still tried to have some fun. George posted a really cute picture of Josh, fast asleep, sucking his thumb, before they all spent some time with their fans, chatting and signing autographs and having pictures taken.

There were so many fans, though, and so little time!

They spent most of the day rehearsing their 'save me' song for that night, although they were all hoping they wouldn't have to sing it. Then it was time for Dermot O'Leary to leap on stage and announce the start of *The X Factor Results Show*.

The acts watched as Bruno Mars sang his new track, 'Locked Out Of Heaven', before superstar Rihanna performed 'Diamonds' on the stage, as a shower of rain gently fell on her from above. By the end of the performance she was soaking wet, but she still looked gorgeous!

After all the excitement, it was time for Dermot to deliver the good and bad news – it was time for the results.

'The first act through is…' he began. 'James Arthur!'

The tension on stage was unbearable and everyone clung to each other in solidarity.

'…then Christopher Maloney!'

Dermot paused. There were three acts left, but only one more would be safe. The audience scanned the stage, wondering who would be in the sing-off. Jahmene and Union J had both given brilliant performances, and Rylan had been his usual entertaining self – who would be the third and final act through to safety?

'The final act through to the semi-finals next week is…'

There was a long and dramatic pause.

'…Jahmene!'

Everyone was completely astonished – Union J were in the bottom two again. And this time they would be singing against Essex favourite Rylan. Whoever went, there would be thousands of devastated fans across the country that night. But first, the two downhearted acts would have to pick up their spirits and sing again for the judges.

Rylan went first, performing a slow and emotional version of Athlete's hit, 'Wires'. Vocally, it was his best performance of the season. There were no gimmicks, no dancing – just Rylan, full of emotion, singing for his safety. But it was bad news for the Union J boys – they could see that it was an amazing performance. Then, while Rylan hugged Dermot at the side of the stage, it was time for the boys to give it their all, singing Snow Patrol's 'Run'.

The pain was clearly etched on their faces as they belted out the track. It was a phenomenal performance with JJ,

Josh, George and Jaymi giving it everything they had. This was the third time they had been in the bottom two – would they survive again?

When they had finished, Rylan and Dermot joined them on stage to face the judges.

Nicole went first. 'Boys, that was a very moving performance,' she told Union J. 'Thank you so much – it was passionate, it was emotional, but it is simple for me. I have to stick with my boy, I believe in him – the act I'm sending home is Union J.'

The boys clapped – they didn't expect anything else. Nicole was Rylan's mentor, and very loyal. Of course she would save him.

Next went Louis, who gave the boys a huge smile. 'Rylan, you're a fantastic guy. You're brilliant fun, you're a great role model, you're a team player, and you're a brilliant performer,' he began. Nobody disagreed with him. 'And I've enjoyed meeting you, and working with you and talking to you – I think you're going to have an amazing career in television and everything.'

Rylan smiled. He knew what was coming next.

'But Dermot, in the sing-off, the boys totally won. As Tulisa would say, they nailed it. The act I'm sending home is Rylan.'

One vote apiece and now it was Gary's turn. The judge had never pretended to like Rylan's act before, but anything could happen.

'Union J, you had a great night last night and also you've just had a great sing-off as well – you're the band everyone is going to want to sign in this competition.

You're going to have the labels fighting over you. Well done on that performance.'

The audience began to chant: 'Union J, Union J, Union J...'

'Listen, Rylan,' Gary said softly. 'You have been an amazing contestant and I'm so glad, because tonight that was your best vocal performance and also, your best song choice – that was one of my favourite songs.'

It was good to hear something nice about Rylan coming from Barlow – but would he go so far as to save him over Union J?

'We've had great fun, none of it has been personal – we've not taken any of it off the stage,' he added.

Rylan totally agreed – he was really happy. Gary was finally making up with him after weeks of slating his performances.

'But the act I'm sending home tonight, I'm sad to say, is Rylan.'

So, it was down to Tulisa – she would have the deciding vote. It was a horrible position to be in, but a decision had to be made.

'Union J, you are four amazing lads – on stage and off stage, and you've given brilliant performances each week,' she said. 'Rylan, you have entertained me the whole of this series. You've made me laugh, you've made me smile, and I have to admire your strength for some of the stuff you've had to put up with, while being in this competition...'

It was time for her to cast her vote.

'Now at this stage I have to go with the act that I feel

has the most potential to sell records in this competition. I'm so sorry, it pains me to say this, but the act I'm sending home is Rylan.'

The sick feeling in the boys' tummies went away and they were left overwhelmed with happiness. They'd made it to the semi-finals! Now they were one step closer to winning *The X Factor*.

Rylan congratulated the boys, who were once again left feeling very guilty. They hated seeing their friends leave the competition, especially when they had been picked over them. But when they left the stage they tweeted: 'We certainly know how it feels to be in the bottom 2! We just wanna make it through to the final now. Thank you to everyone who voted.'

And Sharon Osbourne, who had helped Louis put the boys through in Vegas, was pleased too, tweeting: 'Congratulations to Union J. Well done boys! Big Kiss, Mrs O.'

**DID YOU KNOW?**
**Jade Ellis dated Marvin Humes from JLS when she was 15. They met when they both entered a local talent competition in Southeast London.**

On *The Xtra Factor*, Rylan told Caroline Flack and Olly Murs that he was relieved. 'I feel like a weight's been lifted off my shoulders, like I've been let out of prison!' The presenters laughed as he went on: 'Not in a bad way, I've loved being here – you know what I mean.' Then he said he'd miss Gary, describing him as being like the uncle he never wanted but loved anyway. Gary laughed. The two had definitely buried the hatchet.

Later on, Caroline congratulated the Union J boys on getting through to the semi-finals and Josh said: 'It's quite sad, really – we're chuffed to be here but it's bittersweet to see Rylan go. It was weird being in the bottom two again.'

The boys said they weren't surprised to be in the bottom two because the quality of the other acts was so good. But Jaymi added: 'I think it's going to give us the fight to go all the way, because every time we've been in the bottom two we've really used it.'

JJ revealed he had a tattoo of a heart on his bum before he took the opportunity to tell everyone that the messiest person in the group was Josh, because he had so many clothes.

'Josh has got a ridiculous amount of clothes,' he said. 'I've never seen so many.'

Josh said that Jaymi was the biggest prankster of the group, but they all wound up JJ the most and pulled pranks on him all the time. Poor JJ…

After getting through to the semi-final, James Arthur was so excited that he immediately went out to celebrate at Whisky Mist. When he left – much later on in the night – he had lipstick smeared all over his face! He was definitely being tipped to win the show – could Union J beat him? They could only try…

Before they went to bed, the boys had time for one last tweet: 'Off to sleep ;) going to miss rylan an awful lot…he's such an amazing guy inside and out. Friend for life :) night night josh xx'.

**DID YOU KNOW?**
Union J's Josh would have David Beckham, Rita Ora and Caroline Flack as his ideal dinner guests.

## CHAPTER THIRTEEN

# A NATION DIVIDED

## WEEK NINE – SONGS FOR YOU
1/2 December 2012

What Union J sang: 'Beneath Your Beautiful' – Emeli Sandé and Labrinth/'I'm Already There' – Lonestar

What the judges said:

Tulisa: 'It felt like a really mature performance.'
Gary: 'Good vocals, nice song choice.'
Nicole: 'I loved it – you've grown so much.'
Louis: 'The next big boyband is Union J!'

It had been a shocking weekend for the boys and they now had little time to recover themselves. The semi-finals were less than a week away and they had a lot of work to do.

After having to fight their way through yet another sing-off, it was hardly surprising that their spirits were low. Their Saturday night performances had been exceptional and even Louis was convinced that there was no way his boys would be in the bottom two again. In fact, he'd told them exactly that, moments before they discovered they would be singing for their survival for a third time.

After Rylan was sent home, Josh, JJ, Jaymi and George were all exhausted and emotional. Backstage, George even looked close to tears.

'We're too close to give up,' Jaymi said, when the show was over. 'We've now just got to come back fighting.'

He had given the cameras a brave smile, and put his arms around poor George.

But the next morning the boys were up bright and early, and talking to their fans. They tweeted: 'Good morning! SOOO happy we're still here. Sorry if we let you down this week, we're going to try really really hard this week! George X'.

It was straight off to the rehearsal studio for the four talented boys – who were now just two weeks away from the live final.

And when they got to the studio it was obvious that, after a good night's sleep, they were feeling a bit better.

'You're in the semi-finals!' said Louis, and the boys began to cheer. They had to admit it was a phenomenal achievement in itself, especially against such strong competition.

Louis explained to the boys that this week's theme was

'Songs For You'. They boys could choose any song and dedicate their performance to anyone they wanted. Louis asked: 'Have you any ideas?'

'We were thinking Labrinth and Emeli Sandé,' said Jaymi. "Beneath Your Beautiful'?'

Louis loved the song choice and immediately agreed.

'We really want to dedicate this song to our fans,' the boys all agreed – and George explained why: 'Our fans have been amazing throughout this competition. Sometimes they get in touch with us and let us know some of the hard times they've been going through,' he said.

'Despite where we are now, we've all have struggles with being picked on in the past, so this song's about being beautiful on the inside, and we really hope people can relate to it at home,' added Jaymi.

Being in the bottom two again had really damaged their confidence and the boys would have to work hard not only on their singing, but also on their morale, to keep their spirits up for the long week ahead.

'Being in the bottom two three times is gutting – knowing that the public aren't voting for you, knowing that we did all we could on Saturday night and gave our best and obviously it wasn't good enough,' said Josh.

But deep down the boys knew it wasn't that simple. The country was being divided and there could only be one winner.

It would be a busy week for Union J – but first their mentor had a surprise for the boys...

Louis had always been confused by his act's obsession with the cosy all-in-one outfits they wore when they were

Propelled into stardom. Jaymi Hensley enjoying *X Factor* fame at the film premiere of *The Twilight Saga: Breaking Dawn Part 2*.

Life has changed dramatically for the boys since entering *The X Factor*. JJ Hamblett at the *Cosmopolitan* Ultimate Women Awards 2012.

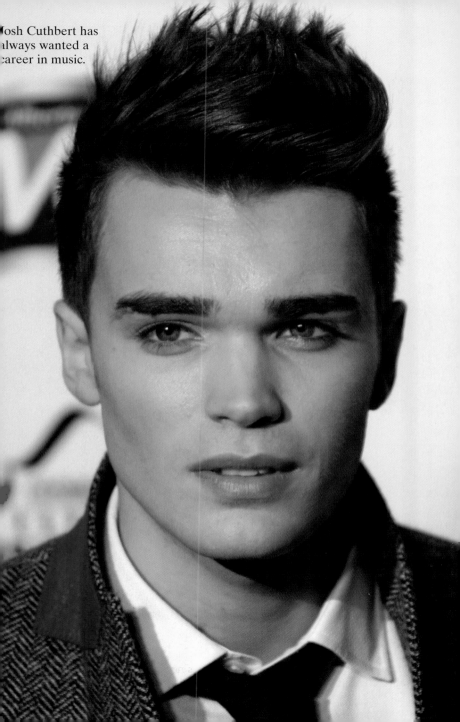

Josh Cuthbert has always wanted a career in music.

A second chance for George.
After auditioning as a solo artist for *The X Factor* and being axed at Bootcamp, George Shelley was asked to join the boys in Triple J, consequently changed to Union J.

A busy day at the studio.

*Above*: Fans wait outside the *X Factor* studios for their arrival.

*Below left*: George at St Pancras International with fellow contestant Ella Henderson.

*Below right*: Arriving at the studio together, ready to rehearse.

Good friends.

*Above left*: Celebrating Rylan Clark's birthday at Mahiki, London, with fellow contestants District 3.

*Above right*: Taking fame in their stride at an awards ceremony.

*Below*: Out and about in London together.

Looking the part. Invitations to big events have become a regular occurrence for the band since being on *The X Factor*.

*Above*: The boys pose at the Ultimate Women Awards.

*Below left*: Taking time out from attending events.

*Below right*: On the red carpet.

With the success of first single 'Carry You' and gigs all over the UK and beyond, Union J look set to rule the charts for a long time to come.

relaxing. 'What's a onesie?' he had asked the boys, after spotting them all wearing them.

George had explained that it was like a baby-grow for adults and Louis had been horrified. He'd told the boys he wouldn't be seen dead in one – unless they got into the semi-finals.

And now here they were, preparing to sing at the semi-finals and the boys hadn't forgotten Louis's words...

'A promise is a promise, so we hope he sticks to it,' Josh told the *X Factor* cameras during rehearsals.

'Louis is more used to wearing suits and turtleneck jumpers,' said George. 'So I don't know how he's going to find wearing a onesie.'

The boys threw themselves into practicing on stage for the live show. Then Louis arrived...

'Hey boys, how's it going?' he asked casually. But when they all turned around they were overjoyed to see him wearing a huge green onesie!

'Yes!' they all exclaimed before giving him a huge hug. Louis still looked unsure about the outfit and asked: 'Is it something like Tulisa would wear?'

'You look like a baby,' giggled George as the other boys fell about laughing. 'I'd do anything for you guys,' said Louis. And with their mentor standing in front of them, wearing a giant baby-grow, they truly believed him!

As well as the usual hours practicing and rehearsing, the boys once more got caught up in the never-ending whirlwind of publicity that goes hand in hand with fame and fortune.

First up was a shoot for *Heat* magazine, where they posed

for some very sexy new pics, and spoke about how they were amazed at the Union J fever sweeping the country.

'I had a girl faint in my arms on Sunday,' Jaymi told the magazine. 'So I kind of just handed her to a friend!'

It was an emotional week, and everyone was feeling a bit vulnerable. George even told the magazine why he hadn't yet posed for topless pictures.

Despite being a complete dreamboat, he revealed that being bullied in his schooldays had left him less than confident about his body.

'I was obese, I'm massively insecure,' he said. 'I won't even take my top off in the pool. It's programmed into my head that I'm fat because I got bullied at school and I can't get it out. If I got changed for PE and took my top off, people would laugh.'

Poor George – hopefully his new hordes of fans were starting to make him feel a little better.

Meanwhile, Ella Henderson was speaking to the media too. After months of speculation over her love life, she finally revealed that she did fancy one of the Union J boys – and it wasn't George. It was Josh!

'Let me explain it like this,' she told *Look* magazine. 'George Shelley is my best friend. Jaymi Hensley is like my big brother, JJ Hamblett is hilarious…'

But how about Josh – how did she feel about him?

'At the moment it's hard to say,' she said. 'He's still in the competition. As soon as we're both out of it, it's going to go boom…I do want to spend more time with him.'

Hopefully it was the words that Josh had been hoping to hear since meeting the glamorous teen. And it certainly looked that way when he posted a very cute picture of him and Ella together on his Instagram, saying: 'FAVORITE @ellahenderson1!!!!!! :D xx'.

It wasn't long since he'd tweeted: 'Gonna miss you Ella! & I'm gonna miss everything we do togetherrrr!'

Maybe the public was finally getting closer to the truth – that in fact, Ella and Josh could possibly become the *X Factor* couple this year!

Josh wasn't the only Union J boy who had tongues wagging that week either. Devoted JCats all over the country were consumed with jealously when the *Sun* newspaper reported that JJ had a new love – a beautiful Brazilian backing dancer called Rithiely Periera.

She was nicknamed 'Rithy' and according to the tabloid, JJ had met her when she was dancing on *The X Factor*.

When JJ had entered the competition he'd been dating a girl he knew from home. But the pressure of it all had sadly caused them to break up. Were the new rumours true? Was JJ loved up with a backing dancer? Only time would tell…

After five days of rehearsals, the boys got on a plane and flew to Dublin – to appear on the Irish TV series *The Late Late Toy Show*, where they appealed for Ireland to get behind them. 'Louis hasn't won for a few years and we want to do him proud,' Jaymi told the presenters.

They were absolutely overwhelmed by fans from the city – from the moment they got off the plane to the moment they got back on it to fly home. Louis had never seen anything like it and the boys themselves were shocked at the adoration they were inspiring everywhere. They just had to hope that everyone they met would be voting for them at the weekend.

When they arrived back in the UK, it was time for the live show.

It was the semi-final of the competition, and the boys knew how close they were to winning. They would have two songs to sing that night – two chances to get their fans to vote for them – and they were ready to give it their all...

The competition was now between Union J, Jahmene, Christopher Maloney and James Arthur – and all the talented acts wanted to win.

In a shock twist, the judges weren't in control of the boys' fate this week. They could have their say, but it was down to the public at home to decide who would stay and who would go. Who would they vote through to the final in Manchester?

'We're not going down without a fight,' said Josh, backstage, as he prepared to sing...

Christopher Maloney went first, followed by Jahmene, both giving emotional performances that the judges loved.

Christopher dedicated his to his Gran, who had been the inspiration for him entering the competition in the first place.

Jahmene dedicated his to his brother, who had sadly passed away a few years before.

Then it was time for Union J to give their performance. George strummed on his guitar while the boys stood on stage and sang to their fans. This song was just for them and they wanted each and every one of them to know that they were beautiful, inside and out. It was a lovely sentiment and one that the JCats appreciated.

It was obvious that the boys had really progressed throughout the competition and Tulisa was the first to notice.

Trying to talk over the screams in the audience, she told them: 'I really, really liked that performance. I tell you what, something felt a little bit different about you guys there – it was almost like there's this maturity about you now, it felt like a really mature performance. It's like we've seen you grow over the competition and now you're standing there saying: 'We're ready, we wanna be in the final and we're fighting for it'.'

Gary was equally happy with the boys and showered praise on them. 'Guys, brilliant performance tonight, what a great song choice. In the past I think you've often sounded like four solo singers in a band but tonight you really blended brilliantly,' he said. 'And you know what, Tulisa's right – there's a calm on stage – you know you're good tonight and it feels really good and I think labels are going to be fighting over you.'

Nicole had only just about got over her tears at Jahmene's emotional performance. But she managed: 'What I love about this group is that you guys are cool, you guys are individual, you're cheese free – a lot of boy groups are cheesy – and Josh, that was a beautiful start to the song. Very honest.'

JJ gave Josh a huge hug – all the boys agreed he'd done them proud that night.

'Everywhere these guys go there's a hysteria,' said Louis. 'You were in Dublin last night – it was like Beatlemania. We've got something great here, guys. JLS came from this. So did One Direction. The next big boyband is Union J!'

Dermot laughed. It was about the hundredth time Louis had said those very words. But surely he was right?

'We respect all of your comments,' said Josh from on stage, 'We're working so hard and we're fingertips away from the final and we want to be there so badly.'

Dermot tried to speak to George next, but as usual the screams from his fans were too loud. George gave up – and instead of speaking, he shook his head and chuckled, leaving Dermot to thank the boys as they walked off stage.

James Arthur was next and he showed the judges why he was being voted in week after week. He dedicated his song – U2's 'One Love' – to his brother and sisters, who had always looked up to him. They were getting mobbed every day because of their now famous brother!

Finally, it was time for Union J to sing again. And after Christopher Maloney had received bad feedback following his second performance, they must have thought they now had a very real chance.

Their friends and family raised their Union J signs in the audience, as Louis announced the band back on stage.

For their second song, the boys had wanted to choose a song that symbolised their teamwork with Louis.

They'd gotten really close to their mentor and it was very sweet to dedicate their final song of the night to him – 'I'm Already There', by Lonestar.

This time George sang first and soon the boys was harmonising together beautifully. They sounded stunning. 'I'm already there, take a look around…'

Whatever happened, the boys must have believed the words they were singing. Even if they didn't win *The X Factor*, they were already where they wanted to be – in the hearts of their fans.

As the music ended and the stage lights found their way back to the judges, the audience began a familiar chant. 'Union J, Union J, Union J…'

The boys huddled together on stage and once more Tulisa was the first to speak. 'Guys, vocally you sounded great tonight, in both performances. But I think you may have played it a little safe with the song choices, because both the songs have been a little bit similar,' she said.

'But at the same time it's about more than just the performances at this stage, it's about all the hard work that you've put in over these past however many weeks and the fight that you've all had. You've been in the bottom two so many times and you're still here, still standing and still fighting and that's the attitude I want to see.'

'Guys, nice performance,' Gary continued. 'Good vocals, nice song choice, but I do agree with Tulisa, it's extremely safe. Are you safe tomorrow night? We can't save you anymore. I think you're at risk now, I really do. But it was a good performance.'

They were sobering words and the boys listened to them with a growing feeling of panic. By the end of his speech, Gary was fighting to speak over the stream of boos coming from the audience. They certainly didn't agree with the two judges – and neither did Nicole.

'I loved it,' she said. 'You've grown so much and being here tonight in the semi-finals, you are already there...'

Louis begged the people watching at home to vote, before Jaymi said the song they'd chosen may have been safe but it meant a lot to them. 'We miss our families so much,' he added, close to tears. 'We all do,' soothed Dermot, before ushering them off the stage.

And that was it. They boys had done all they could do to secure their place in the final. It was now down to their fans to keep them in the competition...

That night, on *The Xtra Factor*, Caroline and Olly congratulated the boys on their performances, and asked how they were feeling. Josh said: 'No one is safe this week and we're terrified. We're really, really scared.'

Then a caller asked whether the story in the *Sun* about JJ and the backing dancer were true – it was clear that fans all over the country were very worried...

'No, it's not – we're just friends,' he said. 'She's a nice girl but it's not true.'

Phew! So many girls at home must have been heaving huge sighs of relief at the news. Especially when he added: 'I'm still single!'

On Sunday, the boys spent the day preparing for the results show. They practised the song they would sing if they didn't go through, and before they knew it, it was time to head back to the studio. It was nearly time to discover their fate...

The show opened with a great performance by all the

acts – accompanied by Rod Stewart! They joined forces to sing 'Merry Christmas, Baby', and all looked like they were having the time of their lives with the megastar. But inside, nerves were eating away at everyone. The waiting was torture. Would Union J make it to the final?

Both Pink and Tulisa took to the stage to perform their new songs for the audience, before it was finally time to find out…

All the acts trooped back on stage. The boys looked very frightened. They desperately wanted to be in the final, even though they had already achieved so much – and would definitely go far whether they won *The X Factor* or not.

They didn't need to win to be successful. Former *X Factor* finalists JLS hadn't won, and neither had One Direction – and both bands were now enjoying mega fame. But the Union J boys had worked so hard and all their fans felt they deserved it…

Walking out with Louis, the boys looked nervous. Their legs must have felt like jelly as they stood with their mentor to hear their fate.

'Okay, it's time for the results,' said Dermot. 'The public have voted and we're about to reveal the three acts going through to next week's final – and the act who received the fewest votes and will be going home tonight…'

The atmosphere was tense, as Dermot wished all the acts the best of luck.

'The first act through to *The X Factor* final is…'

The boys shut their eyes in silent prayer. Christopher looked up to the skies and blinked away tears. Jahmene and James Arthur stared down at the floor.

'...James!'

Hearing his name, James Arthur screamed and nearly collapsed with happiness. Everyone clapped, including the Union J boys.

There were two places left – and three acts hoping to fill them. Who would be next?

'Joining James in the final next week is... Christopher!'

Gary congratulated his act. But Jahmene and Union J could hardly move; they were all so worried.

'Only one more is certain of a place in the final,' said Dermot, speeding up the results. He was conscious that the wait must have been horrible for the two acts left on stage.

'The third and final act through is... Jahmene!'

It was all over.

As Nicole threw her arms around Jahmene, the boys let it sink in: They were going home. They wouldn't be crowned the winners of *The X Factor* 2012.

Struggling to control their emotions, the boys were overwhelmed by hugs from their former fellow contestants.

All the finalists were holding each other so tightly, it was obvious they were all sad to see Union J go. Dermot had to literally drag the boys from their friends to speak to them.

Accepting their fate, Josh bravely told him: 'I'm so happy with how well we've done. We've got so much to thank *The X Factor* for.'

JJ's voice wobbled as he praised the three finalists, saying: 'We wanna wish the guys the best of luck.'

And Jaymi added: 'I can't describe how amazing it's been. We've loved every moment.'

Louis was nothing but positive about his four boys. 'I'm a little disappointed, but we were ready for it,' he said. 'They're going to have an amazing future. They're going to be the next big boyband!'

You could tell by the tears glistening in his eyes that he truly meant every word.

Before leaving the show, the four-piece gathered for one last song – Taylor Swift's 'Love Story'. Brimming with emotion, their voices soared – it was their *X Factor* swansong and they did themselves proud.

The next day the boys had composed themselves enough to travel to the *Daybreak* studios to chat to Lorraine Kelly – and Rylan Clark, who had been given a job on the top show!

Josh admitted he was gutted to leave the show, but had so many fond memories of his time on *The X Factor*.

'We've had an amazing time – we had the best time of our lives,' he told Lorraine.

Jaymi vowed they would continue to perform as a band and said they were on the lookout for a record deal.

'We're going to take a few days off to be with our family, but we will be back,' the heartthrob promised. 'This is not the end for us at all.'

'I've got to say as well, these boys are four of the nicest and politest boys ever, they've got such a good future,' added their buddy Rylan.

The following week, the boys travelled to Manchester for the live final of the show they had all wanted so much to win. They watched as James Arthur was crowned winner of *The X Factor* 2012, and were overjoyed for him.

The *X Factor* excitement was all over for another year. But for Union J it was the start of a brand new beginning. And with their JCats supporting them, the boys had a bright future ahead of them.

*The X Factor* 2012 will be remembered for more than just James Arthur's moment of glory – it will be memorable because it introduced Union J to the world.

## CHAPTER FOURTEEN

# BACK TO REALITY?

The day before their shock departure from the 2012 series of *The X Factor*, the Union J boys had been feeling on top of the world.

They had made it to the semi-final of the country's favourite singing competition, and had thousands of adoring fans following their every move.

They had shown the world what talented musicians they were and captured the hearts of the nation. But most importantly, they had really begun to believe that they could be the next big boyband.

'We don't want there to be any limits on how big we can be,' Jaymi had excitedly told the *Mirror* in early December, just hours before they were booted off the show. 'We want to be as big as One Direction are right now and break America and tour the world. Louis Walsh thinks the sky's the limit.'

It must have been easy for the boys to dream so big after all that had happened to them during their time on the show. 'We will have such amazing lives if we do well,' Jaymi had mused, ignorant of what was about to happen. 'And we will be able to live a life that people dream of...'

Josh had obviously agreed with his bandmate. 'We want to do better than One Direction,' he'd added. 'They finished third and we want to finish first or second. It would be amazing to do that.'

This newfound confidence was a far cry from the low self-esteem that they had all suffered from at the beginning of their *X Factor* journeys.

When the live shows had begun back in September, the Union J boys had been convinced they were the worst act – but they had since worked hard to prove themselves.

'When we got here week one we were the weakest act,' Jaymi had humbly recalled a few weeks before. 'We've worked hard enough to get here on talent alone and not because we've been put together on the show. As much as we are in a boyband we are all songwriters and we play instruments. We want to show that we can go out there and be credible artists.'

But the boys didn't beat One Direction's third place success – instead they had come fourth, and hadn't even made the final.

The lads would have been forgiven for being a little confused – it was obvious that their JCats were devoted fans and there were certainly a lot of them. But they couldn't deny that they had lost because of one simple fact: they hadn't got enough votes. They reckoned it was because a lot of JCats were young and didn't have enough pocket money to vote so many times – unlike Christopher Maloney's nan!

'When we meet all of our fans they say, "we spend all of our pocket money on voting for you but we only get five pounds a week",' said George after their shock departure, as he tried to come to terms with their loss.

Whatever the reason, with *The X Factor* now over, they must have been wondering what would become of them. It would have been easy to feel sorry for themselves and mope around at home, with their families to comfort them.

But as we all know, the Union J boys are made of sterner stuff. They immediately decided that just because they didn't win *The X Factor*, they were in no way destined for the pop scrap heap. Instead the lads took comfort in the fact that history had shown they were in fact more likely to be successful now – precisely because they didn't win. JLS, Cher Lloyd, Olly Murs and One Direction all failed to win *The X Factor* and all subsequently became huge stars. Olly Murs has sold over 5 million records worldwide and has had countless No.1s, despite being runner up to Joe McElderry in 2009.

JLS were beaten by Alexandra Burke in 2008 but have won five MOBO awards, sold more than 10 million records and are the 16th richest reality stars in the UK, with a staggering combined fortune of £24 million.

Like Union J, Cher Lloyd came fourth in 2010, but has since released a hugely successful album. Her third single, 'Want U Back', sold over 2 million copies in America and was certified platinum. She also signed to a major modelling label – all before she turned 19. And One Direction have been credited with reinvigorating the tired boyband genre since their loss to Matt Cardle, also in 2010. They've performed in front of the Queen, sold out a show at New York's Madison Square Gardens and have well and truly conquered America – a notoriously difficult thing to do in the music industry.

But in contrast, winners like Steve Brookstein, Matt Cardle and Leon Jackson all disappeared from the public eye shortly after their triumphant *X Factor* first-place wins.

It appeared that history was on their side, especially since even though the competition was over, the British press was still clamouring for interviews with the lads, desperate to get them to pose up for cool picture shoots and pap them at star-studded events.

**DID YOU KNOW?**
**Josh says his best friend is his kitten, Oreo. He says: 'He's the main J Cat, he's like our mascot.' Josh is determined to get a chocolate Labrador puppy too. Hope Oreo likes him!**

Soon after their loss, Jaymi described the band's thoughts to the *Sun*, saying: 'Nine times out of ten it is actually better not to win. It is exciting times for Union J. We get the option to really work on our artistry.'

The boys were excited about having the freedom to develop their own style, which might not have happened if they had won the show and been locked into a particular recording contract. 'We get the time but not the pressure of being the winners to really sit down and work out what style of music we want to do and make us a brand,' explained Jaymi.

It was obvious that the boys had been thinking a lot about their future and about their *X Factor* experience. 'We have got a lot of positives out of this, and they outweigh the negatives,' Jaymi concluded.

Josh added: 'We hope this is just the start of Union J's career and hopefully we can go on and do what One Direction and JLS have done.'

But they couldn't deny they were gutted they didn't make the final – because they had been looking forward to dancing with their mentor Louis Walsh on stage. 'We wanted to do *Riverdance* with Louis in a onesie!' said George, wistfully. Now that would have been a sight to remember...

Now though, they were determined to sign a record contract and start work on their first album as soon as possible – and so were their JCats, who couldn't wait to hear their first single, whatever it would be.

*The X Factor* and their very first boyband battle may have been over, but the boys would have to prepare themselves for much more musical combat – because forging a name for themselves outside of the show would mean competing against the top quality boyband royalty already out there.

Not only that, but they would have to fend off the many up and coming bands desperate for fame and fortune who were breaking into the mainstream alongside them.

The boys were ready. They knew what they had to do. And they began doing it in earnest...

**DID YOU KNOW?**
**Jaymi's favourite smells are petrol and the perfume Charlie Red. 'It's so good,' he says. 'I just need a bunch of girls around me to wear it. A harem of Charlie Red girls.' Get down to the shops before the next gig, JCats!**

Firstly they admitted they weren't ready to take on the One Direction boys just yet. 'We don't have the record sales or the millions of fans. You can't even compare us to One Direction, they've done so well. We've got to concentrate on getting the first song right.'

It was a good attitude. If they wanted to have longevity in the music industry, they had to concentrate on each step of their careers, and not let themselves focus too much on the distant future.

1D had worked their way up to the position they were now in, and now Union J would have to follow in their footsteps. But Simon Cowell was apparently worried about the boys' future success – it seemed he had high hopes for Union J, and didn't want them becoming as big as One Direction, who were signed to his Syco label.

The *Daily Star Sunday* reported that the media mogul believed that with time, they could even actually topple the mighty band.

On hearing the exciting revelations, Jaymi told the newspaper: 'I loved that Simon was threatened by us. I rang Louis straight away and asked what he said. It's nice that we are still on Simon's radar, even though he isn't on the show this year.'

To find their own style and sound, Union J immediately went on the road, and began to gig up and down the country – performing to the fans they had built up while on *The X Factor*. The shows went down a storm and with each new crowd Jaymi, JJ, George and Josh gained new confidence. As the days passed they were also excited to find out what their fellow contestants were getting up to now that the show had ended.

James Arthur had automatically signed with Syco after winning the competition, and was fast becoming the nation's party king. He was spotted at every big media event, and usually left with a girl (or two!) on his arm. His debut single, 'Impossible', was at No.1 in the charts, and he had become an instant success.

Their favourite little sister Ella Henderson had signed to Sony soon after, confirming the deal on Ireland's *The Saturday Night Show*. 'I'm just so, so excited to go into a studio and finally do what I've already wanted to do,' she told its host, Brendan O'Connor.

And their lovable friend Rylan Clark had been snapped up by daytime TV show *Daybreak* to be their entertainment host, so the boys only had to turn on their television sets to see him almost every day.

Two weeks into their December mini tour, the lads were in Cardiff, performing at a club called Pulse when they made their own announcement: Sony also wanted them on their label. They told the screaming Welsh fans that they would be signing a contract any day and had plans for an album in 2013. The news instantly flew around the Internet, and the foursome knew they would have to somehow confirm the news for all the fans who weren't at the exciting Cardiff gig. So a few days later they bounced onto the *Daybreak* sofa to reveal all.

Christmas was just a week away, and the boys looked very festive in their knitted jumpers. They told the nation that they had indeed had the best early Christmas present ever – a deal with mega label Sony. And they were keen to start work on their first single as soon as possible.

'It's amazing,' Jaymi gushed. 'It's been a crazy week. Obviously when we came out of the show the dream was to get a record deal and we're going to Sony today to sort out all the contracts and stuff. Before Christmas we will have our deal finalised.'

Union J had become the third *X Factor* 2012 act to score a major deal with a record label, and its members were visibly buzzing with excitement.

But George was keen to share that the boys had somehow managed to have a few precious days off since the show had ended.

'It's been nice to have some family time,' he said. 'It's been weird because we've all gone home and we've been in this, like, bubble for three months and there are Christmas trees everywhere and we were, like – when did it become Christmas?'

It had been such a whirlwind few months, and time must have been flying by for the excited lads.

The *X Factor* tour was now just over a month away, where they would be joining their *X Factor* pals in playing to 24 lucky crowds in England, Scotland, Wales and Ireland. It would be exciting but exhausting, especially at such a nerve-wracking time – because the deal with Sony wasn't quite in the bag yet.

JJ's dad Paul told the *Newmarket Journal* the label was still in talks with the band, trying to hammer out the perfect deal. 'They are crossing the Ts and dotting the Is at the moment', said the former jockey. 'They have some shows coming up but hopefully they are going to sign in the next few days. It's going to be big. It's nice to know they are not going to be left high and dry, which a lot of groups often are. They are making their way.'

They certainly were, and in-between their countrywide gigs they even made time to fit in their first trip to a proper recording studio – where they found out exactly what recording an album would involve.

Fellow *X Factor* finalist Kye Sones was putting pen to paper to help them too. 'I've been writing songs for Union J,' he told the *Mirror* in December. 'I did two songs this week for them. They are sounding very exciting and they are a very different band to the boys in One Direction.'

**DID YOU KNOW?**

Jaymi spectacularly fell over, not once
*X Factor.* 'We got through one week an
fell over when they called out our na
it wasn't caught on camera, but he h
of the audience too... 'One time I f
the audience laughed,' he says. 'I
other people fall over but when

Just before Christmas, the boys travelled up to Scotland for a series of shows, where they were supported by local band Supanova and singer Kevin McGuire. They even planned to play a family show during the day, so that their younger fans could get to see them.

It was just the kind of kind boys they were, making sure that every fan got a chance to see them sing, whatever their age. But it was a far cry from the attitude of some of their fellow singers.

Justin Bieber, for example, had recently been turning up so late to his shows that a lot of his young fans were falling asleep in their seats and had to be taken home before he even set foot on stage in front of them. It just showed how thoughtful the lads were when it came to their fans – after all, they wouldn't be where they were without them, and Union J were determined never to forget that.

JJ was excited about their Scotland trip, tweeting: 'Now flying to sunny Scotland. Guna be a wee bit nippy up there. Best wrap up warm ha JJx'.

But George was apparently getting a little confused with all the travelling, and made the others laugh when he said: 'We have a gig in Dundee? I thought Dundee was in Australia?'

'No George that's Crocodile Dundee. Even I know that,' tweeted JJ in response.

George had clearly got over his confusion by the time he spoke to Glasgow's Real Radio, where the hosts pressed him for information on the new single.

'We've been like little puppies in the studio, jumping chewing everything,' he joked, giving nothing away.

about a possible relationship between Ella

Henderson and George had recently begun to die down, and the presenters were keen to find out if romance was blossoming at all.

'Which of the other contestants do you fancy then?' asked radio DJ Ewen Cameron. George was a little lost for words for a few seconds, before he replied: 'Christopher,' making everyone in the studio laugh.

'Someone actually fancies him,' teased Ewen.

'We found someone, finally,' giggled George.

Cameron Craig, from Club Campus in Glasgow, was particularly excited about the boys' imminent arrival at his venue. 'The support for Union J's Scottish tour has been phenomenal, they have played to huge crowds in Aberdeen and we are expecting the same again at Campus,' he said.

The *Metro* newspaper was also very enthusiastic about the gigs, writing: 'Although they've not yet put together their own material, these boys certainly know how to put on a show. With their own spin on pop, chart, dance and R&B classics, Hensley's lead vocals alone are as powerful as any solo artist. Prepare for Union J mania.'

They also offered some advice for parents. 'If you're over the age of 18 or treating the kids to an early Christmas present, please be cautious. Bear in mind that teenage girls can be wild and raucous. I suggest ear plugs to prevent premature hearing loss from thousands of screaming fans.'

Their predictions weren't wrong.

Queues snaked around each venue for the three shows, and inside the buildings the noise was absolutely deafening. They may have lost *The X Factor*, but it was clear they had won the hearts of fans from all over the UK.

**DID YOU KNOW?**
**Jaymi once got suspended for four days, along with his friend Stacey, for hiding all the clocks in his school. 'We thought we'd do it because it was really funny and no one knew what time it was,' he says. 'But we got caught.' He also got suspended for putting a blonde streak in his hair and for wearing an earring to school. What a rebel!**

Back home after the gigs, the boys had a precious few days off and spent them with their friends and family.

Josh went bowling and caught up with his old mates in Berkshire. It had been three months since he'd seen them last and they all had a lot to catch up on.He may have become a famous TV star since they had last all got together properly, but he still knew that his best mates were the ones he had before he hit the big time – and even got quite sentimental at their reunion. He tweeted '#FriendsForLife' on their nights out.

George spent some quality time with his favourite Italian plumber, Super Mario – but he obviously couldn't tear himself away from his fans, because he invited them to play the game with him online.

JJ chilled out in front of the telly, which must have been a nice change to being on it. 'Watching *Face/Off*... wow pretty weird movie', he tweeted. He also managed to watch some classic *Only Fools and Horses* episodes, relax in a nice hot bath and have a McDonalds fix as well as an Indian take away.

And he further proved his down-to-earth credentials when, like the rest of us, he spent a stressful day Christmas shopping – and didn't get it all done in time. He tweeted: 'Well my xmas shopping definitely did not go to plan. Can never find what I'm looking for guess it's going to be round 2 tomos lol JJx'.

Hopefully he managed to get everything by Christmas day, which all the boys spent with their respective families.

But while the turkey was in the oven, the boys gave their fans a special Christmas present – when they went on a huge follow spree on Twitter. #UnionJFollow SpreeChristmasDay trended on Twitter for hours, as JCats ignored their presents and mince pies and tried to get Union J to follow them.

After all the excitement of the day, it was Josh (who got a *Pokemon* calendar for Christmas) who bid everyone a final goodnight. 'Merry Christmas everyone. Hope santa brings you everything you want (you gotta love father Christmas) love you all ;-) night...josh x'.

The boys had one more day off to stuff their faces with roast potatoes and Christmas cake before they were back on the road again.

Bidding goodbye to 2012, they visited Swansea and Shrewsbury and were greeted by packed out audiences in both towns.

When they performed at The Buttermarket nightclub in Shrewsbury, nearly two thousand screaming fans turned up to greet them – including devoted French fan Laura

Chougar, who had flown from Paris just to see them. JCats queued for hours outside the venue to secure the best spot to see the performance, and by 8pm the atmosphere had reached fever pitch.

After their 20-minute set, the boys then went to the VIP area of the club where they chatted to fans and posed for pics. But when it was time for them to leave, their thousands of female fans had other ideas – and surrounded their car, leaving them at a standstill. In the end they needed a police escort to get home!

'A massive thank you to every1 who came to see us in shrewsbury tonight,' Josh tweeted on his way home. 'You made our night that extra bit special. Happy new year'.

@jessclarkex replied instantly, saying, '@UnionJWorld you were amazing tonight and I'm glad I got to meet you again! You're perfect josh, seriously!'

@chrissiebelbs was equally complimentary. 'Tonight was so incredible. @UnionJWorld thanks for cheering me up I appreciate it so much… And you smashed it tonight! Love you xxx'.

Club owner Malcolm Monahan immediately booked them for another gig two weeks later. 'It was electric,' he explained the next day, before saying that the 400 early bird tickets he'd put on sale that morning had sold out in a matter of minutes.

**DID YOU KNOW?**
**Josh once made a girl a Rogan Josh curry – just because his name is Josh! 'It was amazing,' he says. 'Although I think it was a bit of a fluke. She loved it though.'**

## CHAPTER FIFTEEN

# NEW YEAR, NEW START

By the time 2013 arrived, Union J had already played 14 shows and the *X Factor* tour hadn't even yet begun.

The boys were still in discussions to sort out the details of their new recording contract – and hadn't decided on who they would choose to be their new manager either. The boys had parted ways with their old manager, Blair Dreelan, and were now on the lookout for someone to take over.

At first everyone assumed that it would be Louis Walsh. After all, he had championed them from the beginning and was, as the boys themselves had said many times, practically the fifth member of the band. He'd even pranced around in a onesie on *The X Factor* to show his dedication to the boys.

But then rumours began to circulate suggesting that

Union J were looking for someone completely new. And when news got out that they had met up with Oritse Williams before Christmas, JCats began to wonder – would the JLS star be taking over leadership duties for the band?

He was already the manager of girlband VIDA, so it was clear he knew what he was doing. A source told the *Sun* in January: 'The boys had a massive wobble over Louis Walsh. Louis has management experience but Oritse has youth and the knowledge of being in their shoes on his side. People think Louis is past it for a band like this.'

Ouch! Only time would tell who the lucky person would be...

Soon after, Union J were supposed to be heading to Ireland, where thousands of Irish JCats were excitedly awaiting their arrival. But the day before their flight the gigs were cancelled, amid rumours that George was in hospital...

'I love you Georgey...more than life itself,' tweeted Josh, causing fans to instantly start worrying. George then confirmed the situation, by saying: 'So sorry to everyone in Ireland. I have had an accident so won't be able to perform tomorrow so our gigs have been pulled. Sorry, George.'

No one knew what had happened to him, and as a result JCats fell into hysterics, with some even tweeting that he might be dying – or even already dead!

Mark Sutton, from the band's tour management, tried to calm the frantic fans by tweeting: 'Let's put this to sleep

– I can tell you George had to attend hospital after receiving a nasty injury he's not dead or dying as speculated.'

Everyone breathed a huge sigh of relief, but still wanted to know what had happened to their darling George. Whatever it was, he was fully recovered a week later and back on the road with his bandmates.

Next it was Jaymi's turn to shock the fans – by revealing a huge new tattoo on his right arm. He'd had the epic inkwork done in Luton's Adrenalin Tattoo shop, while the boys were between gigs. The intricate artwork blended a musical clef, a 1950s style microphone and a Union Jack and looked like it had been painful.

But Jaymi was thrilled with it, tweeting: 'YEAH BUDDDDY!!! My new tattoo @adrenalintattoo #lovingit #unionjtattoos'.

It also had the number 24 at its centre – just for his long-term boyfriend Olly. 'The 24 is our anniversary,' he explained. 'It's both our birthdays and he was born in the second month and I'm the fourth month.'

But Ireland was set for more disappointment –the band announced that they would have to cancel their forthcoming gigs in Belfast too. They hoped that all their Belfast JCats would forgive them when they heard the reason: the boys were heading into the recording studio to properly start work on their new single.

'Recording our first single!' they tweeted. 'So sorry Belfast but we have to change the gig date, things are moving so fast for us! We'll be back! X'.

There were obviously some big announcements to come, as the boys must have finally signed with Sony and decided on a new manager. But everyone would have to wait a bit longer before the boys revealed the news.

**DID YOU KNOW?**
**Jaymi has an amazing 17 tattoos, while George has none.**

In the meantime, fans speculated on what their debut single would be. Would it be a cover of a famous song, or would they have a brand new one – their very first Union J track?

Their potential winners' single would have been Demi Lovato's 'Skyscraper', but with the guys trying to market themselves as a band with a long-term future, it was likely their first single would be something new and exciting. There was also no news on when it would be released, and JCats everywhere were desperate for more information. But they would have to be patient.

Over a tense January weekend for their waiting fans, they performed at famous London venue G-A-Y., instantly cementing their celebrity status. Lady Gaga, One Direction and Miley Cyrus have all performed at the notoriously raunchy club, which is almost a rite of passage for up-and-coming performers, as well as a well-trodden stomping ground for established stars.

They absolutely rocked the club, singing all their classics from *The X Factor*, while the screaming fans in the pit below reached their hands up hoping for some contact with the lads.

But they didn't let slip any news about their new song.

Finally, on 14 January, the very day the boys were heading into the studio to record their single, they got up extra early – just to share what had been going on behind the scenes with their fans. 'It's what we've always wanted to do for years and years,' said Josh, appearing on *Daybreak* with the band. 'We're so excited to get in there and hopefully record an amazing song.'

It was a big day for the four boys, who just a few months earlier had been only dreaming of the lives they were now leading.

But they revealed they had finally chosen a manager – and it was a surprise choice. 'We've met loads of managers and we love Louis. We did meet JLS's Oritse, it was great to get feedback from someone who's been in a boyband. But we've made a decision and we're now with Crown Management.'

It was a great choice. With offices in London, Los Angeles and New York, the Crown team had been managing some of the world's hottest talent for over a decade. And with names like Jessie J and the Sugababes on their client roster, the boys were in good company.

The boys moved on to discuss the *X Factor* tour, which was by now just days away – the boys were so busy they were working every moment of every day just to fit all their commitments into their tight schedule. Especially since they also had to fit in some rehearsal time for the huge arena tour. 'We're excited to meet everyone again,' they said. 'We've just been to rehearsals to see all the stage and what we've got planned. It's going to be amazing to perform arenas.'

It had only been two months since the boys had been practically living with their fellow *X Factor* contestants, but it must have felt like a lifetime. It was set to be a fun month on the road with their old pals and they couldn't wait to get on the tour bus – even though George was convinced it was going to be very smelly after they all piled on!

Soon after, they also finally confirmed that they had officially signed to RCA records – a branch of Sony. They were joining the likes of Avril Lavigne, Kelly Clarkson, Christina Aguilera and even JLS, who were all already on the label's books. Their new single would be released in June and everyone was now confident they were about to go stratospheric.

Josh told the *Sun*: 'We were told we could chat to any Sony label but One Direction are signed to Syco so we thought it would be good to sign to a rival. We thought they would fight for us more and it would be good for everyone to have a healthy rivalry. RCA have seen how successful they and The Wanted have been and want the same for us. We're recording songs they think will work in America as well as the UK. The plan is to go international quite early on.'

It was a clever tactic and the boys were now keen to get going with their plan of world domination.

With a new single in the pipeline, a record deal finalised and a management team ready to organise their careers, Union J were well on the way to success. It was the beginning of their path to stardom...

But all that would soon have to be put on hold, because

the *X Factor* tour was about to kick off – and it was going to be huge.

**DID YOU KNOW?**
Josh's first love was his PE teacher at school, Miss Worthington. 'She was a beauty,' he says. 'Most of the lads had a sneaky peek when she was playing hockey.' Cheeky!

## CHAPTER SIXTEEN

# THE X FACTOR ON TOUR

With the *X Factor* tour just days away, the boys were on a very tight schedule. Their main priority was to finish recording their first single before the tour began, so they knuckled down and spent every moment they had in the recording studio.

Luckily they still had time to keep their fans regularly updated on how it was all going. 'Love love love how our first single is sounding already!!!!' tweeted Josh from the top-secret location. 'Excited lol'.

JCats were in a frenzy. The boys were being very secretive about their first release, and hadn't even revealed the name of the song. Fans couldn't wait to hear the brand new track and kept a close eye on the Union J Twitter feed just in case they let something slip.

Hearing the lads sing cover versions of some great songs

had been amazing on *The X Factor* and on their mini tour, but now that Union J were recording their very own, brand-new song, no one could wait to hear it – and buy it. Their fans were both ready and waiting to help them conquer the charts.

Finally, the recording was over. 'Early night for me,' Josh tweeted, as they put the track to bed. 'Had a wicked day finishing off the first single. Fingers crossed you all like it'.

They then received a flood of tweets congratulating them all.

'Never been so excited in my life. No joke', said one JCat.

'I'm 999% sure we'll love it', said another.

But though the single had finally been recorded, there was no time for the boys to rest. Instead, Union J were pleased to find themselves back in familiar territory in late January – rehearsing for *The X Factor*. They enjoyed seeing all their old friends again and relished the chance to properly catch up on what everyone had been doing since the show had ended.

For Union J, being on *The X Factor* had been like being part of a huge family. The musicians, crew and dancers had all been so close during their time together, so now that they were back together rehearsing for the tour their excitement was at a record high. Especially because they could see their fans waiting patiently outside the rehearsal studios every day, hoping to catch a glimpse of their idols.

The boys went over their songs and their dance steps.

They even ended up having heart-to-hearts with their closest pals during their breaks.

Josh told *Heat* magazine that the boys had been getting dating advice from tour dancer Danielle Peazer, girlfriend of 1D's Liam Payne. And though the lads were adamant that they were all single apart from Jaymi, Danielle seemed to think different. 'When we chatted to her she let slip that Josh 'kind of has a girlfriend' and JJ 'likes someone',' revealed the magazine.

Fans were sceptical. If the boys themselves weren't admitting they were loved up, there was no reason to panic just yet. However, it didn't stop rumours from swirling, just like they had in the past about George and Ella Henderson, and JJ and Brazilian dancer Rithiely Pereira.

And some hearts were broken anyway, when George told *We Love Pop* that he wouldn't ever date a fan. He explained that it was 'because the fan world is close knit and word spreads really fast between them. And then they'd hate the band and stuff. So it's just easier not to date a fan.'

He then tried to comfort his wounded JCats – by saying, 'But I'm really bad at relationships. I get bored.'

'As long as he doesn't end up dating Taylor Swift,' said one JCat on a fan website, after hearing the news. 'We all know how much she likes brown haired singing Englishmen. Awks.'

Rehearsals for the tour went well, despite one near-accident, when dancer Peazer accidentally tripped Josh up during some complicated choreography steps.

'Careful Danielle, or you'll have to face the anger of JCats everywhere,' joked one fan when they heard the news.

**DID YOU KNOW?**
**Josh always gets excited when he goes to the zoo, which he does twice a year at least. 'The lions are my favourite,' he says. 'I just think they're beautiful creatures. I've never been on safari but I really badly want to.'**

Finally, on 26 January, the 24-date *X Factor* tour began in Manchester. Rylan kicked off the explosive show, before fans were treated to performances by James Arthur, Jahmene Douglas, Ella Henderson, Christopher Maloney, District 3 and Union J.

Only the top seven finalists would be appearing on the tour, leaving the remainder, including Jade Ellis, MK1 and Kye Sones at home.

Rylan had arrived in the nick of time, after being crowned the winner of *Celebrity Big Brother* just the night before. 'Great start to the tour,' he tweeted. 'And all on 45 minutes sleep!!!!'

But it was revealed he had been sneaking out of the *Big Brother* house to rehearse for the tour. Naughty Rylan.

Jahmene was celebrating signing his record deal with RCA, the same label as Union J, and had announced that his first album would be released in May. He was scheduled to start recording it as soon as the tour was over.

The Union J boys must have been relieved that they had already done their first recording. *The X Factor* tour was going to be hard work and they would be exhausted when it was finished.

But it was going to be a lot of fun in the meantime...

A week later, spirits were still riding high as they arrived in Liverpool to play at the Liverpool Echo Arena.

With a few hours spare in the day Jaymi and Christopher Maloney sneaked off together with Rylan Clark – to famous tattoo parlour L1NK. Maloney tweeted: 'Just arrived to get my first tattoo! Hope it doesn't hurt'.

But Jaymi, a veteran of the tattooist's needle, wasn't just there for moral support. Once inside the cool parlour he couldn't help but get involved. Though his latest ink was barely a month old, Jaymi grinned as he had two extra small lines of beautiful script tattooed onto his inner arm.

Maloney was in the chair for over six hours, because he was getting a 'full sleeve' tattoo, which covered his entire left arm. It was a very brave choice for his first tattoo, as it must have been extremely painful. He designed the image himself, which featured a microphone, a date, a rose and his late grandfather's name, James O'Brien. He explained to a local radio station: 'The microphone and the date is from my first audition live in front of the judges, because obviously that changed my life and I needed something to commemorate that.'

The rose was for his beloved granddad James, and he included it because as a youngster he had sung Bette Midler's song 'The Rose' at James's funeral.

Rylan whiled away the hours he spent waiting by chatting with Jaymi and the two boys both kept Chris company as he had the mammoth tattoo done. The outing was important because it dispelled a series of nasty rumours that had been surrounding the tour – that Maloney's fellow finalists hadn't wanted him there at all.

He had definitely been the most controversial star in the competition. Despite coming third, ahead of Union J, the Liverpool singer had apparently refused to sing in the finale of the live shows, and had reportedly launched into a foul-mouthed tirade at Carolynne Poole that had left his fellow contestants both stunned and upset.

Carolynne told the *Sun* that Christopher had arrived at their hotel after turning up late for the final rehearsal and called her a terrible name. 'Everyone heard it,' she said. 'Even Jahmene who was upset.'

Maloney had apparently refused to sing because he was angry he had only been given one line in the group medley. But it was reported that later he had changed his mind and begged to be included.

A source told the *Sun*: 'He showed up wanting to go on stage but they had to turn him away as they were already on stage and he missed the dress rehearsal. Everyone is completely fed up of his behaviour. He was abusive to the production team and other contestants.'

As a result, British newspapers were reporting that the other finalists were asking to have Kye Sones replace Maloney on the tour – and the acts seemed to confirm the rumours by taking to Twitter to show their support for talented Kye.

James Arthur tried to get Kye trending, by tweeting: '#getkyeonthexfactortour', while Ella Henderson posted:

'@kyesones1#getkyeonthexfactortour want u there big bro!!''Bring my boy @Kyesone1 back!'tweeted Rylan, followed by Union J posting: 'wud (sic) love @kyestones to be there. Spread the word peeps much love x'.

But whatever had happened, it was all obviously water under the bridge by the time the finalists found themselves performing together on the tour.

And JCats had too many exciting announcements from their favourite boys to wonder about any bad blood between the finalists for very long – especially when Union J shared the news that they would be going on their first major solo tour at the end of 2013! The band had steadily been announcing bookings at every major festival over the summer, including Chester Rocks, where they would be supporting The Wanted, and the London Gay Festival, with Rita Ora and Katy B. They would even be supporting *X Factor* heartthrob Olly Murs at a special event in Peterborough.

It was a sign that they were being taken very seriously by the British music industry.

But their own tour was the most exciting thing ever for Union J and their JCats – as the boys would finally be singing their own songs!

It was a long way off, however, so for now fans would have to be content with seeing them on the *X Factor* tour, singing Carly Rae Jepson's 'Call Me Maybe', Taylor Swift's 'Love Story' and James Morrison's 'Broken Strings' – all songs they performed in the live stages of *The X Factor*.

For the whole of February, the acts travelled up and

down Britain, entertaining their fans. While in Glasgow, Rylan tweeted a very controversial picture of him and JJ – where they were both topless and looking very cosy! 'Sorry girls,' he said. 'Me and JJ have something to tell you...'

The pic proved very popular indeed, with 2,413 retweets and 1,814 people favouriting it – but it was only a joke, no matter how good they looked together!

It was around this time that George started to notice that his pants were going missing. It wasn't the first time that George had had his belongings stolen – his laptop had been taken from his room at the Corinthia Hotel while he was on *The X Factor*. (It was later retrieved.)

But there was a difference between an expensive laptop and some pants – had some super keen fans managed to get into his room unnoticed? The mystery was solved when Jaymi bent over one day in front of him, and George recognised a distinctive pair of undies...

'Jaymi "borrows" my clothes,' he later explained very diplomatically to *Top of the Pops* magazine. 'He'll bend over to pick something up and I'll be like, "Are you wearing my boxers?" Then he'll just say, "Oh, are they yours? Sorry, I didn't realise...".'

You always read stories about band members being really close and spending a lot of time together – but this seems a bit too close for comfort even for our boys, who are all besties! Hope George wasn't too 'bummed out' about it...

Being on tour was exciting for Union J, but it's not all glamour when you're on the road for so long. It can be exhausting spending so much time with other people and having to be upbeat and friendly – all the time. Staying in a hotel is fun, but there's nothing like your own bed for a good night's sleep, and it's easy to get run down and a bit sick when you're away from home for so long. Couple that with smelly tour-bus toilets and endless fast food and you can see why halfway through the tour JJ tweeted: 'Wow…not feeling too healthy. Off to bed I think. A massive early one is needed!!'

And Josh got so sick of the loo situation that he had to share the following with the whole Twitter world: 'There's nothing better than a coach toilet that smells of wee…lol!'

But in the end it was a small price to pay for an experience like *The X Factor* tour. Besides, the tour bus wasn't exactly shabby. Along with comfy seats and marble furnishings, the bus had a spacious kitchen, with a posh coffee machine and even an oven and microwave. Perhaps George decided to relive his café coffee-making days for the rest of the boys!

Despite their heavy performing schedule and long bus journeys, the boys did manage to finally give their JCats some twitcam activity, as they'd promised months previously.

'Sorry it's taken us so long to do a twitcam,' said Josh, live to his fans. 'We used to do them all the time but we've been really busy in the studio.'

He then explained how they wanted to entertain everyone for the next half hour – by pulling some cheeky pranks on their pals. First they decided to call JJ and pretend that they were a fan who had somehow got his mobile number. They put the call on speaker so that everyone could hear, and giggled excitedly. But JJ didn't answer and instead the phone went to voicemail... 'This is the Vodafone voicemail service for 0-7...'

George started squealing as he realised that the whole world was about to hear JJ's number and it would give fans a chance to make the harmless prank a reality. Luckily he ended the call just in time. It's safe to assume that if he hadn't, JJ's phone wouldn't have stopped ringing all night!

It was Rylan's turn for the comedy duo's next prank attempt. George looked through his contacts for the number. 'It's actually under 'Rylan – my boyfriend', because he put it in himself,' George revealed.

They chuckled to each other like naughty school-children as they waited for Rylan to pick up. 'Jaymi and Rylan are out with a mutual friend,' George said, secretively. The 'mutual friend' could very well have been Katie Price, who was a close pal of Rylan's and had instantly hit it off with Jaymi when they met.

But Rylan didn't pick up either. 'Guys, I'm really sorry about the technical difficulties,' joked Josh, before they quickly decided that Jaymi would be their next target.

The phone started to ring but almost instantly went to voicemail – the boys were foiled again. Maybe everyone had grown wise to their mischievous schemes...

'Right, I'm gonna call Jahmene,' said Josh, getting frustrated. 'I know Jahmene's gonna pick up and I'll pretend to be in a lot of pain.'

Jahmene did pick up, and an excited Josh immediately

put on a sickly sounding voice. 'Jahmene, man,' he told him. 'Can you come over here...I've stabbed my shin.'

George tried to keep his giggles under control as Josh pleaded with Jahmene for help. But it was obvious Jahmene wasn't being fooled. 'It feels like a cactus is inside it,' Josh tried, hoping to convince him. But Jahmene just laughed. 'I'm guessing you're still on your twitcam,' he said.

The boys finally admitted defeat.

### DID YOU KNOW?
Josh has actually milked a cow. 'I was on a school trip to an organic farm and because I was a bit of a class clown I offered to do it,' he says. 'Now I feel as if I've got an emotional bond to this cow, wherever she is. She was nice. I did it for, like, five squirts.'

Back on tour, both Union J and their mates from District 3 gave an awkward interview to *Top of the Pops* magazine. Both bands were asked who gets the biggest screams on stage, and after an uncomfortable silence, Jaymi was the first to speak up.

'Us maybe?' he tried. 'It's a bit awkward but yeah, I think so.'

JJ tried to soften the blow by blaming it all on George. 'I would say that our fans definitely scream the loudest,' he said. 'Everyone loves George, he's the little cutie in the band.'

It must have been hard for both bands. They were all mates but Union J had definitely won the battle between the two boybands. But Josh was very honest about which band he thought would do better in the future. If both bands released a single in the same week, Josh had no doubt that Union J would get more airplay and sales. 'If we did [release songs in the same week] it wouldn't matter,' he said. 'That sounds really arrogant but I do genuinely think we have better songs.'

But the confident singer then pointed out how that he was aware that District 3 weren't their only rivals in the ongoing battle of the boybands. 'It's not just D3 we need to compete with,' he added. 'There's The Wanted, Lawson, 1D and JLS!'

Both groups were keen to say there was no war going on between them. 'There's definitely no rivalry between us,' said Dan from D3. 'We're more like a group of seven good friends.'

And Jaymi was quick to compliment the band – on their looks! When asked who was the fittest, Jaymi instantly replied: 'District 3. Dan's body is like a cheese grater.'

Micky chipped in, 'I can't say who's fittest because I haven't seen Union J's bodies! I'm sure they're ripped under there.'

The D3 lads obviously aren't as eagle-eyed as our Union J boys – because while they were all on *The X Factor*, they had plenty of opportunities to check each other out.

They even all had a spray tan together, and posed for pics in the tanning booths. Dan and Micky from D3 were the least shy, showing off their buff bodies for the camera, while JJ and George peeped from inside the plastic pop up parlour, giving fans just the teensiest glimpse of what was under their clothes.

Not only that, but the Union J lads had even hidden JJ's clothes and pushed him on their balcony naked. 'JJ came in from his spray tan in nothing but a gown,' said Jaymi. 'So we nicked it, stripped his pants off and chucked him on the balcony.'

So District 3 are either blind, or extremely polite – let's hope their good relationship stays intact when both bands inevitably battle it out for chart supremacy in the future…

Everyone enjoyed the tour, and the Union J lads were spotted in high spirits throughout. They became very adept at posing for the paparazzi – grinning broadly, picking each other up and even photo-bombing their fellow contestants.

Travelling all over the UK to perform to such huge crowds was an amazing experience, but for the lads it was when they returned to the O2 arena in London that they felt the proudest.

It was the place where all their dreams had begun to first become reality, because it was where their *X Factor* auditions were held. Back then JJ, Josh, George and Jaymi had been nervously waiting among the other thousands of hopefuls for their turn in front of the judges to come around.

They had no idea that less than a year later they would be singing on the same stage to the sound of deafening screams from the audience. Screams that told them they were now famous and would only get more so, as they continued on their path to stardom.

It must have been a very emotional homecoming for the boys.

'Just got to London O2!!!!!!' tweeted Josh. 'So excited for tonight's show...this is what I have been wanting to do my whole life!!!'

When they stepped out on the stage the crowds were overwhelming. Nearly twenty thousand people had come to see them sing and were all screaming their names. It was a deafening noise, a sound the boys had waited all their lives to hear.

'Wow the O2 was amazing tonight,'tweeted JJ, after their first London show. 'Nice to be back there again and seeing how far we have come since then.Seems ages ago.'

'I had the most amazing time performing for everyone who came to the London O2 tonight,' added Josh. 'Thank you to everyone who supported us!'

Throughout February the *X Factor* tour visited Dublin, Birmingham, Belfast, Aberdeen, Glasgow, Cardiff, Birmingham, Nottingham, Brighton, Manchester and countless other towns and cities. It may have been Union J's first big tour but it definitely wouldn't be their last.

## DID YOU KNOW?

JJ once killed a fish. 'I caught a salmon and I had to hit it over the head with a wooden spoon so we could cook it. It did taste amazing, but I felt so bad.' We now know which Union J member we'd want to be stuck in the wilderness with...

# CHAPTER SEVENTEEN

# A SPOOKY INTERLUDE...

George's joining Triple J, to subsequently become one fourth of the band, was more than just good luck – it was actually almost spooky...

As we all know, JJ, Josh and Jaymi were in the band Triple J before George joined them and they changed their name to Union J. Their former manager, Blair Dreelan, has since explained that the band first began when he met Josh Cuthbert in 2006, while he was auditioning as a solo artist for *The X Factor*. Josh was just 14 years old at the time.

'I literally just spotted him when I was walking through the crowd and I thought he had a really good look about him – he looked like a pop star. I stopped him and I asked if I could hear him sing. He sang and I thought he had a great voice.'

Dreelan began to work with Josh on a number of

different projects in his recording studio in Swindon, and apparently the pair became as close as brothers.

Next Dreelan met JJ – in a hotel reception.

'We had a mutual friend and we just started talking,' Dreelan told *Sugarscape*. 'I really liked the way JJ looked. He reminded me of – not his actual look but the way he is – Johnny Depp when he was in a series called *21 Jump Street*. That was the series that actually launched him and made him like a teenage heartthrob. In my head he had a 90s teenage heartthrob look.'

Josh knew Jaymi from the Sylvia Young School, which they both attended on a Saturday, and when they were introduced, they got on with JJ immediately.

Triple J was formed just a month before Jaymi applied for the group to be on *The X Factor*. So the band were brand new, and possibly even felt deep down that they were missing something – or someone. When Triple J got through the auditions and came back from the first stage of Boot Camp, Jaymi showed Dreelan a picture he'd composed on the computer – of him, his bandmates and a floppy haired boy they'd all bonded with. He'd told his then manager: 'There was this kid at Boot Camp that was amazing, he just looked amazing.'

That floppy-haired 'amazing' boy was George Shelley. It was the first picture of George, JJ, Josh and Jaymi together – long before they had any idea that their futures would be so entwined. Soon after, George was kicked off the show and Dreelan got in touch with him. He saw potential in the good-looking singer, and wanted to manage him separately from Triple J.

'I just thought he was great and looked like a pop star – I thought he could be developed into a pop star,' he says.

But when *The X Factor* called him and proposed the idea of adding a fourth band member to Triple J, Dreelan was shocked by who they suggested.

'They were like, "how do you feel about putting a fourth member into this band?" I said "it really depends on who it is", and they went "we've got this kid called George who got kicked out the show…" I said, "well I've got this kid now called George who got kicked out the show".'

Both sides were amazed. Dreelan says: 'They were, like, "180,000 people entered this show, it can't be the same George".'

But when he emailed them a picture of George Shelley their suspicions were confirmed. It was the same boy Jaymi had pictured in the band when they had met at Boot Camp.

It was an unbelievable coincidence, and one that sealed George's place in the band. George and Triple J spent three days rehearsing before they went to the Judges Houses. The rest, as they say, is history.

But unknown to the rest of the boys, fate had actually stepped in a second time to make Union J happen…

'The *X Factor* producers wanted to put me in MK1,' George revealed to *We Love Pop* during the *X Factor* tour. 'But Charlie, the female singer in that band, wouldn't let me. She didn't think I'd fit in. So the producers said I could either go in GMD3 or Triple J. Triple J made sense.'

## A SPOOKY INTERLUDE...

Now the boys are enjoying the beginning of a long and successful career as Union J. But what if Dreelan hadn't spotted George? What if Triple J hadn't made friends with him? Or what if MK1 had accepted George into their band? JCats everywhere might not have their beloved Union J today. It doesn't even bear thinking about, does it?

**DID YOU KNOW?**
George's earliest memory is from when he was three. 'My mum told me to put my head on her belly and she said, "That's your sister".' Aw!

## CHAPTER EIGHTEEN

# JAYMI BECOMES AN ICON

When Jaymi Hensley bravely came out as gay on *The X Factor*, his fellow band mates were quick to support him. His brave decision helped lots of his young fans to voice their struggles with their own emerging sexuality and he quickly became an inspiration for the gay community.

He had in fact been in a long-term relationship with his boyfriend Olly, who was justifiably proud of the young singer's decision to out himself and their relationship to the public.

So in late February, Jaymi was only too pleased to be part of a new documentary on Radio 1Xtra about 'coming out'.

Hosted by DJ Adele Roberts, Jaymi was joined by series of other celebrities who had also made the decision to share their sexuality with their fans. The aim of the documentary was to discover whether the whole process of coming out had changed over the past decade.

The boys were excited about the documentary and wanted as many of their fans as possible to listen to it.

They tweeted: 'Don't forget – BBC Radio @1Xtra in one hour at 9pm for Jaymi's #comingout documentary!'

It was very revealing and heartfelt. Jaymi opened up to the presenter completely, telling her all about his early life and his experiences of dating.

'I've always known, always,' he said. 'I had girlfriends and experimented with girls and stuff and I never used to be happy.'

As much as Jaymi got on with girls better than boys and liked doing girly things, he just didn't want them as girlfriends. It was confusing, until he realised why. 'I think I was about 14 and one of my friends went to the Sylvia Young School in London and he was talking about someone who was gay and I was like, "oh my God – that's what it is!".'

Jaymi also shared his experience of coming out to his family, which he did when he was 14. And for him, times had definitely changed since he made the decision. 'I've got a very normal – what people would say was a 2.4 children – life. And that's because I came out when I was young, so my family, as much as they are amazing, have had time to deal with it. Time to realise that it's not going to be as easy as "I'm going to get a girl pregnant and you're going to have grandkids". We'll have to have a talk about how we're going to do it [have a family].'

Jaymi was also fully supported by the *X Factor* crew and production team, who always knew he was gay. They thought it would be for the best if he was honest about everything to his fans, and encouraged him to openly admit his sexuality. But even so, it wasn't them who finally inspired him to come out to the public.

'What pushed it was a young gay kid messaging my mum on Twitter saying how depressed he was and how his family was never going to accept him,' said Jaymi. 'He read an interview with me when he thought I was going to come out and he got his hopes up.'

It had prompted Jaymi to think about his own experiences and he began imagining how helpful it would have been for him to have had someone to look up to – someone young who was gay and in the music industry.

'I would have loved to have been able to look at maybe JLS when I was 15, someone with that boyband image and be, like, "that one's gay, I can fancy that one". And if I can do that for a kid and the week after he messaged my mum he says, "I've come out to my mum, it wasn't easy at the start and my dad's struggled with it a little bit but my mum's come round to the idea and we went shopping the first day" – that's nice. You can come out at 15 and start enjoying your life.'

He also revealed that his band mates had told him: 'Just be you and don't let anyone change you because one day, someone will love you for that one thing that you thought made you different.' It was wise advice.

For Jaymi, coming out was the best thing he ever did. And as a result he's a great role model for his fans, whatever their sexuality, because he is a confident young man, comfortable with who he is as a person. It's inspiring to think he's become the role model he always wanted to have in his teens.

After the interview, JCats all over the world tweeted their congratulations, and Jaymi trended for a full day on Twitter. 'Thank you everyone sooo much for the amazing messages and worldwide trending all day whoop love you guys,' he tweeted.

Maybe Christopher Maloney had been listening in on his tattoo buddy's interview too, because after the *X Factor* tour ended, he had some news of his own to share with the world.

Speaking to *Now* magazine, he was at first a little thrown when his interviewer asked him if he was gay. But he decided to answer the question honestly and openly… 'Do you know what? I'm going to admit it. Yeah,' he said.

He went on to sensationally tell the magazine that he had actually been in a relationship with his boyfriend for three years, just like Jaymi.

Revealing why the public didn't already know, he said: 'Honestly, I've never denied it or anything like that. It's just that with the show it was always an inappropriate time or people just asked inappropriate questions.'

He suggested that his time on the show and on tour had been difficult for his relationship, as spending a long time apart can often put a strain on couples. 'The tour and everything else is only to make a better life for us,' he said. 'I've tried to say that to my partner – I'm not just doing this for me. I didn't speak about my love life [before] because I didn't want my partner to be dragged through this. It wasn't to gain votes or anything.'

Maloney also said he'd struggled with being on the show, especially since he'd received Twitter abuse and even death threats. 'I had a breakdown,' he admitted. 'I went home the Monday after the show finished and a psychologist came to see me. I wasn't struggling because I was a sore loser, but because of all I'd had to endure. It was hard to keep a grasp of reality.'

Luckily the Union J boys had each other to help one another through any tough times on the show. And their friendship only grows stronger and stronger.

**DID YOU KNOW?**
**Jaymi's boyfriend is called Olly and everyone calls the two of them 'Jolly' when they're together. Sweet!**

Whilst on tour, the band revisited one of their favourite venues, The Buttermarket in Shrewsbury, to perform a special gig for their JCats. Super fan Emily Rawstron from Blackpool had saved up especially for the gig, and said it was a dream come true to meet her favourite boys.

'There were a lot of screaming girls,' the 17-year-old said. 'Most had bought presents like Coco Pops because Josh loves them, and balloons for Jaymi, because it was nearly his birthday.'

She revealed that when one girl threw some of her (clean) underwear on stage, Josh picked it up and threw it back out into the audience. But unfortunately the cheeky present landed on a young child who had come to the gig. Oops!

Emily had taken a beautiful hand-made sign along to the gig, like many of her fellow fans, and she couldn't believe it when JJ pointed at it during 'Call Me Maybe'.

'George gives the best hugs,' she said. 'And Josh always thanks us for our support.'

So there you have it – if you're ever lucky enough to meet them, head straight to George for one of his epic hugs.

On 2 March, the *X Factor* tour came to an end. The boys all agreed that they'd had an amazing month, filled with some incredible new experiences. Jaymi and Josh had even got to momentarily fly the plane on their way back from the tour's Belfast gigs, and posted a picture of themselves in the plane's cockpit to prove it. It was now time for Ella, Jahmene, Christopher, James, Rylan, Union J and District 3 to concentrate on their own careers.

But before the really hard work began they still had time for one last silly moment with their *X Factor* pals – so they raided Ella's wardrobe to find new outfits for their last song of the tour. Josh wore a sparkly blue top and stilettoes, while George wore a girly Adidas jacket and gold parachute pants. They tweeted a picture of their new clothes, saying: 'This is how we dressed for the final song on tour tonight!!! Hahahaha!!! Yes.... Josh is wearing Ella's outfit! Heels and all!'

Poor Ella – being the only girl on tour must have been hard enough without having the boys rooting through her clothes...

The lads were very excited when they were next asked to be part of Comic Relief 2013, which raised a record £75 million for charity.

'@JessieJ has dared us to eat some horrible foods for @rednoseday #UnionJ4RND', they tweeted, after they were told what they would be doing to raise money.

In fact, the boys had three nasty food challenges to endure to do their bit for the charity.

The first was a suspiciously simple looking item.

'Oh, it's just an egg,' George said when he saw the plate. He even sounded a little disappointed.

But when the lid was removed from the dish, a noxious substance wafted all around them – because the eggs were pickled in vinegar.

Josh nearly fainted in fear. He staggered back dramatically and said: 'Urgh, I can't eat egg! This is like my worst nightmare. I'd rather eat a donkey's b******s.'

But while the rest of the lads coughed and spluttered, JJ simply reached for his knife and fork. 'Do you know what? I actually like egg and I like pickles, so let's do it boys.'

Tucking in, he made it look easy. Bet they'd be glad to have him in the jungle! After a lot of protesting, everyone followed his lead and ate the smelly eggs.

What followed made everyone wish for more pickled eggs – because their next dish probably had come straight from a jungle somewhere.

Heaped on the plate were three piles: of worms, crickets and scorpions.

Everyone began squealing and even the previously brave JJ was jumping up and down like a big baby.

Josh tried to pretend he preferred them to the eggs, but when he put one in his mouth and screamed, it was obvious he had quickly changed his mind.

JJ decided to sample a cricket and sniffed it delicately before declaring it smelt like barbecue. He popped it in his mouth and just like Josh, began to scream.

George picked up a scorpion and giggled. 'Jaymi, look,' he said, thrusting the tiny harmless creature in his friend's direction. Jaymi backed away, not even wanting to be close to the tiny eight-legged arachnid.

'George, George, George,' everyone began chanting, egging him on. Taking a deep breath, he threw it in his mouth and swallowed, before giving himself a round of applause. The boys were gobsmacked. Especially when he picked up another and swallowed that too. Everyone was impressed – baby G was clearly the bravest of the bunch!

Jaymi eventually sampled a worm, and followed it with a huge glass of Ribena. 'It's got legs,' he whimpered.

JJ tried an insect combo, by munching on a worm and a cricket at the same time. And he would have been fine if Josh hadn't grabbed his glass of drink and kept it out of arm's reach.

Jaymi thought it was hilarious as JJ staggered around after Josh and the all-important drink. But eventually they gave him a huge round of applause for his efforts, and George threw his arms around him for one of his special hugs.

The third and final challenge was by far the worst for the band. Dare-mistress Jessie J must have been in a really mischievous mood when she came up with her final idea: jellied eels.

A delicacy for Londoners, the gelatinous fish dish is still served all over the capital, especially in the East End. But for the boys the mere sight of it caused them to gag.

'I know it's for charity, I love Red Nose Day but that is disgusting,' said Josh.

JJ put a tiny bit of the offending jelly onto a spoon and gave it a sniff. 'We can't do that,' he said shaking his head.

Josh began to get goosebumps at the very thought of eating the eels, and showed JJ his arm to prove it.

After much deliberating, they came up with a plan – to all eat it at the same time.

They all raised their spoons... '3-2-1...I love you boys,' said JJ. But as he put it in his mouth the others chickened out and watched him as he went on to visibly gag on the food.

They may have been laughing but they knew they all had to do it, so one by one they followed him. And one by one they gagged and fell to the floor, retching.

Challenge complete, they were proud of themselves. After all, it was a small price to pay for the charity to raise so much money.

But for George the taste torment wasn't over yet. He and Leigh-Anne from Little Mix had been given a separate challenge – to eat a spoonful of cinnamon.

It's actually a lot harder than it sounds, because as yummy as cinnamon is in cakes and biscuits, it feels like your mouth is burning when you eat it neat with no cakey goodness to dilute it. George went first and put the spoon in his mouth, before spectacularly spitting it out in a huge orange cloud. Leigh-Anne actually managed to swallow hers, but she certainly didn't look too pleased about it.

**DID YOU KNOW?**
Josh once wore girls' knickers on a night out clubbing. 'I've worn a thong before,' he explains. 'Three of my friends did it too. We pulled our trousers down to show them off. It was extremely uncomfortable.'

# CHAPTER NINETEEN

# LIFESTYLE CHANGES

After such a busy month on tour it was only natural that the Union J boys should have a well-deserved rest.

George went home to his family and indulged in some long country walks in the crisp March air. It was the perfect way to unwind after a hectic touring schedule.

JJ went to a country music concert at the O2 Arena and Josh went to the cinema to watch *The Croods*.

Then it was back to the recording studio for the four boys, who still had lots of songs to record for their album.

There was still no news for JCats about the title of their new song, or even when it would be released. The boys were definitely still staying tight-lipped about their first foray into the charts. But then a video appeared on YouTube, which caused mass hysteria among fans. Called 'Miss U – Union J', it appeared that a demo of their long-awaited first single had been leaked without them knowing.

Thousands of fans listened to the upbeat and catchy tune, and declared that they instantly loved it. 'I can't wait for the album! I'm so excited,' wrote one fan. 'Oh my God this is actual perfection,' said another.

But everyone was confused, because the boys still weren't tweeting anything about the song, or its accidental leak. And there was still no official word about the new single, leaving some fans feeling very suspicious.

Was it just a hoax on Union J's poor JCats?

Eventually the truth was revealed. It wasn't a hoax exactly, but it sadly wasn't Union J's new song either. It was a song written and recorded by musicians Roland Lubrano and Jason Thompson, who had the boys in mind to sing it. They had uploaded it to YouTube in the hope that JCats would like it and pass it on to the boys, so that they could consider using the song on their album.

It was an awesome track – but not picked up by the boys. JCats would just have to wait a little bit longer for the new single.

In the meantime, George told *We Love Pop*: 'We've been in the studio with Steve Mac and Wayne Heffner. They've written everything, like JLS's 'Beat Again' and One Direction's 'Gotta Be You'.'

It was an exciting revelation. If such big names as Mac and Heffner were involved in the new album, fans would have some great music to listen to in October, when it was released.

It also showed how seriously the record company was

taking the band's future. So many people were working hard to help the boys become successful – they must have felt honoured.

But it would all come down to their own talent in the end. Without their fabulous voices and vibrant personalities the best song in the world wouldn't make it into the charts.

With the pressure on to live up to the hits churned out by JLS, The Wanted and One Direction it was unsurprising that they were working with such seasoned professionals. And they really wanted to be involved in the writing of their future hits, too. 'It's massively important,' said Jaymi.

JJ says he often attempted to write songs when he was younger, but fans shouldn't expect any old Hamblett numbers to be revived on the album.

'I wrote some bad songs as a kid about horses,' he says. 'Me and my pony, giddy up, giddy up,' were just some of his unique lyrics.

On Twitter he has shared another classic from his songwriting youth. 'When you knock *knock* on ones dooooooooorrr, you don't feel like, you don't love me anymooooore.'

George was quick to evaluate his band mate's efforts. 'JJ that makes no sense!'

Maybe JJ should stick to singing for the time being...

March was an exciting month for Union J, for a number of reasons. But the biggest reason of all was that it was the month they all moved into swanky new million pound flats in the centre of London.

'Such a fun day organising and decorating my flat!' tweeted George as he settled in to his new home. 'It's going to be so cool when it's done! Who's coming to dinner?'

It was lucky that their addresses were being kept top secret, or else the lads would have been feeding a lot of hungry girls that night.

Now that their fame was growing, it was time the boys began living the lifestyle of a famous band – and their new record label had been busy helping them adjust to the world of celebrity.

'It's been a crazy few months but we are loving it,' Jaymi told the *Daily Star* soon after. 'We've been given a taste of what our lives could be like. We've all recently just moved to London and become neighbours.'

The boys had become so close, almost like brothers, and were used to eating, sleeping and breathing together from their time on *The X Factor*. It made sense for them to live together too. 'Me and JJ live together and George and Josh have their own places in the same block,' Jaymi said.

George claimed that JJ and Jaymi had actually turned into husband and wife since the move. 'They're like my nan and granddad,' he said. 'When we get in the car in the morning, they're, like, 'Have you got this, have you got that?'

The boys had been excitedly decorating their new places and buying furniture and cool gadgets for their swish lads' pads.

'We've pimped our apartment out with 55-inch TVs,' Jaymi said. 'We have four TVs at the moment, one each in the bedrooms and one in each lounge.' Two lounges? The flats sounded very posh indeed, but not nearly as posh as the cars that they said would soon be parked outside them: matching Mercedes A-class motors, a gift from their record label.

The fancy cars cost £20,000 each and the boys were excited to get the keys and take them for their first drive. But they were all waiting on George to pass his driving test first.

'They have put me through an intensive driving course,' George explained. 'Hopefully we will get the cars as soon as I pass, so the other guys are wanting me to hurry up and get my license.'

Poor George. Moving house, recording an album, learning to drive – he must have been rushed off his feet with all those things to sort out.

The boys were working 15-hour days to get the album ready for their fans, and were often so exhausted they went straight home to bed at night.

But they were so excited they couldn't stop gushing about the new motors. 'Jaymi and I are getting white ones and George and JJ want black ones,' said Josh. 'I can't wait. I am so embarrassed to be driving my clapped-out Citroen at the moment. It's about ten years old. It's silver but it's so dirty it looks like I wipe my bottom with it. All the fans keep telling me a pop star can't drive a car like that.'

The Mercedes certainly sounded cool, but the boys would have a long way to go before they began to rival Harry Styles' car collection. The 1D heartthrob had just bought a £100,000 Porsche to go alongside his 1970s Ford Capri, Audi R8 and Range Rover.

And with their history of driving, who knows how long the cars would last anyway – all the boys have been involved in crashes shortly after they learnt to drive.

'I wrote off my first car after just two weeks!' JJ admitted to the *Daily Star*. 'I was driving too quick on a wet road and crashed into the back of an 80-year-old man's car with a little dog in the back. I burst into tears!'

Both Josh and Jaymi have both also had accidents in the past, and warned of the dangers of multi-tasking at the wheel.

'I was eating a pain au chocolate when I skidded on black ice and crashed my first car,' Josh admitted. 'I did a 360-degree spin, hit the curb, flipped over and hit a lamp post.'

'I crashed just after passing my first test,' Jaymi added. 'I tried to change my Whitney Houston CD and that was that.'

Nonetheless, the new cars and luxury flats were an impressive start to their new celebrity lifestyles and they were on a high with all the excitement. But was the pressure of being the next big boyband getting to them at all?

'What pressure?' Jaymi grinned. 'We are having the best time of our lives. We are getting free cars, we live in amazing apartments and we get to sing every day. We could be living in council houses with no jobs. We certainly don't have anything to complain about.'

Jaymi had worked in some truly rubbish jobs before

appearing on *The X Factor*. 'The worst was working in a factory,' he says. 'It was awful. I was working there the week before I went to Boot Camp. You stand at a conveyor belt, pick up things and put them in boxes. It's non-stop.'

Though he was now probably working harder than he ever had in his life, Jaymi was finding being a recording artist easy in comparison to his former jobs.

Hard work can seem less so if it's something you love doing. Jaymi was so grateful for being allowed to explore his passion as his career, he was willing to work every minute he could – as were all the boys.

**DID YOU KNOW?**
**JJ hasn't yet found the hoover, iron, or the washing machine in his flat yet. He doesn't know how to use any of them, says Jaymi. And if the loo roll runs out in the toilet he'll just use a different toilet. Lazy JJ.**

While they were moving house, the boys must have spent hours sorting through old belongings like photos and letters, which can often make people feel a bit sentimental.

It certainly made Josh a bit nostalgic, because he tweeted a super cute picture of himself as a baby soon after the move. Sporting a huge grin and sticking his finger in his mouth he looked a proper little angel in his funny looking tracksuit. (Thank goodness *The X Factor* had stylists!)

Soon the boys had some even more exciting news. As a

new band putting together their first album, having some support from established music industry stars is both great for your confidence and for your credibility.

But they could never have dreamed of a collaboration with an artist whose personal fortune is valued at $500 million and who has sold over 50 million albums worldwide – especially so early on in their careers.

But that's exactly what happened when it was announced that rapper Jay-Z had reportedly agreed to do a duet with the boys, laying down some lyrics for one of their new tracks. Apparently the rapping royalty was given the choice of doing a duet with The Wanted, who were already well-established, or taking a gamble on new boys Union J – and he chose Union J.

Various gossip websites reported that Jay-Z felt the Union J boys had more of an urban vibe to them than The Wanted, and that his vocals would sit well with their harmonies.

It was a big blow to The Wanted, who had been hoping to collaborate with a big American artist for a while. But it was great news for Union J, as a song with Jay-Z would give them instant access to the huge American market, which they aimed to one day break into.

Maybe it would happen sooner than they ever dreamt...

As an exciting and busy March drew to a close, George allowed himself some time for reflection. On the 25th he celebrated a poignant personal anniversary, and shared it with the band's Twitter followers.

'A year ago today I was getting on that train to go to my very first xfactor audition!!' he wrote. 'What a year!!!'

He could never have imagined how much his life would be changed by that short train journey. Far from living in his parents' home and working in a coffee shop, he was now sharing a swanky central London pad with one of his new bandmates and recording a hotly-anticipated album. Far from being bullied at school over his weight, he was now bringing girls to tears on stage as the definite 'little cutie' of the group.

No wonder he felt he should acknowledge the first anniversary of the day his life changed forever.

Some JCats were moved to tears by the tweet. 'How emotional, tears are streaming down my face,' said one.

'And so much has happened since and even better times are ahead,' said another. It was a good point well made.

**DID YOU KNOW?**
**George's favourite food is spaghetti bolognese and his favourite song is Tulisa's 'Live it Up'.**

## CHAPTER TWENTY

# THE WAIT IS OVER

Finally the date JCats everywhere were waiting for was announced. On 2 June, Union J would be releasing their first ever song and it would be called 'Carry You'.

The boys revealed the song's name during a webchat with their biggest fans, as they wanted them to be the first to hear the song's title. 'It's a great pop song and we're excited to be performing it – it's very catchy,' said Jaymi.

The boys would become the first *X Factor* artists from the 2012 series to release original material, despite only coming fourth on the show. Being forced to leave the recording studio soon after must have been a wrench for the workaholic Union J lads. But they couldn't help but be excited, because there was a good reason for the time out. They were about to film their first music video!

It was freezing cold in Nottingham when they arrived in

the city to begin shooting their scenes. It was snowing outside the tour bus, and Josh had to snuggle up to a hot-water bottle to keep warm. But nothing could dent their enthusiasm. Whatever the weather, making a music video would be a whole lot of fun.

George was especially pleased to be filming in the Northern city – because it's where his dad lives. Being so busy and now living in London it must have been a while since the pint-sized star had some precious dad-time. So George was pleased he could fit a much-needed catch up into his shoot schedule.

The boys stayed at the Lace Market Hotel, and visited lots of local landmarks for the video.

'We didn't want to use locations that had already been used in other videos,' George told a reporter from the *Daily Star*. 'It's weird and it's great. It's different and has lots of quirky areas like the Jam Café and the Vintage Shop.'

All the boys were enthusiastic about the video. 'There's a lot going on and people everywhere,' said George. 'We're all a bit tired and cold but pumped and very excited to get it out there. It feels like a dream to be doing this. A year ago I was at university doing my graphics course and leading a normal life.'

He also finally explained what the song was all about.

"Carry You' is about getting support from people around you. The fans are helping us and we are helping them. It's a good upbeat pop tune we hope everyone will love.'

As each scene was filmed, it became clear what the

music video was about – it was the story of Union J's rise to fame.

In the initial scenes JJ, Josh, Jaymi and George were each doing their own thing, before meeting up at an open mic night and playing to a screaming crowd.

'It's about how we were individuals with our own identities but came together as one band,' the boys told the waiting reporters, almost in unison.

JJ added: 'We all came from four different places to sing together as one band. Josh is the worrier and serious one, George is the computer geek and the creative one, Jaymi is the parent and the demanding one. I'm just the laidback one. We all bicker but we've got so close it feels like we're brothers. Arguing is healthy I think.'

Even though it was cold and wet and exhausting, the boys still found themselves dreaming about the future. 'I would love to be No.1, even if just for one week,' he said. 'It would be amazing for the single to do that well. I would have to spend the next week recovering!'

But Jaymi was more cautious. 'Every band to come out of the *X Factor* has gone straight to the top ten with their first single. We'd hate to be the ones that didn't.'

'It's not a race to bring out a song but we are glad to be first,' he added. 'James Arthur and Ella Henderson's releases won't be for a while and Jahmene Douglas's will be after us. Our album is very diverse. Some songs sound a bit like 1D, some sound a bit like The Wanted and some sound like neither. We want to make our own sound and our own avenue and have ballads. 'Carry You' is a good pop song to come out first.'

After the shooting was over, it was up to the film editors to cut together and polish the video. All the boys could do was wait. 'That's a wrap!' said Jaymi, as darkness fell on the second and final day of the shoot. 'That was the best two days of our lives.'

'Bye bye Nottingham,' they finally tweeted. 'Been such a crazy few days! Can't wait for the next few months.'

Jaymi filled his now spare time by partying with Katie Price and her new husband Kieran Hayler – at their wedding blessing.

Only 150 guests were invited to the top-secret event, which was Willy Wonka themed and held in the seaside resort of Weston-Super-Mare.

Jaymi joined singer Michelle Heaton, fellow *X Factor* star Rylan Clark, members of the *TOWIE* cast and WAG Danielle Lloyd for the bash, which included a gospel choir and mountains of sweets for the guests to munch on.

Katie serenaded her new hubbie at the event with a version of Vanessa Williams's 1992 hit 'Save the Best for Last', and gave all her guests a copy of her version on CD.

'I didn't see her sing at the wedding but she did record the song in a studio and hand out the CD to everyone.' Jaymi said. 'Maybe she can sing at my wedding if I ever get married.'

Back in London, the boys tried to figure out how to cope with all the female attention they were getting from fans. 'Some fans tried to sneak in recently as they found out where we lived,' said Jaymi.

'We thought everyone would forget us,' said George.

'Normally there's a calm before you release a single after *X Factor*. But the girls have built up somehow. I'm not sure how.'

George went on to say that all the boys were awful at chat up lines, and claimed that they were all definitely single except for Jaymi. (But he was actually hiding a pretty massive secret of JJ's...)

'We're like four geeks,' he said. 'I don't think we'll ever get used to it to be honest. We go back to our normal lives every night and then when we wake up in the morning there is this lifestyle with all these girls. It's weird, we're just normal guys.'

But although they admitted they were struggling a bit with all the attention, they definitely weren't off girls altogether. Especially not Josh, who seemed to develop a crush on every female celebrity he met!

First he admitted to being sweet on Michelle Keegan – and even said he fancied a bit of *Twilight*-style vampire action with the Corrie babe. 'People say I look like Robert Pattinson or a vampire. I've not had any girls asking to bite my neck but I'd be up for it. It sounds kinky. Michelle Keegan can have a nibble any day.'

Not sure her boyfriend Mark Wright would be too keen...

Then he revealed his penchant for older ladies, including Holly Willoughby and Kelly Brook, who are both a decade older than him. 'I know Holly likes the band,' he said, wistfully. 'My mum found an interview where she said some nice stuff about us. She said, "I think Holly Willoughby's got a thing for you".' He added:

'We've been on her show *This Morning* a few times. She's very pretty and really sexy. But she's married with kids. I also think Kelly Brook is really fine. She's incredible.'

But when he revealed to Capital FM that he quite fancied Sharon Osborne, fans began to think maybe Josh had a problem. 'She's sexy, isn't she though?' he asked. 'In a weird way. I think it's the way she holds herself.'

George egged him on, saying, 'I did get a very embracing hug when I met her. It's the red hair and curls that do it for me.'

Enough already, Josh – time to get a girlfriend!

**DID YOU KNOW?**
**The boys had the choice of a few songs for their debut single, but chose 'Carry You' because they thought it was the most catchy. 'It was the one we were all walking round singing,' says George.**

Time was passing and it wouldn't be long before 'Carry You' was revealed to the world. The waiting was torture though, and gave the boys time to worry about things. 'If the single doesn't go well then all of the other projects we've got in the pipeline are pointless,' Josh told the *Daily Mirror* during one moment of uncertainty.

The boys spent an evening raising money for Cancer Research UK, when they attended the Jog-on to Cancer event at London's famous Kensington Roof Gardens.

It was the first time the lads had been to a celebrity event for a long while, as they had been so busy with their music. Word had quickly got out that they would be attending, so when they arrived there was already a crowd of screaming girls waiting for them – including WAG Lizzie Cundy, who apparently rushed over to the boys as soon as she saw them.

Dressed in jeans, shirts, black ties and grey blazers and wearing poppies on their jackets, it was clear they were enjoying letting their hair down for such a good cause.

The boys also busied themselves with domestic chores to fill their time. They did their usual food shopping in Tesco: 'Walking round Tesco with Jaymi and Olly! #Jolly Shopping lool!'tweeted George.

Josh tried to deal with some pressing cat issues: 'I need to get a bigger bed because my cat Oreo takes the whole flipping thing up when I'm sleeping!'

And JJ and George had a very awkward encounter while they were wandering around London. 'Ha! JJ and I just got asked if we were interested in being models for Abercrombie and Fitch, then she realized we were in Union J! Awks!'

Well at least the model scout had good taste!

As the days passed, the boys grew more and more restless. 'Today is Saturday, tomorrow is Sunday. We we we [sic] so excited, we so excited, Carry You goes on air Monday,' rhymed George on Twitter, three days before the world was due to hear the song for the first time...

Finally, six weeks before the single was officially released, 'Carry You' had its first airplay – on the Capital FM breakfast show.

Fans all around the country were up early to listen to the new song, which they'd been waiting months to hear.

It was poppy, it was upbeat and it was sentimental, all at the same time. It was an instant hit with fans because it was so catchy, and Twitter was quickly awash with people calling it the song of the summer.

While it was understandable that JCats were getting emotional at finally hearing the long-awaited tune, everyone was shocked to hear that JJ had literally wept while he was listening to it on the radio for the first time.

'JJ's eyes kinda started to melt,' Josh told the radio station. 'We all started crying,' JJ quickly added, trying to save his blushes. 'I was looking at all the tweets after and the support and what people were saying was so nice. It just kinda made me bawl a bit.'

While JJ and Josh were too emotional to really be interviewed properly, Jaymi managed to hold it together to say: 'The message of the song is that we've been on a massive rollercoaster the last year, with each other and it's about being there for each other. It's there for the fans, we really wouldn't be here without them.'

Just a day later, the track had made its way to number five on the iTunes pre-release chart. Fans had instantly put their hands in their pockets to pre-order the track, over a month before it was even released! The boys began to get excited: could they actually break the Top Ten with their first single?

George decided to give his fans an added incentive to buy the track: he promised them that he would sit naked in a bath of baked beans if they got to No.1 in June, when the single was officially released.

'We'll have a massive party,' he told the *Sun*. 'And I've

said I'll sit in a bath of beans. Pictured and everything. You have my word.'

Josh also promised to do something crazy if they got to number one – although it wasn't quite as enticing as George's offer. 'I'll eat my toenails off, on stage at Wembley Stadium,' he said.

It's safe to assume most fans would prefer George's promises to Josh's...

When the 'Carry You' music video was released a week later on Capital TV, fans were once again quickly to praise it, describing the video as 'perfect'.

Featuring the boys skateboarding, riding bikes, shopping for records and riding in taxis, it was like seeing a day in their lives unfolding on screen.

'This might be sacrilegious,' wrote one reviewer, 'but as far as we can tell, British boyband Union J could give fellow *X Factor* alumni One Direction a run for their money in the charm department. It's pretty adorable.'

And 4Music wrote: 'One Direction have some stiff competition nipping at their heels, that's for sure!'

Fellow celebs were keen to share in the Union J love fest, showering the boys in a hail of congratulatory tweets.

'Big congrats to @UnionJworld on their new single, 'Carry You'!!' tweeted Nathan Sykes from The Wanted. 'Everyone check it out'.

He was closely followed by former *X Factor* judge Tulisa, who had always been a fan of the group. 'Loving Carry You guys. Very proud of you all!'

**DID YOU KNOW?**
George used to have a bit of a temper – especially when it came to *Pokemon*. 'When I was about 10, I threw my brother's brand new games console across the room because I was angry,' he says. 'It was something to do with *Pokemon* – I think it was that he wouldn't give me a card.' A word of advice for Josh: you'd better share that *Pokemon* calendar you got for Christmas!

## CHAPTER TWENTY-ONE

# BOYBAND WAR

As Union J eagerly awaited the release of their first single, the rest of their boyband competition had what can only be described as a full on meltdown.

First One Direction and The Wanted – both bands that Union J admire– reignited their simmering rivalry in a very public war of words on Twitter. Relations have never been easy between the two band camps, as they vie for their teenage fans' affections and compete for world music domination. But in April their constant bickering finally turned into an all-out war, which had the music industry more than a little confused. Especially when their girlfriends got involved in the online slanging match.

Who could have known that when One Direction auditioned on *The X Factor* with The Wanted's debut single playing softly in the background, that the boys would grow to have such a bitter rivalry?

For some reason, the two bands have a long-running feud, which has included such horrible moments as Zayn Malik calling Max George 'chlamydia boy'. The playground insult resulted in Max offering to meet Malik for a fight. This never happened.

But it was a case of 'manbags at dawn' after Louis T apparently made some comments about The Wanted during a 1D gig, causing Tom Parker to get in touch with him on Twitter. He tweeted Louis with a video of the One Direction singer's *X Factor* audition, which had happened way back when 1D didn't even exist. (This is, of course, a time that is hard to imagine…)

'You even talk about us at your own gigs. Are you that upset you didn't get in this band?'tweeted Tom.

'Pal, we both know I wouldn't waste my time auditioning for your band,' replied Louis, before tweeting a link to a *Metro* interview Tom had recently done. Tom had admitted to the newspaper that he was 'shattered' after being rejected at a first stage *X Factor* audition when he was just 16.

The Wanted had formed in 2009 as the result of a nationwide hunt for a new boyband that was led by Jayne Collins, who also created The Saturdays and Parade. But Tom had auditioned for *The X Factor* a few years before and told the newspaper it had been a traumatic experience. 'You don't meet Simon [Cowell] at the first audition, you sing for a director. He told me: "It's a no" before I finished the first chorus. I was 16 and it shattered me. I didn't sing for two years.'

It seemed like Louis was saying that whilst he himself had got through the *X Factor* auditions to become a member of 1D, Tom clearly hadn't made the grade. Ouch.

Back and forth the insults flew, with Louis saying: 'You clearly spend too much time on Twitter. Funny that face-to-face you act like a little girl. Goodnight old friend.'

'Hey Tom,' began Liam Payne, wading in on the argument. 'Let's talk about your singing – your amazing tone pierces my ears with every note. Ps tweet out when you have someone to speak to. Our drummer has more followers than you.'

It was another low blow. The 1D boys may have over 10 million followers, but The Wanted have a very respectable million fans on Twitter. 'I also heard he wets the bed,' added Louis, clearly back in the playground again.

'Aw bless!' said Tom, sarcastically.

'Ah I know it's embarrassing when you're sh*t isn't it?' shot back Liam. The whole thing was descending into farce, with both sides starting to look a little silly.

The Wanted's Jay then stepped in, presumably to try and stop the Twitter madness from getting any worse. But his long message didn't help matters one bit.

'Dear Louis Tomlinson, please stop mentioning us in your gigs, we certainly no long mention you and it's time to let dead dogs lie. Your passive aggressive style of speaking makes me cringe, and I wish you'd either have the b*llocks of some of your co-workers to speak truthfully, or the class of the majority of them to be silent.'

He went on: 'I'm not sure what's happened since we

saw you at the *X Factor*, but you've done a sterling job of becoming one of the most overrated, arrogant and not to mention insincere people around.'

And finally: 'Your shocking lack of talent will only be forgiven by lots of humility and no-strings-attached friendship among your band. Louis, don't measure your worth in followers or money, because they're fickle, and when they go you might just feel worthless.'

The message provoked an army of fans on both sides to step in to defend themselves and their favourite boys, and their Twitter feeds practically imploded under the strain of it all.

Then the boys' girlfriends got involved, with Tom's girlfriend Kelsey Hardwick retweeting a message that said: 'Louis spends more time tweeting Tom Parker than his 'well deserved' fans.'

This was followed by Louis' girlfriend Eleanor replying with '#nipslip' – in reference to a recent picture of Kelsey on a night out with Tom. Let's just say she'd had a slight wardrobe malfunction in front of the paparazzi.

'Awwwww Bless ya!!' replied Kelsey, clearly not embarrassed in the slightest. 'Did ya wanna see more!!Xxx.'

The girls' intervention seemed to finally stop the boys from continuing the spat, but the damage was done. The bands had publicly shared their dislike of each other once again, and behaved very childishly in the process.

The Union J boys, along with the rest of the world, had watched the two bands trade insults with each other with rising disbelief. And in the end they decided they wanted to help end the feud and get the boys to make friends once and for all.

Union J are all about peace, love and togetherness and wanted the two bands to come together to sort out their differences and make up.

'We're hoping we could bring One Direction and The Wanted together and get them to make friends again,' said Jaymi. 'We'll stand in the middle so they don't have a scrap,' he bravely offered. 'Us boybands have to stick together. We need love and lots of hugs – not fighting.'

It was typical of the boys, who are all all-round nice guys, to wade in and try to help. But sadly even Union J couldn't get the two warring bands in the same room for a much-needed hug-out.

'It's really random,' said Josh, clearly as confused as the rest of the world. 'But I'm not taking sides. I'm team boyband.'

The boys went on to reveal they never fight or argue, because they're too soft at heart. 'The most physical we get is hugging,' said George.

**DID YOU KNOW?**
**Though he doesn't exactly agree, lots of people think George looks like Harry Styles or a young Johnny Depp. But he gets very confused indeed when fans liken him to Miranda Cosgrove from *iCarly*. 'We have the same smile, apparently,' he says.**

Another group who were astonished at the silly word war were chart-toppers JLS. 'It's childish and unnecessary,' said JB. 'They're both nice, we've never had any issues. There's enough room in the industry for both bands.'

But his words would prove to be more than a little ironic, just a few weeks later – when the boyband world was dealt another crushing blow.

JLS announced that they were going to split up.

In the years since they came second to Alexandra Burke on *The X Factor* in 2008, the popular boys had dominated the British charts and enjoyed all the trappings of a rock star lifestyle. They'd had 10 Top Ten hits, including five No.1s, and even won two Brit Awards in the process.

But now they had made the difficult decision to go their separate ways. They explained in a statement that they wanted to leave on a high, instead of fading away into obscurity, and announced that their tour at the end of the year would be their last as a foursome.

When they appeared on Alan Carr's *Chatty Man* a few days later, they were still obviously devastated about their decision. As Oritse Williams tried to explain their decision, he broke down in tears and had to be comforted by his bandmates.

JB Gill put his arm around his pal, and said: 'It's Oritse's baby, effectively, you know. He brought us all together.'

As the group tried to contain their feelings, Marvin Humes explained: 'It's an emotional decision, we're best friends, we're brothers, the bond between us is indescribable. We've been through so much since we first came together and no one would have dreamed what we achieved could be possible, and of course for it all to end was a massively emotional decision and it wasn't one that was taken lightly.'

He added: 'We wanted to go out on top and not be that act where people are like, "Oh bloody hell it's JLS again".'

JLS have had the kind of *X Factor* success that the Union J boys were dreaming of. They had their own range of dolls and condoms, and even a charitable foundation in their name, which, they were keen to point out, would continue.

It was a shock to everyone, including the Union J boys.

One Direction's Louis Tomlinson was among those who aired their sadness on the morning of the news.

'Sad to hear about JLS. Wish them all the best of luck in what they go on to do,' he said.

And TV presenter Mark Wright was on the verge of tears after hearing about the group's demise: 'Not gonna lie, my eyes watered a little bit reading that JLS are splitting. Sad article.Congrats to all your success boys.'

The Union J boys told reporters that they were genuinely upset about the split, with George saying: 'They're an amazing band, I'm really said about it.'

Jaymi confessed: 'I found out on Twitter and was genuinely gutted and upset. I've not been this upset about a band splitting since Steps. Girls Aloud and JLS in one year...I'm not sure I can take any more splits this year. George came up to me and said, "You know, their hearts won't beat again", and I literally cried!'

They also said they really wanted to support the boys on their farewell tour, by buying tickets to the gig – and even said they'd be keen to be their support act.

But it must have been with a mixture of guilt and satisfaction that they received the news that the split may have partly been their fault...

The *Daily Star* reported that although JLS had said they had split because they wanted to pursue solo projects and not outstay their music industry welcome, there was an entirely different reason behind the shock split.

They claimed that JLS felt they were unable to compete with the younger boybands they had paved the way for – like One Direction and Union J. And their record labels had reportedly turned their back on them to focus on the new wave of boybands.

JLS's last single 'Hold Me Down' had failed to break into the top 100, and a source revealed to the *Daily Star*: 'They weren't prepared to hang around singing the same old songs at lesser venues or on stale television shows. That's the route you take to Butlins and the holiday park circuit. If they could no longer fill the O2 Arena, they felt it was time to go.'

According to the newspaper, the boys felt they were being neglected by their label as their bosses were investing more time with Union J as they prepared to release their first single.

It was bittersweet for Union J. They were devastated that JLS were no more, but must have been excited to hear that their record label felt they had so much promise.

It meant that their bosses believed they could be as big as the top pop band – or even bigger. And when it was announced that Union J had signed a lucrative deal worth £200,000 to release their memoirs, it was yet more proof that the four boys were well on their way to super-stardom.

The boys would be singing alongside JLS at Ponty's Big Weekend in Wales, so at least they would get a chance to have a heart-to-heart then with the guys, who they are reportedly already close with. 'It's been really lovely to meet them,' said Jaymi. 'They've been around since I was 17, 18, so they were the massive boyband when I was younger. To get to know them personally was amazing. They're going to be amazing what whatever they each do because they are such amazing guys.'

With JLS gone and 1D and The Wanted seemingly intent on destroying each other in the media, there could just be room for Union J to slip in and safely take over the world... Watch out boys!

**DID YOU KNOW?**
**JJ was a chatterbox when he was at school and always got told off for talking. Once he made his cookery teacher so angry she threw a pencil at him. 'She told me to be quiet and I didn't listen. Miss Foster, if you're reading this, I still remember. And now the nation knows,' he says.**

## CHAPTER TWENTY-TWO

# COUNTDOWN TO 'CARRY YOU'

It had been over a year since Union J began their *X Factor* journey, but although they were now a super hot band with their first single on the way, their loyalties still lay with the show. It had, after all, been the vehicle that finally launched them all into the public eye – after years of wanting to be pop stars.

They had loved every moment of the exciting experience and would forever be grateful for the opportunities it gave each of them – and for introducing them to their beloved George, of course.

So when uber-cool Scottish singer-songwriter Emeli Sandé publicly stated that young singers should avoid singing competitions like *The X Factor*, the boys were moved to defend the show.

Sandé has written songs for *X Factor* contestants Cher

Lloyd, Leona Lewis and Ella Henderson, *Britain's Got Talent* singer Susan Boyle and even *Popstars: The Rivals* alumni, Cheryl Cole. She wrote her first song aged 11, for her primary school talent show, and four years later took part in Choice FM's Rapology competition. She went on to win Trevor Nelson's BBC Urban Music competition and was actually offered a record contract as a result of the win, before the deal was cruelly cancelled by the management company in charge.

She was, therefore, no stranger to singing competitions and the exposure they can give new starters in the music industry.

It was a bit of a surprise then, when she told the *Daily Star* that she would never have considered *The X Factor* herself.

'I find it quite depressing,' she said. 'I find it sad that four people are judging these people and really knocking their confidence.

'I don't think I would have considered appearing on the *X Factor*... The kids who need music in their lives should just focus on their craft.'

Giving her own advice to the UK's singing hopefuls, she added: 'I'd say don't be in a rush. The pressure they put on kids is for it to happen right now, but your talent will always be there.'

When George heard about the comments, he told *EntertainmentWise*: 'I think it's one of the best decisions that I've made personally in my life.'

Josh was quick to put his opinion forward too. 'It's made so many people's dreams come true,' he said. 'You will not be able to listen to a radio station for a day and not hear a song from somebody who has had success coming from the *X Factor*. JLS, Little Mix, One Direction...'

Jaymi said that it was a 'tough world out there' in the music industry, and to make it as a credible artist without some kind of platform or stepping-stone was very difficult indeed.

Sandé may have though that singing shows were cruel to judge new acts and knock their confidence, but sending off demo tapes and getting no reply, or struggling to even get a gig at a local pub – surely that was just as bad?

'If you're lucky enough to make it without a platform like that it's fine and she works really hard and whatever,' Jaymi said. 'But I struggled for seven years, sending demos off to everywhere. It doesn't cheapen the fact that we've made it, because we've worked just as hard.'

Josh tried to explain further, as he had also spent years attempting to break into the industry through the standard channels. 'People who make these remarks very often don't understand what these people on *X Factor* have done before the show,' he said. 'They just think that we've just turned up – like we've gone, 'yeah I'll do *X Factor*, I fancy having a go at singing, I think I can sing' – but we've been trying for years and years.'

The boys used last year's winner James Arthur as another example of a success story, and described how he had definitely been put through his paces before appearing on the show. They were adamant he deserved every moment of success that he was now enjoying.

'James is a real artist,' said Jaymi. 'Whereas we are a

boyband. We were manufactured by *X Factor* at Judges Houses – we are that lane of artist and we're not denying that. James is a real, down to earth artist and his music is fresh. He struggled for years and had been in a bedsit, he was on the breadline. And there's only so many times you can say, I'm going to do it the "right" way. He did *X Factor* and it changed his life forever.'

Jaymi made another great point when he talked about the intensive training they had all received on the show. 'You'll never get a ten week intensive boot camp of how to be a popstar in the real world,' he said.

Plus with all the publicity that the show gave them, the boys were extremely happy that they chose to enter the contest, and would never deter anyone from wanting to follow in their footsteps.

**DID YOU KNOW?**

**George had a pet hamster when he was a kid – called Steven. 'He had really long hair,' he says. 'Then my sister got a hamster called Gloria. They mated and we had loads of little baby hamsters. It was so cute!' A long-haired boy who's a hit with the ladies? Sounds like someone else we know, George!**

Jaymi may have been honest about the band's beginnings by admitting that they were manufactured by *The X Factor*, but it was nothing to be embarrassed about. The boys certainly proved their credibility when they performed for the BBC Radio 1 breakfast show, in Bangor, Wales.

Union J joined DJ Nick Grimshaw to kick off the first ever Breakfast Show Tour, which revisited cities all over the country that have hosted Radio 1's Big Weekend.

The location and line-up had at first been shrouded with secrecy, but students at Ysgol Tryfan school, which was eventually revealed as the first location, were more than excited to see Union J appear on their stage.

They began by stepping from foot to foot and rolling up their sleeves nervously, as a delicate piano tune began to play…

It was the first time ever that the band had performed 'Carry You' live, and both teachers and students began screaming and cheering them on. It was a historical moment for the boys and one they would remember forever.

'That was really good, you should be singers,' joked Grimshaw once the song was over. But the boys weren't finished showing off their singing skills yet. In an astonishing departure from their usual 'poppy' style, the boys went on to sing an acoustic version of Bastille's No.2 hit 'Pompeii'. The stripped-down version of the song gave them a chance to properly show off their voices – voices that had, after all, earned them their ticket to the *X Factor* live shows.

There was no choreography, the boys just sang their hearts out – especially Jaymi, whose voice soared as he shut his eyes and lost himself in the song. The crowd was silent as they performed. But as the last note was struck the audience showed their appreciation by screaming loudly. Girls in the front rows reached their hands out to the boys on stage, and George gently touched all their fingertips.

'We love you Bangor!' shouted Josh over the noise, as they walked away.

It had been a great set. They had promoted 'Carry You', and proved to everyone that they weren't just a manufactured boyband – they truly deserved their place in the music world.

When a video of the event was put on YouTube, it was viewed nearly a hundred thousand times and sparked a debate about the band.

'I've never really like Union J,' read one post. 'But this is actually really good.'

'Some people are saying that Union J sing much better than 1D,' wrote another. 'But let's see in a year or so...'

'If you think that One Direction can sing better than Union J live you're so wrong,' responded one girl. 'I like both bands but seriously One Direction have been around for what 3 years and even with their vocal training they still don't sound as good as Union J.'

So even Directioners – who were by reputation fiercely loyal to their boys Liam, Zayn, Louis, Niall and Harry – were beginning to fall for Union J...

Someone else who had fallen for Union J was Caterina Lopez – JJ's new girlfriend! Yes, sorry JCats, but JJ had actually been quietly dating the beautiful international model and actress since early in 2013, although it's not clear exactly when they first met.

It wasn't hard to see why JJ had fallen for Caterina – with a killer body, the face of an angel and a sexy

American accent, the brunette bombshell was pretty much the perfect woman. And there were rumours that she was actually Hollywood megastar Jennifer Lopez's cousin, which meant she was related to pop royalty.

At first there were tears among fans, who were gutted their boy was in love. But Caterina soon won them over with her all-round friendliness and support for Union J. She was just like JCats all over the world and wanted to see them do well. 'We need the boys to hit #1 with 'Carry You' – do what you do best #JCats,' she tweeted in April.

She dances to Union J songs for 30 minutes a day to keep fit, and makes a daily effort to get the band trending.

Some fans even admit to having a bit of a girl crush on the 25-year-old, who wanted to be a rapper before she became a model. And once the pair began tweeting pics of their cosy life together, a chorus of 'awww' went round the Twittersphere.

JJ must have been relieved – he didn't want his JCats to be upset or jealous. But he obviously wanted the fans to know that Caterina was very important, because she soon became a firm fixture on the Union J Twitter feed.

Caterina regularly reveals JJ's romantic side to the world, and keeps fans swooning (and jealous) by posting exclusive pictures of her boyfriend at home, relaxing. He sends her flowers for no reason at all, which she tweets pictures of too. 'I have the best boyfriend ever', she often says, and JCats agree.

He even shares her clothes, which Caterina isn't too keen on. 'I hate it when my boyfriend wears my clothes,' she fumed one day. Wonder what he was wearing!

Fans soon began to call them Jaterina, as a sign of their couple status – as we all know, name combining is practically marriage in the world of famous people.

Of course, the perfect name combination would have been JCat – but that name was already taken by Union J's fans.

Caterina has become a conduit for fans and often passes on messages and pics to JJ for people. She's good mates with the rest of the band and constantly supports them by sharing what they're all up to on her Twitter feed.

In May, the couple became proud parents – to a little pug! They went puppy hunting together to find the very special new family member, and as soon as they brought her home she was introduced to JCats as Lola.

Caterina refers to JJ as Lola's 'daddy', and Lola as 'Daddy's little girl', and tweets about their antics. Pictures of Lola and JJ are by far the most popular for retweeting. Various pics show them watching telly together, going for walks in the park and sharing milkshakes.

Lola even sits on JJ when he's on the computer talking to JCats. The tiny puppy already has lots of fans, and even stars in her own YouTube videos.

The other members of the band love her too, and George even babysits her when JJ and Caterina go out. Ella Henderson adores Lola and reckons she would make firm friends with her own dog, Trixie. 'I'm in love,' she tweeted to Caterina soon after Lola arrived. 'Need to set up a puppy date...'

If having a puppy together wasn't proof enough that they were a serious couple, Caterina got every JCat overexcited when she retweeted a message, which said: 'Retweet if you think that JJ and Caterina will get married.'

Could our first Union J wedding be happening soon?

With JJ now happily settled, and Jaymi engaged to Olly, it means that only George and Josh remain single. Wonder which lucky ladies will snap them up...

**DID YOU KNOW?**

JJ always cries when he breaks up with girls. 'It's the hardest thing to do,' he says. 'I don't want to hurt them and it's horrible. They start crying and then I start crying.' He stays friends with all his exes though – once he dries his tears.

# CHAPTER TWENTY-THREE

# A MILLION
# FANS UNITE

With just a month to go before 'Carry You' was officially released, the boys must have been literally counting down the days. To break the Top Ten in the UK charts would be an amazing achievement, and they were doing everything they could to make that happen.

Their new life was a mixture of working hard and playing hard, and they were thoroughly enjoying all the attention they were getting.

But the tables were well and truly turned on the band when they were invited to the premiere of *Star Trek: Into Darkness*, at London's Leicester Square.

The boys had all been secretly excited at the prospect of director JJ Abrams new movie, so much so that they couldn't keep their usual cool on the red carpet (which was actually white for the event) – despite the fact that they were all wearing sharp suits and looking extremely polished.

At first they posed for pics and signed autographs for fans, and even took the time to record a message for their fans via Absolute Radio. 'Without you guys we wouldn't be here, you're making our dreams come true,' said Jaymi, as George made a heart with his hands.

But when the stars of the film arrived and the crowds began to scream, the lads couldn't concentrate on anything other than catching a glimpse of the Hollywood actors and actresses, including Benedict Cumberbatch, Chris Pine and Zoe Saldana.

The boys admitted they were definitely 'Trekkies', and George tweeted from the white carpet: 'FAN DUDEING AT THE STAR TREK PREMIERE!!! White carpet was soo soft! #trekkie George!'

After all the excitement was over, Josh added: 'Star Trek was incredible!!!!!! Such a good film! Josh x'.

If the amount of exclamation marks in their tweets is directly proportionate to their excitement then the premiere was certainly one of the most exciting moments of their year so far.

After pics of the quartet at the event were released to the media, famous celeb gossip website Holy Moly was moved to make an official announcement. First they posted 15 pictures of the boys at the event and titled the sequence: 'Look! It's pics of Union J at the *Star Trek* Premiere. Because they have nice faces.'

Then they wrote:

*We have a difficult relationship with fans of boybands. We used to be ok with the McFly fans but then one of us said an album they made wasn't very good and it all kicked off. The Wanted's fans despise us but that's ok because The Wanted are toilet. So we want to state now that unless Union J make a truly terrible record or say something very wrong then HOLY MOLY OFFICIALLY ENDORSES UNION J...*

It was glowing praise from the popular website, which admitted the boys had well and truly won them over, and promised to be a 'one stop shop' for pictures of the boys from now on.

But despite getting enough positive reviews and praise to make their heads too big to fit through their front doors, the boys remained down to earth.

Excitedly planning their end of year tour, the band were on the lookout for the right support act to join them. 'We're doing a bit of scouting for people to support us, though it's just exciting to be headliners,' they admitted.

In a show of affection for their mums, they even jokingly put them forward for the job, telling *EntertainmentWise*: 'Our parents will probably support us, I think that would be quite funny. The four mums.'

George added: 'My mum did say she was going to do a 'Carry You' cover and put it on YouTube!'

George's family are all musically talented, so it would probably be amazing.

Though they now live in the bright lights of London and hang out with celebrity pals at star-studded events, the boys have always made it clear that they will never forget where they came from.

JJ in particular has kept close ties to his former community and regularly pops into his old school, Fordham Primary, to surprise its pupils – including his little sister who still goes there. In May he donated to them the T-shirt he wore on Comic Relief, for it to be auctioned off to raise money for the school – and he even got his band mates to sign it, so that it would be worth more dosh. The money raised went to improving the school's playground, so that the students would have a great space to spend their lunch break.

It was such a thoughtful thing to do. But not unusual for the caring boys, who are always doing things to make others happy – and their fans certainly do everything they can to return the favour...

**DID YOU KNOW?**
**JJ once tricked his best friend into spending the day with his girlfriend and her friends – even though his mate couldn't stand them.**

**Not only did the poor lad have to spend the day with a bunch of girls he didn't like, he also ended up covered in poo and dressed in a girl's T-shirt...**

**'I told him we were going to see some jockeys but we went to the park with them all,' he explains. The friend, clearly annoyed, went off to play on his own on a rocking toy, but he accidentally broke it and fell over.**

**'He'd landed in dog poo and it was all over the back of his white t-shirt,' says JJ. 'He had to change**

into one of my girlfriend's tops, which said "RSPCA I LOVE DOGS" on the front.' Luckily the lads are still friends – and his mate can now see the funny side of the story. Just...

On 8 May, with their JCats' help, the boys reached a landmark in their careers. Though the single wasn't even out yet, the 'Carry You' video reached a million views on YouTube – a phenomenal achievement.

It prompted a wave of excitement amongst the boys, with George tweeting: 'CANT BELIEVE CARRY YOU HAS 1,000000 VIEWS! Thank You!'

Capital letters are the same as exclamation marks for the boys – the more there are in their tweets, the greater chance that they are about to explode with excitement.

'Everyone that's watched it, every fan's mum's grandma's dog – thank you,'gushed Josh to Capital FM.

'I'm just positive it's my mum hitting refresh,' joked Jaymi.

The boys were pushed to reveal another song title from their album, but they were still keeping it all a big secret. 'Wait and see,' said Josh. 'Cheeky Boys maybe...'

'We're still half way through writing it at the minute,' admitted Jaymi. 'We don't know what's going to be on there, what's not going to be on there, so we don't want to put anything out there that might not be true.'

The boys did say, however, that they thought the album would surprise people. 'I think it's going to be quite diverse – things that maybe people don't expect of us, and the good old stuff that people want to hear,' said Jaymi.

'Like people want to hear ballads and they want to hear stuff that we did on the show, so we're going to stay true to who we were and who we're going to be going forward.'

In the revealing interview, they also said they were in talks with other singers for some amazing collaborations. 'We'd love to work with Jason Derulo,' admitted Jaymi.

They told the radio station that they loved reading all the fan fiction written about them, and owned up to Googling themselves to find out what people are thinking about them. 'I'm addicted to Tumblr,' admitted George.

They said that the video shoot for 'Carry You' was a lot of fun, but they struggled with one particular chilly problem on set. 'Nipples were a really big problem,' said Josh. 'We were wearing these really thin t-shirts and our nipples were the size of this Capital FM studio after being in the cold for six hours. It was intense.'

George admitted to a very hairy moment on *The X Factor*, when the stylists asked if they could cut his luscious locks – but revealed that Harry Styles saved the day by telling him to stay strong. 'I said look, they want to cut my hair off. And they did, they combed it back one week and I was just like – it's not happening. Harry said to just do whatever I wanted with my hair.'

Jaymi said that he is definitely the parent of the group, and he even cleans up after JJ – and Lola. 'JJ's dog pooed on my bedroom floor – I wasn't impressed.'

'They're like an old married couple at home,' said Josh, giggling.

The boys talked about their celebrity crushes – a topic they're always keen to discuss. Josh said his was Jade from Little Mix, George chose Demi Lovato, JJ named Eva Longoria – who looks a lot like his girlfriend – while Jaymi refused to name someone. 'I actually put my foot in it once and met someone I'd admitted to having a crush on and it was really awkward,' he explained.

All the other boys starting whispering and Jaymi went red and tried to stop them – but it was obvious they were saying the name Aston Merrygold. Poor Jaymi!

The boys' banter with each other was very amusing, and it was lovely to see how close they had become. They're always teasing and pranking each other, but are also quick to give each other hugs and support.

Soon after, the boys returned to Nottingham – where they had filmed the video for 'Carry You' – to perform their new song again.

The Hits Radio had invited the band to join their Future Hits Live show, in which they aimed to bring together their favourite popstars – and introduce the new acts that they were convinced would be huge in 2013.

Alongside them were Misha B, Charlie Brown, Nina Nesbitt and the Loveable Rogues – all of whom were tipped for big chart success. It was an amazing event, and the boys were excited to be back in Newcastle so soon after their fun two-day video shoot.

They posed for pics with countless fans, and performed 'Carry You' to a huge screaming crowd.

It made the boys very emotional, as they were still coming to terms with what their future was going to bring. Every cheer and every new fan made them more excited about their possibilities as a band.

It also made them more and more confident that they were going to have a long and fruitful career together – a career that was only just beginning.

'THAT WAS INCREDIBLE!!'tweeted George. 'Love Newcastle, Love my brothers, Love Carry You, Love you All!!'

As each day passed, more and more people, newspapers, websites and radio stations were falling a little bit in love with the four boys and their message of sticking together and caring for each other.

### DID YOU KNOW?
**Josh's favourite TV programme is *Deal or No Deal*, his favourite cartoon character is Shrek, and he can sing 'Hero' in Spanish.**

Mark Owen, member of super-boyband Take That, was just one of the people encouraging this attitude, when he singled them out for praise in an interview with music channel MTV.

He said that the boys' rise to fame reminded him of the exciting initial days of Take That, and included them alongside One Direction in their fame and popularity.

'I think it's exciting when new acts come along and people get really into them like One Direction and Union J,' he said. 'You look at them and you're reminded of when you started and when you were younger so it brings back memories.'

The boys must have been very excited to read the pop veteran's words. To remind him of Take That in their glory days must have meant that Owen thought very highly indeed of the band. And he was definitely hopeful for their future.

'You just wish them well really and hope all goes well for them. We've met them a few times, out and about doing stuff, and they all seem like nice and decent guys so I just wish them well.'

It was almost as if he was passing over the boyband equivalent of the Olympic torch – giving the next generation of boybands his approval and backing.

He had one piece of advice for the boys. 'I think they should always look after each other really as they'll be going through an experience that not many other people go through apart from when you're in the band. I think that's the same for any band… just look after each other in that set up. That's the only advice I'd ever give.'

Union J are as tight as can be, and they're always saying how much they admire their fellow boybands. They have always acted respectfully, whether to their friends, their family or other singers. It's just one of the reasons that their growing fan base was faithfully supporting them – and tipping them for the top.

Soon they would find out whether all that support would get their debut single to No.1 in the charts. A nervous few weeks were ahead for the boys…

### DID YOU KNOW?

JJ's alarm ringtone is 'Wide Awake' by Katy Perry, and if he was a girl he'd want to date George.

## CHAPTER TWENTY-FOUR

# CHALLENGE UNION J

It was obvious that excitement was rising amongst the lads as the day of their single release approached.

To keep themselves and their fans occupied until the big day, they began a new series of videos, entitled: 'Challenge Union J'. They invited fans to submit challenges to perform for the cameras, with the first one being: 'Expand Your Mind'.

'We asked you guys to send in your ideas,' said Jaymi. 'And each week we're going to be facing different challenges, set by you, the JCats....'

The boys didn't know what to expect when they were handed the envelope that contained their first challenge. 'You will be hypnotized by the incredible Ben Dali,' read JJ. 'Who will induce you into a trance like state and explore your full boyband potential.'

Josh looked sceptical, but JJ was overjoyed. 'I've always wanted to be hypnotised!' he said excitedly.

Stage hypnotist Dali talked to the boys as they sat with their eyes closed on the sofa. Once he was satisfied they were 'under', he convinced the boys that they were first extremely hot, then really cold. George and JJ were left clinging to each other for warmth, even after Dali brought them back round.

At this point it became apparent that Jaymi and Josh were impenetrable to Dali's mind-bending skills, so they stepped away. But JJ and George were apparently totally under his control, so Dali continued with the challenge.

'When you wake up you will find that you are a champion jockey, and you have to do whatever it takes to finish that race,' Dali told the two boys, still slumped in their chairs.

JJ began galloping in his chair very convincingly. His past as a jockey was very much evident and he went to great efforts to win the imaginary race.

George's technique was a little less honed. He slapped his thighs over and over, while wearing a big grin on his face. It's safe to assume he won't be winning any horse races in the near future.

Josh and Jaymi fell about in fits of laughter as they watched their friends from the doorway.

After it was over, JJ said: 'It was a bit weird, but great fun though, because I've always wanted to be hypnotized. Although I knew I was doing it, it felt like I didn't care I was doing it. You feel like you're in your own little world. I'd definitely do it again.'

**DID YOU KNOW?**
**JJ's favourite boyband when he was younger was the Backstreet Boys, and his favourite movie is *I Love You Man*.**

The next challenge was called 'Liar Liar'.

'It's the red envelope of doom,' said George ominously, as he opened the envelope. 'Boyband rules state that honesty is always the best policy to a long and fruitful career. You will each have to take a lie detector test, to find out who is Mr Goody Two Shoes, and who is telling porkies.'

The boys started off with some simple questions like asking each other their names. Then Jaymi asked Josh: 'Have you ever done anything inappropriate whilst in the band Union J?'

Josh decided that honesty was indeed the best policy, and said that yes, he had. But he wouldn't say what.

Then George asked Jaymi whether he was in Union J. 'Yes, I am in Union J,' he said. The machine whirred, then gave him a small electric shock as it decided he was lying!

Jaymi looked confused and asked his friends: 'Am I not in Union J?'

'I don't know, apparently not...' said Josh.

'Is it true that you wash and style your hair before bed so you don't have to do it in the morning,' asked Jaymi of Josh.

Josh looked embarrassed, but knew he would be caught out in a lie if he didn't admit it. 'I do that occasionally,' he said carefully.

'You're so difficult to trick!' said Jaymi, who was frustrated that he was the only one who hadn't had a shock from the portable lie detector machine.

'Do you like the way you dress?' the boys asked JJ. 'No,' he replied, only to receive an electric shock. The machine knows, boys!

It was Jaymi's turn again next, and Josh asked him whether he had ever kissed anyone he shouldn't have. 'Yes,' he said instantly. But the machine was adamant he was lying. 'You lying child,' admonished Josh. 'At least he's faithful,' said George, putting his arm around his friend.

Josh finally fell foul of the machine when he was asked how many brothers and sisters he had. 'Six,' he replied confidently, only to fall off his chair when the machine delivered its punishment.

It was left to Jaymi to sum up the challenge. 'I don't think it worked for me – it said I lied about everything. I was asked if I was in Union J, and I said yeah, and it said no you're not.'

He looked puzzled and ever so slightly scared, as he added: 'So I dunno, we're going to have a little bit of a chat in a minute – maybe they know something I don't.'

**DID YOU KNOW?**
**JJ says the three things he can't live without are family, girls and horses.**

Their third challenge was an endurance test. The boys had to each run 200 metres and whoever did it in the fastest time would be pronounced the winner. 'Sometimes with even the best fans in the world a boyband needs to make a quick getaway,' read Josh from the envelope the boys were handed. 'This challenge has been devised to test your endurance in such a scenario.'

As his band mates cheered him on, Jaymi was the first to take the challenge, finishing the sprint in a respectable time of 01:11.

Next up was JJ, who had a focused and determined look on his face as he ran as fast as he could – finishing in a speedy 01:06.

Then Josh sauntered up to the treadmill, looking relaxed as he raced through the 200 metres in a very swift 00:59 – less than a minute!

It was looking like he would be the clear winner, but then George took to the treadmill…

He was grinning as his little legs pounded the moving floor, and looked so relaxed nobody would have guessed he was going to win. So everyone was astonished and started to applaud when he came in at a time of 00:57 – knocking two seconds off Josh's previously winning time.

'I came into the gym thinking that I would lose, but I won,' said a beaming George. 'I beat Josh by two seconds so – ha ha!'

**DID YOU KNOW?**
**George says the three things he can't live without are computers, music and coffee.**

For their fourth challenge, the boys found themselves back firmly on solid ground. 'We're outside and we have no idea why,' said George, as the boys were handed the now familiar red envelope. 'You've all recently moved to London,' read Josh. 'And with your new single 'Carry You' out next week, what better way to promote the band than with the great British tradition of busking.'

George looked horrified, as he and JJ chorused, 'Noooo!' Josh also looked slightly concerned, while Jaymi just looked confused. 'I don't want to busk,' moaned George as someone handed him a guitar.

'At least it says good luck,' joked Josh. 'That's fine. That makes it all alright.'

Standing in the cold outside South Kensington tube station, the boys decided to play Bastille's 'Pompeii'. It was a song they knew they could do without any extra backing music, and it was one they knew all the words to.

People stopped and took pictures on their phones as they recognised who was entertaining them on the street. Josh started the song confidently, while George played the guitar and JJ and Jaymi giggled. But they soon got into the familiar rhythm of performing together, and sang the song beautifully.

Passers by started smiling and tapping their feet to the music, and were obviously impressed by the lads. In just a few minutes a large crowd of people had gathered to listen to them.

As the song came to an end, Jaymi said: 'That was the scariest thing we've ever done but we love you guys!'

They looked proud of their achievement, especially since the experience must have felt terrifyingly similar to their *X Factor* audition – standing up in front of strangers and singing for their approval.

'Whoever sent that challenge in, thanks, it's been freezing, it's been great,' George said, before the boys escaped the crowds to get warm…

**DID YOU KNOW?**
JJ sleepwalks and sleeptalks and has tiny feet – a minuscule six and a half!

## CHAPTER TWENTY-FIVE

# KISSES, TATTOOS AND PLAYDOUGH

If you have ever wondered what it would be like to snog Union J, then reading *Heat* magazine in May must have been like an answered prayer: because in it the boys described exactly what kissing style they use when wooing lucky females.

JJ revealed that he liked to start off a romantic session with a bit of face stroking. 'I slowly touch her face,' he said, before Josh interrupted, with: 'Back of the ear!'

It was a suggestion that got heads nodding all round amongst the lads, and JJ agreed that his exes had very much enjoyed a bit of ear licking action.

'Some girls like their ears being licked,' he said. 'It's a really "thingy" place, isn't it?'

He meant to say 'erogenous', which means a sensitive

area, but he obviously couldn't remember the word. Maybe it was all that talk of kissing girls that was putting him off...

Jaymi stayed quiet for the whole conversation, obviously unimpressed with his bandmates' techniques. Eventually he rolled his eyes and laughed, before saying: 'I'm so happy I'm gay, honestly...'

It was a much more low key kind of kissing that the boys next indulged in – when just days after the revealing Heat interview they were invited to attend The British Soap Awards.

Heading up north for the biggest event in the British soap calendar must have been exciting for the four lads, who walked the red carpet to much screaming and applause.

Josh looked smooth in a black suit with satin lapels, while JJ and Jaymi wore matching beige chinos and George dressed down his shirt and tie by accessorising with a denim jacket.

But they weren't there to just soak up the celebrity atmosphere andmeet their favourite stars – instead they had been given the very serious task of presenting the most important award of the night: Sexiest Female.

Appearing on stage to announce the award, the boys all looked super cute and just a little bit nervous. Especially when they realised that they would be giving the award to Josh's fantasy girl, Michelle Keegan.

Michelle plays Tina McIntyre in *Coronation Street*, and it was her fifth consecutive win of the award. She had wolf-whistled the lads when they first appeared on stage to announce the finalists in the category, despite being with her boyfriend Mark Wright at the event.

Like a pro she ascended the stairs to the stage wearing a beautiful cream dress, and gave each of the boys a kiss on the cheek before accepting the award. It must have been one of Josh's finest moments!

As the applause rang out, the boys left the stage with Michelle and then went on to party the night away in celebration of the awards.

It must have been a late night, because the boys enjoyed a long lie in the next morning – until the hotel cleaner gave Josh a very rude awakening. 'Now that was an incredible lie in until house-keeping just comes in when I'm butt naked!!! Not the best situation I've been in,' he tweeted the next day.

Luckily he recovered from his embarrassment in time to join the rest of the boys in performing at Victoria Park in London – for the As One In The Park event, held at the end of May.

The sun was out for the day-long festival, which saw Katy B, Conor Maynard and Holly Johnson take to the stage in front of the packed crowds. Billed as a 'very special guest' act, Union J were greeted by a huge roar of cheers when it was their turn to sing.

Among the thousands of fans in the crowd were three very special JCats – Jaymi's fiancé Olly, JJ's girlfriend Caterina and little Lola, who had come to see her daddy perform.

Caterina was excited, because it was a special day for JJ in more ways than one. She tweeted: 'Celebrating my sweethearts bday today and going to see Union J perform for the first time with LOLA! Happy bday JJ!'

It was the perfect way for JJ to celebrate turning 25 – the sun was shining, his little family was in the crowd, and he was singing on stage in front of thousands of people. 'What a beautiful day to perform, woop!' he tweeted.

Because he was be working on his birthday, JJ had given himself an early birthday present two days before – a tattoo by celebrity tattoo artist Kevin Paul.

The ink king has previously worked on Harry Styles and Ed Sheeran, and is a total pro – staying up till three in the morning to finish off the huge and intricate design for JJ.

He tweeted pics as the design progressed, and a tired JJ even managed to smile for the camera – despite the long hours he had spent in the chair undergoing the painful procedure. Covering most of his left arm, the image featured an angel and its wings, and JJ was happy with the result, which highlighted his bulging bicep.

**DID YOU KNOW?**
**George is a little bit OCD. 'I don't have a three-second rule when it comes to dropping food on the floor,' he says. 'If it touches the floor I put it in the bin. But then I have to wash my hands, even if my hands didn't touch the floor.'**

For the rest of the three-day-long weekend, JJ relaxed and indulged in junk food – specifically pizza and milkshakes.

When he arrived home on bank holiday Monday afternoon, with an ice-cold take-away from his favourite Milkshake City, Jaymi was so jealous he immediately went out and got one too!

Holy Moly stayed true to their promise about providing multiple pictures of the boys, and posted a whopping 31 shots of Union J performing at As One In The Park on their website.

'Are Union J the best looking boyband of all time ever?' the headline read. Holy Moly journalist Tim Chipping then explained:

> We all know how boybands work by now. There tends to be two good-looking ones (one boyish, one manly), a gay one, a weird one and the ugly one who can sing. Sometimes they just have one good-looking one (or in the case of The Wanted – none). But Union J seem to be the first ever UK boyband where every member is poster material (Take That don't count as they never managed to be good looking all at the same time). We say this as an entirely hetero male but... blimey. Would, would, would and would.

The press were becoming more and more supportive of the boys and they must have blushed with pride when they read what the gossip website had to say.

But the press could also be a burden, which is what the lads discovered when they picked up the newspapers that same day.

One Sunday paper had reported that JJ had become smitten by soap actress Wallis Day, and had even got a friend to ask her out at the British Soap Awards after party.

'JJ couldn't keep his eyes off Wallis. She's tall and has a gorgeous smile,' a source had apparently told the paper. The story went on: 'As she was dancing, he was totally captivated by her. His band are about to take the world by storm and you'd think he'd have the confidence to chat up a pretty young actress – but he was totally in awe of her.'

According to the paper, the pair had chatted and swapped numbers – and had even been in contact after the party.

JJ was mystified by the romantic report, which quickly began to spread around a multitude of other Internet gossip sites. After all, he was happily loved up with beautiful model Caterina, and they even had a puppy together.

Caterina was dignified and completely ignored the rumours, except to say: 'I have never really watched *Hollyoaks* before, but maybe I should now...'

But JJ used Twitter to address the story head on and completely denied it. 'Just wanna say again that the rumours between me and Wallis are indeed false. As u all know im in a relationship with cat woop,' he tweeted, setting the record straight.

May continued to be an exhausting whirlwind month for the four boys, as they travelled around the country on a radio tour to raise support for their new single. Josh's phone got stolen in a petrol station, the boys got stuck in a lift, they all ate vast quantities of Nando's chicken and they even made Playdough versions of themselves when they got bored while travelling between towns.

But it wasn't just British radio channels who wanted a piece of Union J action – radio station *The Hot Hits* were excited to interview JJ for their Australian show, proving that Union J fever had begun to spread far beyond the UK.

JJ revealed that he used to live in Mornington, near Melbourne, so he already regarded himself as an honorary Aussie. And he satisfied Union J's growing fan base 'down under' by announcing the band's ambition to perform in the country.

'As soon as they book the flights,' he promised. 'As soon as possible. That's the place where I'd like Union J to break, if we could. It would be wicked if we could.'

It was a tough but exciting month for the boys, who admitted to feeling a little exhausted and even ill at times during the month.

'Movie and chocolate cake after a looong day is heaven,' tweeted George at one point, prompting Josh to call him an 'old man'.

'Feels like I have man flu coming,' tweeted JJ a few days later. 'Not good. Need a hot chocolate and an early night methinks.'

But they hoped it would all be worth it when 'Carry You' was finally released.

**DID YOU KNOW?**
The boys have a group hug before they go out on stage
– to calm their nerves. But only after Josh has gone to
the toilet. 'He sits on the toilet for 20 minutes playing
*Pokemon*,' says Jaymi.

## CHAPTER TWENTY-SIX

# GIGGING AND COOKING

As May drew to a close, the moment they'd all been waiting for was nearly upon the boys – Union J's debut single, 'Carry You' was so near to its release that Josh, Jaymi, George and JJ were a bundle of nerves.

So it was lucky that they would be so busy in the days leading up to the important milestone in their careers.

With ten days to go, they told Glasgow radio station In:Demand: 'It seems so long since *X Factor*. We've come such a far way in such a short time. We're very nervous. We're absolutely pooing ourselves.'

'We want to do as well as we can,' said JJ.

Jaymi said that he'd had 'Carry You' stuck in his head for weeks and had been finding himself singing it in some very unlikely places – like the supermarket. Josh added:

'It's when you're grabbing the broccoli and it's almost like you're singing it to the broccoli.'

Four days before the release, the boys were invited as VIP guests to watch the *Britain's Got Talent* semi-finals – along with Rylan Clark. It must have been strange to revisit the *X Factor* studios, where *Britain's Got Talent* is filmed, and see it looking so different.

They gave some much-needed support to the contestants because, after all, they knew exactly what it was like to be facing a panel of judges live on stage and hoping for the public to vote for them.

Appearing on the aftershow, *Britain's Got More Talent*, they sang a snippet of 'Carry You' and the audience all clapped along to the catchy song.

The next morning, they were up bright and early to head to their favourite *Daybreak* studios where they caught up with presenters Kate Garraway and John Stapleton.

'It's not bad going is it? When you've got nearly a million Twitter followers, nine million hits on YouTube, a book deal – and not even a song released yet,' said Kate, obviously in awe of the band's achievements.

'It's a big, big weekend for us, so we're very excited and very nervous at the same time to see how it goes,' said Josh.

They took the opportunity to thank their record label and everyone who had been involved with 'Carry You', because they said that they were the people who had helped make their dreams come true.

Then they performed a stonking version of 'Carry You' in the studio – it was a great accompaniment to everyone's breakfast! They also took part in yet another challenge for the morning show – a 'jelly-off'. With cute bibs tied around their necks, the boys tucked into platefuls of the wibbly-wobbly treat, to see who could eat the most.

Josh tried to pour most of his onto JJ's plate, while George could hardly eat his after he had cast his eye over his fellow bandmembers. 'It just came out Josh's nose,' he sniggered.

While the others moaned about the task, JJ got straight down to business, and cleared his plate long before the others. Josh and George immediately loaded Jaymi's plate with the remainder of their jelly and held their plates aloft in triumph. Cheats!

On the day of their single release, the boys must have woken up with severe butterflies in their tummies. They had three gigs to perform that day, which on its own would definitely be enough to cope with. But then at midnight, the moment would arrive – Union J's 'Carry You' would be officially available to buy.

First they made their way to Birmingham's LG Arena, for the Girl Guiding Association's Big Gig.

'Carry You will be out in less than 12 hours!!!! #nervous,' tweeted George as they made their way there.

A pop concert for Girl Guides from all over the country, the Big Gig brings together the UK's best singers to perform for the Girl Guides, many of whom are JCats.

'Just performed at LG Arena in Birmingham, best feeling ever seeing everyone sing along to Carry You,' tweeted George.

Once that performance was over, the boys went straight back to the bus to make their way to the Madjeski Stadium in Reading, for the All Starz Summer Party.

The Reading gig would be a particularly special gig for Josh, because the well-known stadium venue was right in the middle of his home turf.

'I am very, very excited. I am a local boy, so to be doing a big concert in Reading is a dream come true,' he said.

'I have been to the Madejski Stadium a couple of times so it will be amazing to be performing there.

'I grew up in Bracknell and spent a lot of time in Reading, shopping and going to the cinema, and I am a huge football fan so to perform in a football stadium is exciting.'

As a local, he was anticipating lots of support from the people he grew up with and he had been looking forward to the gig since it was announced earlier in the year.

Back then he had told his local paper: 'As it's local a lot of my friends and family will probably be in the audience but hopefully everyone will give support because we are a local act.'

He wasn't wrong. When the boys sang 'Carry You' to the crowds, they were greeted by a cacophony of cheers and screams.

They had joined Jessie J, Lawson, JLS and Amelia Lily for the gig – all well-established acts – and they more than held their own.

'The vocals of this boyband were stunning with perfect harmonies and the boys, especially Josh, had great banter with the crowd,' said reviewer Becky Barnes, for the *Reading Post*.

The sun was shining and life was good for the boys.

**DID YOU KNOW?**
**Jaymi is always trying to lead the boys astray – by trying**
**to get them to stay out super late when they're**
**partying.**

Finally they headed back to London, where they were due to go on stage at G-A-Y at 1:30am. They had a few hours to reflect on what the evening would bring, and they were equally excited and apprehensive.

'George and I are sitting here nearly speechless at the thought of us officially having a single out in just over an hour!!!! Crazy,' tweeted Josh.

Most JCats spent the day promising their support for the boys on Twitter. 'You've carried us and now it's our turn to carry you! We won't fail you, pinky promise!' said one. 'Us JCats will do whatever it takes to get Carry You to No 1,' said another.

As the minutes passed, the boys counted them down on Twitter until, finally, it was midnight.

'OHHH WOW,' they tweeted. 'We officially have released a single!!!!!! I am speechless!!!! If you all download it then we have a chance of doing well!'

The instant it was released, the song began to climb the UK iTunes charts, which was a great indication of how it would fare in the official UK charts a week later.

Minutes later the boys tweeted a picture of it at number 78, where it didn't stay for long. Little by little, it crept its way closer to that elusive No1 spot.

With all the excitement, the boys were buzzing as they took to the G-A-Y stage in London. It had been such a whirlwind day that they hadn't had time to change their clothes between gigs, but nobody minded.

They were in high spirits. Their first single had finally been released, and they had high hopes for its official chart position.

They joked around with the crowds, even signing mock contracts to say what they would be willing to do if 'Carry You' reached No. 1 in the official UK charts.

JJ's said that he would have his legs waxed on stage, Josh's stated he agreed to wear a nappy and Jaymi's promised that he would sing a version of Dolly Parton's '9 to 5' while dressed in drag. They were good dares, but none of them beat George's initial promise to bath in baked beans, which he insisted would still go ahead.

The boys appeared to have boundless energy as they bounced around to 'Carry You' in the early hours of the morning. But when the night was over they all flopped exhausted into their beds to get a few hours kip.

'Awkward moment when you're so tired you get in the shower with your pyjamas on,' tweeted George, when he finally woke up. The poor boys must have been running on adrenaline after such a hectic few days.

'16 and climbing!!!' he added, keeping everyone informed of their iTunes chart position. 'Love you millions!'

Thousands of people were downloading 'Carry You', including their pal Jahmene Douglas, who struggled with a dodgy Internet connection but made sure he purchased the track. 'Wooo, so proud,' he tweeted.

The boys had another busy day ahead of them. First they joined the *Sunday Brunch* team to appear on their Channel 4 show. They talked about the gigs they had performed the day before, and admitted that they were exhausted, but said that it had been an amazing day.

'We did the Girl Guides gig and there were about 15,000 girls under the age of 18, screaming,' said Josh. 'So it was absolutely amazing. It was one of the best feelings ever.'

Mark Owen was on the show alongside the boys, and he congratulated the boys on their recent success. 'We used to do five or six gigs a day,' said the Take That band member. 'And finish up at G-A-Y. We used to have fun.'

The boys bonded with the pop veteran over their shared experience of the music industry, and the boys even got the older singer to buy 'Carry You' while they were on the show.

**DID YOU KNOW?**
**Jaymi says his signature dish is Domino's pizza, or Tesco Finest sausage and mash. We don't think that's what the question meant, Jaymi...**

JJ and George tried their hand at some cooking while they were on the show, and admitted that none of the boys were very good in the kitchen.

'We tried to do a BBQ once, and we started it at 1pm and only got the burgers on at 7pm,' explained George.

'I just stood there fanning it for three hours,' said JJ, before saying that he lived on Nando's takeaways.

'I struggle with ham sandwiches,' added George. 'Just ham butter bread and I don't know.'

The presenters, both talented chefs, look stunned and told the lads to start having baking competitions at home to hone their skills. 'Or you could just go out partying,' they joked. They worked together with the hosts to make a tuna pie, with George making the pastry and JJ doing the chopping. JJ struggled with getting the pastry to line the dish, almost dangerously wielding the knife at one point.

Jaymi was shaking his head in mock disappointment as he looked on from the sidelines. 'I just want to apologise to everyone out there in the music industry who likes cooking and is good at it,' he laughed.

As they cooked, they said that if they reached No. 1 they would all get tiny No.1 tattoos to celebrate. But George sounded slightly frightened at the idea of going under the tattooist's needle.

The dish looked yummy by the time it was finished. They tucked in to the pie and looked surprised as they said: 'Oh my God that's amazing!'

With full tummies, it was then time for the boys to head over to the Vodafone Big Top 40 radio studios, to find out how their song would unofficially chart on its first day out.

The Big Top 40 is based on iTunes download sales only, and wasn't the official UK Top 40, which 'Carry You' wouldn't enter until a week later. But it was a great sign of how the song would do, and the boys wanted 'Carry You' to place as high as possible.

'Carry You' had risen to No. 9 on the iTunes chart show during their time on the *Sunday Brunch* show – where would it end up?

While they waited for the chart announcement to begin, they answered questions from their fans in a live webchat on the show.

They said that even though they were now huge pop stars, they were still the same boys as they were a year ago. 'We always said we wouldn't forget where we came from and would always keep our feet on the ground,' said Josh. 'And we won't forget our friends and family that's why whenever we get spare days we're always seeing our friends and close family.'

Jaymi added: 'This is work. We love our job, but I got the best advice from Vanessa's boyfriend from The Saturdays. He said she's always kept work, work and life, life. She socialises with her work friends, and then again with her friends from home. That's what we do – we just watch soaps and play X Box.'

Jaymi revealed that he still goes back to his hometown of Stopsley to see his Olly and his family every week.

The boys said that when they hear their fans singing 'Carry You' back to them from the crowds, it always makes them emotional. And they declared that they truly loved their JCats. 'They're so loyal,' they said. 'And they're bonkers like us!'

As the hours passed, 'Carry You' kept climbing the Vodafone charts. It was incredible to watch and the boys stayed in the studio to track their progress.

'Number 7! We're literally so happy right now!' tweeted

George in the afternoon. 'You are making our dreams come true!'

But soon after, it had jumped again. 'AS IF IT'S NUMBER 6 NOW!' he wrote. 'Woah! I'm becoming speechless!'

The boys went into a near meltdown when they next passed some of their stiffest competition...

'Guys totally blown away by ur support we've past the milestone that is daft punk #4,' tweeted Jaymi.' I know u guys can keep us climbing love you.'

More precious minutes passed, and 'Carry You' remained at No. 4. It was agonising to watch and wait for the 6pm cut-off point, when the iTunes UK charts positions would be finalised for the week.

'Still at number 4! If u haven't downloaded Carry You please please do! Let's get it to number 3 before 6pm!' they wrote.

Finally, just before the deadline, the boys made it, overtaking Passenger's 'Let Her Go', Jessie J's 'Wild', and even Olly Murs''Dear Darlin''.

Only Robin Thicke's 'Blurred Lines' and Naughty Boy's 'La La La' were ahead of them, and they'd both had more time to chart – Union J's 'Carry You' had only been out for 18 hours.

'NUMBER 3!! Thank you so much everyone! Today has been my favourite,' tweeted George at the end of the hectic weekend.

It had been an epic six months since the end of *The X Factor*, and everything they had dreamed of was finally coming together.

Sitting pretty at No. 3 on the iTunes charts, the boys were in a great position to place well in the official UK charts a week later. But with seven days to go until then, the boys had a lot of work to do yet to make that happen.

**DID YOU KNOW?**
Jaymi says the coolest gift he's ever been sent from a fan was a bulk load of South African sweets and chocolates from her hometown.

# CHAPTER TWENTY-SEVEN

# UK CHART SUCCESS

Despite all the excitement and drama of their busy weekend, the boys had no time to rest.

They woke up bright and early on the Monday morning, raring to get outside and carry on promoting 'Carry You'. With six days to go before its official chart entry on Sunday 9 June, they wanted to do everything they could to get it to a high position.

'What an amazing day yesterday,' tweeted Josh. 'Let's keep it up people... we can push for that number 1 spot by end of week!'

'Waking up to see Carry You still at number 3 and the sun shining makes me sooo happy!' added George.

After getting ready for the day, the boys got into a taxi to take them into central London. But it was no ordinary black cab: instead it had their band logo and a picture of them all emblazoned on the side!

The cab was one of two that had been specially decorated for the boys, and lucky fans who spotted one of them had the chance to win dinner with Union J if they jotted down the registration number and sent it to Union J HQ.

The boys would be riding in the cabs all day, visiting London's most famous landmarks – for an impromptu series of singalongs, organised to raise money for the British Legion Poppy Appeal.

They announced their busking plans early in the morning on Twitter, leaving thousands of JCats to frantically plan last-minute journeys into the capital.

Amongst other places, they went to Leicester Square and the London Eye, where they found themselves mobbed by crowds of screaming fans. Luckily they had a huge, burly bodyguard to stop things getting out of control.

At each venue they sang 'Carry You' and 'Call Me Maybe', causing pandemonium on the city streets. But after tearing around the capital, followed by a trail of eager JCats, they still had huge grins on their faces when it was time to go home.

The next day they furiously began tweeting their fans again, to ask them to keep downloading 'Carry You'. But they still had time to wish good luck to everyone who was doing their school exams.

Josh also showed his sensitive side when he helped a feathered friend to safety. 'Just helped an injured pigeon on the side of the road,' he tweeted. I actually helped it fly off. SO happy with myself.'

Then they made their way to *Heat* magazine's headquarters, for an interview with their radio station.

Sitting on a comfy sofa eating chocolates, the boys answered a variety of questions from their fans, including one about what they would like to be if they weren't in a band. With his mouth full of sweets, Jaymi said: 'I'd like to be a professional food taster. I like my job, but I'd like a job that actually entitled me to eat rubbish food.'

George decided he would be a shoe designer, before changing his mind and saying, 'astronaut' – at the exact same time as JJ!

They both looked shocked, and JJ said: 'I swear on my life I was going to say astronaut, how weird.'

Josh decided he would be a footballer, and JJ then said he'd be a scientist. He'd look good in a lab coat...

The boys were all in high spirits, laughing and joking with each other on air. JJ admitted that romantic movies were his guilty pleasure, while Jaymi said that he was a sucker for a musical. They all did hilarious impressions of each other, then fell about laughing at themselves.

They had so much energy, it seemed like the presenters had fed them far too many sweets during the show!

**DID YOU KNOW?**
**Jaymi says the three things he can't live without are his phone, his family and chocolate.**

That night, they appeared on Nick Grimshaw's BBC3

show *Sweat the Small Stuff*, where JJ let Grimmy and George physically hurt him. Calm down JCats...

Brave JJ had agreed to have his arms waxed, and it was the radio DJ's job to carry out the procedure, with a little help from a giggling George. As JJ looked nervously on, the duo warmed the wax strips in their hands, before laying them gently on his arms.

JJ looked terrified as they counted down to pulling the strips off, and screamed in pain when they finally did it. It was yet another price that the boys had to pay for their fame.

As the days passed, the boys were getting more and more excited. With packed schedules, the week was slipping away and they had no idea how well their single was doing.

All they could do was promote their song and hope for the best.

Later in the week, they made another exciting revelation to the *Daily Star* – their swanky new flats were once inhabited by other famous pop stars.

'JJ and I are in Cheryl Cole's old apartment,' explained Jaymi. 'We didn't want to live on our own. Josh is in Nicola Roberts's and George is in Zayn Malik's.'

The boys truly were following in the footsteps of band royalty. One Direction and Girls Aloud had both spent many an evening in those homes, back when they themselves were beginning their fledgling singing careers.

The Union J boys must have hoped that sleeping in the plush pads would bring them good luck.

But they weren't doing much sleeping in the week leading

up to their first chart entry. Instead they were performing, appearing on TV and radio and posing for photos for magazines. They hardly had a minute to themselves.

They told the *Daily Star*: 'Once we have the chart position, we can relax. That's when we'll throw the biggest, craziest party.'

There was a lot riding on their first single. If they broke into the Top Ten with their first song, they would know if they had a chance at a successful career together as Union J.

They knew that although they had a million Twitter followers and countless fans, unless people bought their music, they wouldn't be able to continue on their Union J journey.

Josh told the *Yorkshire Evening Post*: 'I'm realistic, and we've all done other things before this band, so we understand the industry, and I think that helps us. We're really happy about this new single, it's a great song, and I don't think we'll be "that band from *The X Factor*" much longer, just Union J, a great band with great songs. We have high hopes.'

He said that the boys had nearly finished their first album, and that they planned to release it after their second single – but everything was dependent on how well 'Carry You' did.

'If it does well, it might mean it's the start of a successful career, so there's an amount of pressure for it do well,' he said. 'But another pressure that if it flops, we'll have to go back to our old jobs. It's crazy to think we've got this opportunity.'

The boys would be performing to 80,000 people as part of Capital's Summertime Ball at Wembley when the chart news was announced – it would be incredible if they could celebrate good news with their fans while on stage.

Especially since they would be with Taylor Swift, The Wanted, Will.i.am, Jessie J and Robbie Williams when it happened.

Veteran *X Factor* alumni Olly Murs could see that the boys were nervous, and gave them some advice, via the *Daily Star*. He had got to know them all well when they were on the ITV show, and he himself knew the music industry well. 'Carry You' was battling some heavy duty chart classics for a spot in the Top Ten, including Robin Thicke, Jessie J and Passenger.

Olly was confident that Union J would be the band who filled the void left by JLS retiring, but he wanted the hard-working boys to keep grounded and enjoy the experience for as long as it lasted.

'The first single is the worst – it's a tricky time,' he said. 'I wish Union J all the success in the world and hope they can create something for themselves. But pop music is always changing, and you never know how long your success will last, so they should just enjoy it.'

Olly himself was already in the Top Ten with his single, 'Dear Darlin'. Union J could only hope that they would join him there.

The boys were overwhelmed to receive support from all over the world. Mark Wright announced that he had bought 'Carry You', and urged his fans to do the same, while their boyband rivals, The Wanted, told the new singing sensations that they were behind them all the way. 'Good luck this week @UnionJWorld,' tweeted Tom Parker. 'Rooting for you!'

### DID YOU KNOW?
JJ is the worst dancer in the band, and the boys all agree Josh is the 'meanest'. JJ himself has often joked that he is 'pretty bad' when it comes to his stage moves, while George says that Josh is the one who is constantly flinging around jokey insults at everyone.

But the most exciting message of support came from Disney princess Selena Gomez, and left George blushing in amazement.

It's no secret that George has always fancied the cute brunette. He once admitted: 'I've got an undying crush on her, it's the whole Disney thing. I love her.'

So when the boys appeared on CBBC's *Friday Download* and were shown a video message from the American star, George could hardly keep still with excitement.

They didn't know anything about the secret message, so when it began to play, his mouth fell open with amazement.

'Hey George, it's Selena,' she began.

'Shut, up, no,' said George, clearly in shock.

'I was in London for a bit and I'm actually bummed I missed you so next time, maybe give me a call?'

JJ started clapping, while George was obviously chuffed to bits with the flirty message – especially since she was now single after splitting up with Justin Bieber.

Maybe he would now have a chance with his dream girl...

The next day, the boys were up early again to rehearse for the Summertime Ball. They were excited to be performing at the huge event, and especially excited to finally find out how 'Carry You' would place in the charts.

After a tiring day of practise, they all went home to watch the final of *Britain's Got Talent*, and George even found time to put his newfound cookery skills to good use.

'I'm attempting to make chilli,' he tweeted. 'I'll let you know how it goes!'

Two burns and a messy kitchen later he tweeted a picture of the result, and it didn't look half bad. He must have been grateful to the *Sunday Brunch* team for showing him the basics, just a week before.

'Can't concentrate on anything but tomorrow's chart show,' tweeted Josh, a few hours later. 'ONE more push guys! We can do this!'

It must have been a sleepless night for the boys, but they were all full of energy when they woke up on Sunday.

It was the day they had all been waiting for.

After months of hard work, they would finally find out what position 'Carry You' would enter the charts at.

They made their way to Wembley Stadium for the Summertime Ball, where they were announced on stage by none other than Justin Timberlake. They danced and sang in front of the screaming 80,000 audience members, and the atmosphere was electric. They could hardly believe it was all real.

'I have been in the audience of the Summertime Ball for

the last 5 years,' tweeted an emotional Josh when he came off stage. 'To think I performed today is a dream. Thank you to everyone.'

Finally, that evening, the boys discovered that 'Carry You' had entered the charts in the amazing position of No. 6.

They had placed higher than Jessie J, David Guetta, Demi Lovato and Bruno Mars – all established pop stars with successful track records.

It was a phenomenal achievement for the band, who less a year before hadn't even existed. It wasn't the No. 1 spot as they had all hoped and wished for, but it was very close – and it was an indelible mark on the music world, showing just how much they had achieved since leaving *The X Factor*.

When Take That debuted in 1991, their first song, 'Do What U Like', only reached No. 82 in the charts. It took them four more song releases before they broke the Top Ten with 'It Only Takes A Minute', which entered the charts at No. 7. And it was actually their ninth single, 'Pray', that finally secured them the top chart spot.

Waiting so long for a No. 1 certainly didn't do them any harm. In fact, it made them work even harder to get to where they wanted to be, and it made their subsequent staggering success (they're arguably the most popular boyband of all time) all the more sweet.

'Honestly I am the luckiest boy in the world,' tweeted Josh, after he heard the news. 'Today has been 1 of the best feelings ever. I am overwhelmed and so grateful for everything.'

After months of dedication and hard work, the boys

had taken another huge step on their journey to becoming the biggest boyband in the world. They understood how much further they had to go, and were ready for the challenges that would surely lie ahead.

But together, they were confident they could make it.

Over the next few months, the boys continued to work on their first album, which was due for release in October.

But in September JJ announced an even more incredible achievement – he and Cat were expecting their first child together.

The boys, who only a year ago had been fresh-faced and nervous at the *X Factor* auditions, were growing up so fast. Now a new baby JCat would soon be born, and would join the boys on their exciting journey through the music world.

'Guys I want you to be the first to know that I've got some big news… I'm going to be a daddy…' he tweeted, to his amazed fans. 'My girlfriend and I are super super excited and the boys can't wait to be uncles! They are already thinking of names beginning with J.'

The boys couldn't wait to meet their new little niece or nephew, and began planning its first onesie right away. The months and years ahead were set to be exciting ones.

Only time will tell what the future has in store for our Union J boys.